LOSING VENICE

a novel

SCOTT STAVROU

·ROGUE DOG PRESS·
Port Richey

ROGUE DOG PRESS

LOSING VENICE

For permissions, media & press inquiries contact
info@RogueDogPress.com

*This is a work of fiction. Names, characters, businesses, organizations, places,
events and incidents either are the product of the author's imagination or are
used fictitiously. Any resemblance to actual persons, living or dead, events, or
locales is entirely coincidental and unintended. Of course, many of the best parts
of Venice live primarily in the imagination and La Serenissima has long been the
setting of many inexplicable coincidences.*

Book and cover design by Rogue Dog Press Design
Cover Photo by Marco Ceschi

Library of Congress Control Number: 2018941387

ISBN: 978-1-7321956-8-4 (Paperback)
ISBN: 978-1-7321956-2-2 (ebook)
First Paperback Edition: April 2018
10 9 8 7 6 5 4 3 2 1

For my mother, who taught me that life should be an adventure. And for Lisa, who makes it one.

Perhaps I am afraid of losing Venice all at once, if I speak of it, or perhaps, speaking of other cities, I have already lost it, little by little.
Italo Calvino, *Invisible Cities*

ONE

CROSSING THE GRAND CANAL

Arrived Venice. Streets full of water. Please advise.
Robert Benchley, telegram

I DIDN'T MOVE TO VENICE to become a thief or a drunk though there is little question that my flair for achieving the latter was a catalyst for the former.

Boredom was an occupational hazard of being far from home in a new town; mischief mixed with alcohol had seemed the antidote for my ailment. It was a cure I'd used before with some success in other times, in other places. When you don't know how exactly to move yourself forward, you generally fall back on the old tried and true remedies.

It's surprising how pensive you can be while rowing yourself across the Grand Canal with a broom in a stolen gondola. Especially if you're tucked snugly beneath a heavy blanket of winter fog that leaves you, your black boat, and dark thoughts aimlessly adrift in the still hours of the night on the world's most prestigious strand of water. My surroundings were perfectly matched for my mind-set.

I was trying to work out how to use the broom to its fullest advantage as an improvised oar when a big splash of brisk water swept over me, all grimy and bracing cold. I shivered. The waters of the Grand Canal may be the stuff of postcards and poets when gazed upon from the lofty heights of the Rialto Bridge but when you're down at canal level and a drunk Irish guy in front of you scoops up a cold slice of the Adriatic with a dustpan and it sprays you all about the head, face, and feet, well it's not so damned pleasant or poetic at all. Life is like that. Note to self: when stealing gondolas in the fog of a winter night in Venice, always sit in the front of the boat. Or at the very least, try and find a gondola where the oars aren't all chained up and you don't have to resort to using the broom and dustpan in the bottom of the boat to row yourselves across the canal.

Perhaps it'd be enough to just be a bit more discriminating in your search for crew mates. More rigorous that is, than the selection process I'd used, which was merely the only other drunk guy in the single Irish pub in Venice that happened to speak English and also wanted to get to the other side of the Grand Canal after the bar had closed. Mischief loves company and many had shipped off together on the basis of less, I'm sure.

"Hoist the mainsails," I said, for something to say.

"Aye, aye, Captain. An oar, my kingdom for an oar."

The sound of our voices in the stillness of the night made me all too vividly aware of being where we probably should not be and doing what we definitely should not be doing. I was speculating how much longer it could take us to get across the canal. It wasn't that wide, after all, and even though it couldn't have been more than a few minutes so far, our endeavor seemed earmarked with the portent of an ill fated three hour tour. You don't have to be as smart as the Professor or as wealthy as Mr. Howell to know how those ended up. All you needed was a TV and an excellent selection of cable channels showing the American classics. I wondered briefly if I was indeed the first person in history to have been deep in reverie about Gilligan's Island while rowing across the Grand Canal and couldn't decide if that would have been a good or a bad thing anyway.

I was unsuccessfully trying to use the broom as both rudder and oar when I realized I was spinning us and our purloined craft off-kilter. My partner in crime had stopped rowing and forsaken his dustpan to reach into his overcoat.

For a brief second, I could see his face through the fog when the flame of his lighter threw a small spotlight on his head, making a hole in the murkiness. Then it disappeared again and was replaced by the steady but less pronounced glow of the tip of his cigarette which burned brighter when he inhaled.

"Ahoy there, Seamus, excuse me for asking, but what the fuck are you doing?" I asked, in what was meant to be a curious and amicable tone, just friendly seafaring banter.

"Steady on, mate. I just wanted to savor this moment a bit. My last night before going home and all. Smoke?"

What the hell. Petty larceny and Guinness mixed with liberal doses of "what am I doing here and why do I do the things I do?" is a compelling cocktail. Life offers up only so many such moments so I decided to drink it up. I placed my broom back in the bottom of the gondola where it dripped more cold water on my feet and leaned forward and took a smoke and a light from my shipmate. As I settled down in the back of the boat, it rocked from side to side and small swells of water lapped hungrily at the low edges of the gondola, which was clearly not so well designed for the quiet savoring of moments in midstream. I inhaled and blew out the smoke, watching it stir itself into the mist and fog.

"You ever hear of a TV show called Gilligan's Island?" I asked. He hadn't.

What was it they said? Two countries divided by a common language? That was England though, and I knew enough to know not to mix up the Irish with the English. Still and all, I couldn't help but feel strangely pleased there were indeed some limits to America's cultural hegemony. Pleased and surprised, which was not my general reaction to limits of any sort. Many of which I've been made aware of in the past, few of which I've been eager to abide by.

I was singing the theme song to myself in my head, thinking about how they could build a radio from a coconut but not repair the S.S. Minnow, when I looked around as I heard a new sound: the hum of a motor churning through the waters. The fog was so thick you could hear the boat though not see it. The deep-throated growl of the engine reverberated off the palazzos on both sides of the Grand Canal, ending both the silence and our inactivity.

Beer and petty larceny had earned me a seat in the smoking section of a stolen gondola with a motorboat bearing down on us from points unknown. Suddenly mischief making was less charming. I looked toward where the throb of the engine seemed to come from and made out a red light making steady and altogether too rapid progress toward us.

A quick slideshow flashed through my mind: crash of motorboat on wooden gondola, two drunk guys in dirty, cold canal water, Italian police, fines, jails, desperate calls to embassies, losing a new job, being deported my first week in Italy. None of them were inspiring. I couldn't help but be annoyed at whatever had incited that intruder to be out motoring around on the canal at this time of night. He probably wasn't even going anywhere important.

I could see tomorrow's headline: "Inebriated Foreigners Mowed Down in Stolen Gondola, Wielding Broom and Dustpan." It's not the kind of clipping you want to send home or add to your resume.

I hastily flicked my cigarette into the water and picked up my broom. At least it would be an interesting way to go. I'd always felt bad for those people pictured in the history books, buried in lava from Mount Vesuvius, captured in mundane still life poses for all eternity.

Drunk, in a stolen boat with the wrong implements, utterly in the wrong place at the wrong time. At least it would've left something interesting for the reporters and the historians if we had died then and there. It would have, I thought, left lots of interesting questions. But I had enough questions, just not enough answers. The one I did have was human nature at its most instinctive: pure preservation.

I shoved my broom deep into the water and started rowing in a sudden urge to not be tomorrow's headline. You ever have that feeling? Sometimes it's the little things you never planned on doing that enable you to step back and appreciate the larger things.

We managed to make it across the canal without being broadsided or arrested, but a lot of lights flashed on us when the foghorn sounded again, closer this time. While we frantically rowed our very best with our makeshift implements in an effort to get out of the way, we were helped along by what I took to be words of encouragement in Italian I didn't understand. Very stern and serious encouragement.

The boat passed us by with a last angry blast of its horn just as we finally made our way to the far bank of the canal, leading us to our next little challenge. What to do with a stolen gondola once you've made your safe crossing and the dangers are over?

I was able to use my broom to pull us along the edge of the canal by placing the brush end inside the balustrades of the boat decks of the palazzos. The problem was all the little docks led only to the private entrances of the palaces. We maneuvered clumsily along past two palaces, the way you drag yourself on the edge of the pool before you can swim, until at last we located a gap in the homes of Venetian old nobility. There was a small pathway about six feet wide where the level of the water had risen just up to the second highest step. Seamus stepped out and helped pull me along so I could follow, and the place had been made to order for our purposes. By the glow of his lighter, we found a thick old metal ring anchored deeply into the cobblestones. Worried about the gondola drifting off to sea, we dragged it up to street level as far as we could and tied it up securely to the old cast-iron ring that was waiting there for two people such as us and probably had been for centuries.

"The good lord looks after cowards and drunks, my da always told me," Seamus said.

"Which are we?"

"Touch of both, I wager," he said.

"Or neither. The motorboat sobered me right up," I said.

"It's a shame after all that good effort, too. Least you're not after lack of trying."

I would've liked to have seen the gondoliers face in the morning when he found out his boat wasn't exactly where he left it, but at least it wasn't too much the worse for wear. I hoped whoever he was he had a suitable sense of intrigue. Who knows, he might have even enjoyed telling the tale to his gondolier pals.

We walked along and I felt a bit better with each step that took us further away from the site of our criminal expedition. Seamus and I said our farewells on a dimly lit street near the Accademia museum, where I could now see the wooden bridge we could have walked across, had we been so inclined. It looked pretty pedestrian after the past few minutes.

"Do you," I asked, "feel a bit guilty about that?"

"Fuck's sake. For borrowing a boat? Hell, no. It'll be a good tale for the boys back home at the pub."

I admired his conviction even though I wasn't heading home and no one was awaiting my stories.

Seamus had his course set: he was going back to Dublin tomorrow with no regrets and plenty of stories from his travels. I was newly arrived in Venice with lots of regrets and unsure of how my story was going to unravel. Somehow opposite trajectories, emboldened by too many pints of Guinness and a need to get to the other side, had helped us forge a moment of balance in a stolen boat.

The way I'd been feeling of late, a moment of balance was a good start.

TWO

UNDER A SANTA MARGHERITA SKY

I MADE THE PERENNIAL MISTAKE of all amateur criminals when I went back to the scene of the crime in the light of day.

But it was all business as usual, nothing to see. No drunk Irish guy, no stolen boat, just Venetians going about their normal business. I was even a bit disappointed I couldn't discern exactly which boat we had absconded with. Probably it was off shuttling tourists around the Canal. Daytime was rush hour for the Grand Canal, even if the procession was imbued with more elegance than stalled traffic on an interstate back home. As I walked back to the nearby Campo Santa Margherita, I was thinking about how best to chart a course in unfamiliar territory.

There are reasons people go other places. Some people use maps, some follow signposts and some explore uncharted lands. There are different people, assorted places, and various reasons, but the places and the people and the reasons, the whole equation really, stays the same. Many a man's folly is determined by the fervent belief that discovering what is out there might help one chart the insides, the soul, the being, the self. On a map, there is always a scale at the bottom explaining the size and dimensions of what is charted; in life there is no scale to tell you what is what.

I had my reasons: a woman who was another man's wife, a life that didn't feel like it fit well and an urge to be elsewhere. An older woman, a new job, an airplane: Marco Polo International Airport. It was a simple equation, even if others did the sums for me.

I added it up again and wished I remembered something more about algebra and imaginary numbers while I sat there in the sun of the campo sipping prosecco outside of the Café Rosso. It was January 12, early in the twenty-first century but late in the afternoon, and a chill wind whistled around the campo, but still people sat outside eager to pretend sunshine meant good weather, despite the wind and the thermometer's evidence to the contrary. Then there was a thump on my right shoulder. I looked back quickly, only no one was there and it wasn't a thump. It was a blob, really a smear, of pigeon shit impertinently plopped on the right shoulder of my new green winter overcoat, an obscenity of droppings from the sky.

For a fleeting moment I was disgusted. Then I looked around; no one had seen me befouled. Everyone went on pretending it was a beautiful winter's afternoon. Sometimes reality must be railed against despite the evidence. And suddenly I realized that I had been very lucky indeed. Had I been sitting even two inches to the right of where I was, had the wind been a bit stronger or had the pigeon made just a slight adjustment of wingtip, the unlucky plop from the heavens would have landed right on my head.

Yes, that day in the Campo Santa Margherita in Venice, when a plop of pigeon shit fell out of the sky onto my right shoulder, I was lucky and I knew it. If I had been anywhere else or done any other thing, everything would have been different. I finished my champagne, gestured to the waitress and ordered another glass to celebrate my good fortune.

"Encore prosecco, per favore."

That's how it was then in Campo Santa Margherita. The square was cold and bright and filled with people clutching onto the lingering holiday feeling, making plans for Carnevale, and looking forward to the great things that would happen to everyone in a new year, all of us lucky to be alive and to be sitting there and not somewhere else.

Yes, I thought, it was a very simple equation. If you were sitting here and sipping prosecco in the wan winter sun, it meant you weren't somewhere else. You weren't in Afghanistan being raided by fighter jets, you weren't in Somalia or Liberia being persecuted by machine gun-toting tribal chieftains, you weren't in New York staring at the gaping hole left by people who thought their god and ways better than another, you weren't selling cookware door-to-door in Terra Haute, you weren't in a long line at the DMV or the DMZ, and you weren't back home in San Francisco in another man's bed. There were lots of good places not to be and I was glad not to be in any of them. At least that's how it felt as I finished the second glass of champagne, celebrating my hereness.

It might have been just as good, or maybe even better, to be in another place with other people, doing other things, but I wasn't then, so I didn't know. At thirty-five, I was just beginning to grow wise enough to realize how many things I wasn't and the immensity of the unwoven tapestry of the things I didn't know and had not done. And perhaps to even appreciate the imprudence of the things I did know and had done.

Later, I went back to my large furnished apartment behind the Church of San Trovaso and stared at the yellow lights of the church before turning on the TV to Stazione Due where two mustachioed Italian men spoke about soccer, er, football, while three barely dressed women danced to trendy Italian pop music in the background. All three were very buxom, having bountiful breasts was seemingly a prerequisite for being on Italian television, and strangely, all six breasts hung a bit lower than any of the Baywatch breasts ever had, and I thought how long it had been since real breasts held center stage on a television or movie screen I'd viewed. I had grown accustomed to a celluloid world turgid with silicone and the unnatural had started to seem natural, making the real suddenly seem strangely false to my American-trained eyes.

Lacking the presence of anyone else to persuade me to stop ogling foreign bosoms on late-night television or to eat dinner or change for bed or follow any of the conventions that constituted good living, I stared at the shifting and slowly bouncing breasts until I fell asleep in my clothes on the couch to the sounds of singing in a language I didn't understand.

When I woke up, cold and stiff, there were still breasts on the TV, only they were different, this time the breasts, still barely concealed, were selling rugs and jewelry—home-shopping Italian style. Everyone the world over nursed at the teat of commercialism and it was a hungry world, a ravenous world. I went to bed and I was hungry too, but more sleepy than hungry, and I kind of missed the wondrous six breasts that had gone from the screen and wondered where they were now and if anyone was looking at them or playing with them.

In my sleep, I drifted along a canal in a gleaming black gondola with a beautiful woman whose face was shrouded in the mists and we made love to the gentle lapping of the water and the rhythm of our bodies beat a melody on the water. Beneath the fog, the waters of the canal grew silent, and I missed the musical sounds we'd made and kept wishing they would come back but I couldn't hear them. I wondered how we'd get to the shore without an oar or even a broom. She told me not to worry, but I did.

Awaking in the morning, I shed sleep and illusion but remembered the dream as I fixed myself a coffee and dragged out my English-Italian dictionary. To dream: sognare.

It was time to get ready for work and stop dreaming; they were mutually exclusive pastimes. So I took a shower and then shaved. Living alone and less rushed had allowed me to spend, or waste, more time on myself and I'd purchased a shining brass and gold shaving dish and badger hair brush at a store in San Polo and had taken to giving myself hot foam in the morning in attempts at making a mundane morning ritual something more of an event.

It occurred to me while looking in the mirror that morning, my face smeared with the warm creamy foam, that my reflection, unlike myself, was left-handed. All these years of shaving, staring into mirrors, how could I never have taken this left-handed aspect of myself into consideration? My reflection and I even parted our hair on different sides.

Was what I saw in the mirror the reality or what I knew to be true, or thought to be true? While I scraped the night's new whiskers from my face, I tried to remember who it was that said, "Beauty is truth, truth beauty." That would be all you needed to know.

THREE

EVERYONE GOES TO VENICE

BEING ALONE IN A FOREIGN LAND, I had many solitary days to read stacks of reports, many of which had been re-translated so many times as to make the bureaucratic English even more ludicrous than usual. I read them, digested their facts, figures, and faulty language and worked on what was and wasn't expected of me in the new role I had been cast into.

My position in the small office of the Venezia Tourism Council was tenuous. I was the hired gun in the western town that well knew how to handle their own affairs and didn't want outsiders meddling, only maybe, since things were bad, they would tolerate having someone around for awhile. Someone who would help out with the mess and get things back to normal so they could get rid of him and forget he was ever there and deny they'd ever wanted or maybe even needed him. I knew I was not really wanted and didn't feel essential, but there I was all the same.

I sat down in Signor Contarini's office.

Like most of the interiors of the old palazzos, it was richly paneled in dark woods and ornately over-decorated with the signature opulence that was Venetian décor.

"You know, of course," he said, in his smug, heavily-accented but highly-polished British English, "Venice was the world's first tourist destination. The first travel guide in history was published about Venice, over a thousand years ago. We had tourism police here in Venice before anyone even thought of America. In America what you call history is what, two, three hundred years? It is trivial against a thousand years. Venetians have always gone to the outside world and the world has always, forever, wanted to come to Venice. There is no other place like Venezia. Solo una Venezia. Solo una. La Serenissima."

"Of course, there's no place like Venice," I confirmed, since he seemed to expect me to do so.

On his desk was the marble lion that symbolized Venice and books in various languages lined the left wall of his office from the richly veined marble floor to the dark wood ceiling. The Venetians loved their books and their lions and their home. I came to learn that there is a particularly strong trait in the Italians to impress upon you the grandeur and glory of their history, faded and museum-like though it was, in the way that the washed up high school quarterback still tells the tales of the same old games of years before, they being more important to him than to you. But most things people told you, I reflected, were more important to the tellers than the listeners. Not everyone was listening, anyway. Empires, like high school quarterbacks, find it hard to let go of their more glorious moments, no matter how far in the past they lay. They lived and breathed their lost greatness every day.

As if I hadn't listened closely enough, I was reminded that there was no place like Venice. There's no place like home, right Dorothy? Was there any place like any other place? Of course no place was like Venice, no place at all. Well, there were lovely canals in Amsterdam and Bruges. Bangkok was the Venice of the East. Wasn't St. Petersburg the Venice of the North? And Stockholm, it was all on water and equally canal ridden. Still and all, there was only one Venice and people would come to it as long as it kept afloat, as long as the hole in the ozone didn't get too big, the glaciers didn't melt, the seas didn't rise, and the Fascists didn't take over.

Hell, even after the Fascists and during the war they had all wanted to come to Venice. Allied commanders vied for the right to be first in Venice. A New Zealand General got there first and commandeered the Hotel Danieli as his HQ, it being where he'd spent his honeymoon some years before during the world's collective sigh of relief just after the Great War, the war to end all wars, but before World War II, its inevitable sequel.

Unlike most sequels, World War II was far better cast and much more enthralling than its predecessor. With a great flair for showmanship, some Nazis even capitulated by wearing those imposing black uniforms; Patton slapped a scared soldier silly then strapped on his white pearl-handled six shooters and led his cavalry of tanks to the rescue. You knew who to root for then. Terkel was right, World War Two was the last good war. Another of the many things I didn't understand about war was the way people abbreviated the big ones, WWI and WWII, saying "dou-ble-u, dou-ble-u, one or two," which is not much of a successful abbreviation, after all, since actually saying "World War" takes less syllables than the aforementioned abbreviation. Oh, how unlucky to have been European and been born in 1900, just old enough for the first world war and still, if alive and whole, young enough for the second world war. Unless you liked wars and killing people, then how very fortuitous. Everything is relative. This, I believe, we have from the man who helped us understand splitting the atom. Even the lowly atom had its place in the big wars. Few were excluded.

Of course there had been good wars and bad, or maybe they were all bad, it depended on who you listened to and which movies you watched or which god you prayed to and which generation you were born into.

Venice had weathered the stormy seas of war and peace, empire building, and irrelevance. Merchants, Crusaders, Explorers, Jews, Greeks, Christians, Moors, Muslims, Popes, Ottomans, Turks, Austro-Hungarians, Lombards, Romans, the Vatican, the Plague; they'd all been either for or against Venice at some time or another in the long and sordid history of the world's fateful ships of state.

Venice, when she was a success, the supreme power in Europe and Lord of the Seas, was never loved, always different. She was perched half on land but lived on the seas, the gateway between East and West, between Christianity and Islam, but committed only to herself and her business, which was trade. Now her empire had been traded for tourism and her battles were fought for the trade of tourists' pocketbooks. She was, in the end, a living museum, though they did not like to think of her that way.

And through it all, it seemed to little matter to Venice herself, who, though she sank slowly into the soggy marshlands of the lagoon, was ravaged more by the lapping of the Adriatic than by the power brokers that dictated the course of human events. Even with the world at war, people wanted, needed, to see Venice.

"The problem," Signor Contarini said, "is not getting people to come. We do not need the EU to help us make people want to see Venice. All people want to see Venice, it is a fact, of this you can be sure. It has always been so."

Italians had a strong sense of history; in the Venetians it was paramount.

Things were done that way because they had always been done that way, so it was the right way. The historical weight so common in Europe was particularly ponderous in Venice, where the Venetians knew that their way was the right way.

It wasn't explicit that yours, being different, was necessarily the wrong way, just that you probably had not yet learned, or thought of, the right way. Once you understood Italian well enough, you couldn't learn the Veneziano dialect—not if you weren't Venetian, and there weren't many left—but with some Italian, you would be surprised to discover that a gondolier might tell you to have caution, the Venetian water was particularly slippery, as if no other water shared this trait, as if the precious waters that flowed up the Adriatic and into Venice's Lagoon harbored a particular special quality of slipperiness not shared by other, lesser waters. They all knew at what hour to stop drinking steamed milk in their coffee, when it was time for an aperitivo or a digestivo, when you should eat and when you shouldn't. And when you shouldn't be dining, the restaurants closed. They knew what kind of film you needed for your camera; little did it matter if it had been made in Germany or Japan.

The Venetians were comfortable in the smugness of their elegant cloak of superiority and it was a costume that fit them well. Or to which they had grown into, at least.

Signor Contarini wore a smartly-checked, double-breasted suit and a shiny silk red tie and even a boutonnière, something I'd previously seen only in old movies and at high school proms. He had ruled his Ufficio Turismo for so long that he was ill at ease at having an outsider brought in, one whose paycheck was signed by bureaucrats at the EU in Strasbourg rather than by him.

As a Venetian, he was, of course, particularly well-suited to the task and there weren't so many real Venetians left, a fact I often heard him lament. Yes, everyone should come to Venice, they just shouldn't come and stay too long, only just long enough, you see. A functionary, an outsider, who was me, chosen by someone else, could be of little use in this game. Though I wasn't sure in what boardroom or on what conference call the decision had been made to toss my piece in the game, neither of us bothered with whatever distinction had gathered us both in his office that morning.

"They all want to see Venice. You know how it is," he said, leaning forward and perching his elbows on the back edge of his desk and making a steeple with his long fingers.

That was another thing; the Venetians were always building churches.

I had no idea how it was really, but people were always telling you that you knew how it was. Whether you did or not. I'd found it generally meant you were supposed to recognize that the way it was, was exactly like the person speaking to you said it was. That was about all I knew about how it was. That, and that most people liked to talk more than listen, whether or not they had much to say.

"Of course they do," I said, having quickly gleaned that my role in Contarini's office was to agree with everything he said, to reassure him. My father had well-prepared me for the role of minion, though it presented itself more than I would have liked.

"The problem with all this talk of war, with the U.S. imperialist agenda," he said, "is that Americans are becoming too afraid to travel. And this is crazy, preposterous."

I wondered where and when he learned a word like preposterous. It was a pretty damned good word to know for a third language, or maybe it was his fourth or fifth, I knew his mom was from Murano and he spoke dialect, and of course Italian and English, and I knew there was some French and German. Contarini was a Venetian first but a modern European also, and as the singer of Venice's siren song abroad, he was often required to hold forth abroad, trips he complained about making.

"Of course," he continued, "the people will still come. But Venice can only hold so many people and it is important Venice attract the right sort of people."

Everyone wanted the right sort of people. Only I didn't know who they were, to me they were just people. But for the good places; like the Guggenheim Museum or Slim's Nightclub South of Market in San Francisco, the golf course at Augusta, or Willard's Whizzer Roller Coaster at Six Flags, there was always a line or a gate and someone to tell you whether you were well-dressed enough or tall enough or rich or cultured enough or testosterone-ridden enough to get in. It was all about getting in. Good sorts, bad sorts, it didn't seem to matter to me. Everyone was some sort. If you weren't in, you wanted to be.

"Twenty years ago, the average tourist stay in Venice was two weeks. Ten years ago it was almost a week. Now it is one day. Solo un giorno. The people herd onto the trains, like the cattle, and they go stampeding across to the Piazza, they see the Doges Palazzo, Piazza San Marco, perhaps they ride in a gondola once, and then they go, thinking they have seen Venice, when they have not.

"The French and the Germans, they will always come to Venice and they will stay for a weekend, again and again, this we know."

How long ago was it that Italy had first been allied with Germany against France and the world, then with the U.S. against Germany? It seemed a long time, but the business of tourism, like most businesses, depends much more on bank accounts than on nationalism or prejudice or even wars. Traveling is the ultimate democratization, the great equalizer; even if people only went somewhere else to be reassured of how different others were than themselves, to reassure themselves that different was neat to see but still different and therefore probably wrong. Business was the piston that powered the world, and travel and tourism were its output. Or perhaps its oil, depending on how you looked at it. I didn't have time to figure it out as the illustrious Contarini spoke down to me from across his desk again.

"The Americans, they do not stay long enough now, you see. They do not spend enough time. Or enough money," Contarini added with emphasis, pleased at having put his finger precisely on the problem.

"It's absolutely preposterous," I said, wondering what English words I could use that would send him to a dictionary. He was not the type of man who would ever ask what a word meant. Antidisestablishment. I knew that was in the dictionary, I'd looked it up more than once. Xenophobia, that was another big one but for all its prevalence, its tangled roots would have gone beyond Latin and all the way to Greek. Besides, it didn't really apply. Not to the highly-touted tourism gem of Europe. That set me to pondering when and where the last person to speak Latin as his native tongue or to truly believe in Zeus had died, but since I didn't have the answers, I kept the questions to myself.

"So you will work on this," Contarini commanded, as if I held America's missiles and bank accounts in my back pocket, which I was pretty sure I didn't.

∞ ∞ ∞

I left his office patting my pockets, no missiles no bank accounts, thinking that in the world community, America was like the annoying guy in college, the pompous ass no one really liked but they invited him to all the parties because he had good drugs or brought along a bottle of Swedish vodka. No one really wanted him there, but everyone wanted what he had. Or some of what he had, anyway.

It occurred to me that perhaps America was like George W. Bush. Not too bright, not too savvy, but rich and with a long legacy of prestige and power. Someone to invite to the party because he might hook you up with something. The founding fathers hit a home run of life, liberty and pursuit of happiness, and America and George W. were perched there on third base. No one ever stole home anymore though. Almost never. Jackie Robinson had, you'd seen it on SportsCenter Classic. But he had to. He wasn't born anywhere near it.

I had never stolen home either. Barely even had a place to call home. But I understood about people wanting to see other places, the restlessness was rooted deep in my soul. As the son of a Marine, I had learned that you had to go where you were sent, everyone did. It was a habit I had detested, new schools, new people, the same struggles in different settings. With each move, I managed to delude myself into thinking that in a new place everything would be different. But I came to learn that mostly everything was the same, most everywhere. Everyone was busy not having anything to do.

I managed to make and leave behind many new friends back beyond the enemy lines that were my past, most of whom seemed irreplaceable but, nonetheless, always had to be replaced. I had grown accustomed to being the outsider, to leaping off the high dive that was the first recess on the first day at a new school. New kids hate recess and you can spend more time underwater on a dusty playground than in an aqua-tinted pool. Children, like Marines and mobs, are a critical bunch and invariably tough judges. This was not the type of grievance I could take to my father, so instead I protested about it loudly to myself throughout my childhood. The U.S. Marines do not complain or hear complaints. Semper Fidelis. I'd always meant to look up the Latin for always moving but never had, though it would have been far more appropriate. It was also the thing I understood best. Being elsewhere.

My father had wanted me to join the service, and I failed him. Had wanted me to attend Annapolis, and I failed him at that. Had wanted me to attend a less expensive state school as an alternative, and I managed to disappoint him in this also. Helped along by some scholarships, some student loans, and a son's inherent birthright to fight the will of the father, I attended Princeton. Succeeding at failing my father became a minor hobby of sorts and I got pretty good at it.

It wasn't hard as it was a pattern we had grown used to. You see, I was an only child, but not spoiled. Though all only children say that. But in my case, it happens to be true—though most say that, too. Perhaps it was because I was born to be a second child but my brother had died when I was three and left me alone, so I didn't know any better. And one day we just stopped talking about him, adding him to the long tally sheet of important things we did not understand or discuss together, me and my father. I was not the first, not even quite the only, just barely the second. It's no fun being second best when you're the only one in the contest.

I was even, for a time, inspired to get good grades when I found out how little respect my father had for me learning the wrong things, but then they lost their allure for me too when I discovered that it was really just paperwork. Once I looked beyond the veneer of vaunted reputations and famous professors who mostly left teaching to assistants while they wrote, I realized that no matter how inspiring it was to displease my father, the price of the education wielded little impact on the learning. And though there was so much to learn, there are not always people to teach.

I had sought refuge in academia, believing that it was not only far from my father but also that it would offer me, for the first time in an otherwise itinerant life, a clean blank state. I had been wrong. Princeton was peopled with privileged legacies, guys with III and IV at the end of their names, those who already knew one another from Andover or Exeter or lesser prep schools or yachting camps and country clubs or the Hamptons. The same people who had always been popular were popular still. I began to see that college, like society, is constructed to distill groups down to their purest elements and that everyone wants to sit at the right table, but like the Hamptons, there are wrong sides and right sides and less seats at the right table than there are people who want them. Even at the popular table, someone has to be the least popular. The Ivy League was not as hard as I'd thought it would be, though my academic career was marked with mediocrity. No one sets out for mediocrity, it just has a way of happening to most people.

It wasn't a degree in English Lit from an Ivy-walled university in the cold climes of the East that had set up my life, my career. It was the moving, the urge to be somewhere else, one which I had fought but ultimately come to accept, that had surprised—and saved—me. I was an expert at getting people to go places because other people had always made me go other places.

With the dawn of the twenty-first century, tourism was the world's biggest industry. Huge fortunes were spent on the task of moving people and their money and their dreams, and I toiled well at it.

The Chicago Convention and Visitors Bureau had plucked me out of the East and the ivory towers of higher learning, and I had stopped learning and started working. And I helped make more people come. More pockets swelled and statistics were tallied.

Long after I began to grow weary of the broad shoulders of the Midwest but before I picked up the deep values of Middle America, Las Vegas lured me out west.

Another Convention and Visitors Association: the LVCVA. An oasis of neon in the desert about as far from the values of the Midwest as you could get. A place with almost no values and nothing real, thus beloved in the way that people love illusion and a lack of reality. I helped reposition Sin City as a family destination, helped make it "America's Way to Play."

I was particularly proud of that feat of gamesmanship. Gambling, bars open all night, free drinks, topless women in headdresses and high heels, Siegfried and Roy making elephants and bank balances and everyday morality disappear; sure, wake the kids, phone the neighbors, head off to Vegas.

Barnum was right, there was one born every minute, and on this time-tested principle. people kneeled before the altars of green baize gaming tables and eagerly pushed their colored chips forward and thanked the dealer and had another free drink and waited for the next face card or roulette ball or three cherries to line up. It was all a big game. That was one of the first things I'd been told in Vegas, it was always "gaming," never gambling. People wanted to play games, they just didn't want to know they were gambling. Whether or not they were. That's why there were insurance companies and casinos. So everyone could delude themselves into the powerful mystery of pretending they did not know what might happen. But the same things kept happening, all the same, just to different people.

Then San Francisco wanted me after an earthquake temporarily scared off too many visitors. I went and the people came back. Oh, I knew it wasn't because of me but someone had to work at it and the rewards had to be thrown somewhere, and, surprising me as much as anyone, my skill at restlessness was a valuable commodity, an expertise of sorts. I was as restless as the next guy, hell, maybe more so, but I was well-compensated for it.

The funny thing is, you would think, or at least I had in the beginning, that working on travel tourism would require you to learn much of the place you touted, to explore and find its hidden gems and un-touristed special spots. Rubbish. If one thought that, one would be wrong. It has been my experience that one often is.

Very few people travel to get off the beaten track and discover new places. People travel to collect clichés. Guide books, television, Hollywood, and myriad other mass media had made everything vaguely familiar, and people went to places to more or less confirm that what they'd seen or heard was true. The Golden Gate Bridge. There it stands. Just like in the movies. Sears Tower, tall, just like they said. Used to be the tallest in the world. A pyramid or a castle or even a Venice in the desert. There it sits, even if it shouldn't. This little restaurant Arthur Frommer wrote about, good indeed, just like he said. In the end, the house always wins at games of chance, just like they say. But people play and move their pieces around the game of life hoping to pass go and collect their money once again. And not everyone uses the convention of free parking. There's not much of it in most places.

Hell, even Columbus with his vague plans and sailing westward, an Italian explorer funded by the throne of Spain seeking a path around the world to India, said, yesiree, Indians, just like I thought. He reinforced his mistake with his preconception. As you do.

There had probably been a sailor sitting on the Santa Maria writing away in his cramped quarters at night: "Autumn is definitely the best time to visit the New World. Make sure when you go to pack good walking shoes. And a gun. Try to at least pick up a few words of the local lingo, please, thank you, these things will serve you well, though the native dialect is limited. They don't even have a word for smallpox. Save time for souvenir shopping, as there are some nice trinkets and the best value is all the free land, which they do not own at all, so help yourself. Do make it a point to see the locals in their quaint native costumes which are quite lovely and mostly all hand made. You can see most of the major sights very quickly if you avoid high season, when of course the place grows crowded with the English and Dutch and French, it being chic with such colonial peoples nowadays."

My resume in tourism, or cliché gathering for the various tourism organizations for which I'd toiled, was all blue chip geographical stocks, and unlike the Dow or the NASDAQ, with the addition of Venice to my portfolio, it could only continue to soar.

Yes, I thought, I navigated in some pretty good circles. Though I wondered if life were meant more to resemble a circle or perhaps a straight line. Was it a line with birth and death at either end or a smudged circle of ashes to dusty ashes? Should have paid more attention in Geometry. Mr. Carrol was right about that, though I doubted he'd have proffered any illumination on the geometric shape that life, or a life, should have taken. And anyway, was a line even a geometric shape? Did a life have a shape of its own, or take the shape of its surroundings like gas or water? Or perhaps, and seemingly more likely, have no shape at all? Or happen to be the wrong shape for the proverbial hole? Or was that pegs? I was wholly confused about that.

I should have asked Brent Wilkins, who let me copy off him in Geometry, but he might not have told me. He'd made me promise to never tell anyone he had the highest IQ in the school. He was very private about his knowledge. Nice of him to let me look over his shoulder, though. He got me an A in Geometry. Little good it had done me. Our lots had been thrown together that year in math class due to the alphabet rather than arithmetic. Though behind him in IQ points, I was ahead of him in our alphabetized seating charts. Even though V, the first initial of my last name, Vandermar, is very far back in the alphabet.

For a short time in my youth, my father had tempered my frustration with being so far back in the alphabet when he told me the proud heritage of our name, which meant in Dutch, "Prince of the Sea."

It was years later when I found out it meant only "of the sea," so I was not a prince, nor even of the sea. I was used to never correcting him, so I failed to do so in this instance too. Nonetheless, I took pride in knowing the humble origins of our shared name, however meaningless the knowledge was. Perhaps just for the simple fact that my father, like the Marines, was not a big believer in knowledge for its own sake. There was supposed to be a reason for everything you learned.

FOUR

UNCHARTED WATERS

LACKING FRIENDS IN THE OFFICE or elsewhere in Venice, I spent many days wandering the winding little streets and got lost continually, but always managed to find my way back to the Canale Grande and then you were never too far from home, no matter how far from home you really were.

I took drinks and newspapers in many campos, savored being unknown while sipping a caffè macchiato or a small glass, un ombra, a shadow, the Venetians said, of Valpolicella or Nero Rosso or whatever wine the waiters deigned to bring me. I strolled across the small bridges of the city and worked on tailoring a new costume for my existence, one that I could fit well and which would be my own design.

There was an enchanting freedom in the anonymity of being abroad, a compelling elixir of exile brewed from being outside the culture. No one knew you or expected anything from you, you didn't get junk mail, or if you did, you didn't understand it, so could throw it away with reckless abandon. There were fewer forms to fill out, and while I guess there were just as many societal conventions, you didn't follow them because you didn't know what they were. There was a certain sharp pleasure in not well understanding the things that went on around you, in not being an intrinsic part of them, but participating in them all the same. It was like the delight of being a child in a new setting where you saw and wondered about everything as if you'd never seen it before and might not ever see it again, everything new and fresh and mysterious.

Little was wanted or expected of me by anyone at work and I wasn't sure if I would even try too hard to make a go of it and fight the uphill slope of the bureaucracy and office politics that had converged to consign me to this faraway land, but I enjoyed the freedom of not being expected to be a vital cog in any machine, and particularly in Venice, the alluring absence of machinery. There was a glory in the absence of cars and car alarms and parking permits and all the noises that you took for granted and just a wonderful absence of distractions, albeit a clear lack of focus.

My biggest decision the first month was which café to call my own. A man's bar is an extension of his personality, and it's every bit as important he choose the right bar as the right friends or the right mate. For a long while, I'd had all the right friends but then they became boring to me, or I to them. Too many conversations included talk of mortgage rates or new babies, too many people told you on the phone that someone else said hello to you and waited for you to say, "Tell so-and-so I said hi, too." You had to do it no matter how inane you found it, and it made you start being frustrated with them and then with yourself for being bothered by the few people who crossed your own life's path so regularly.

I had made many wrong choices, but in the matter of the bar, I picked well.

Truthfully, I hadn't picked it myself at all. I had been lost, again, and slowly making my way in the direction I thought was toward my apartment, but had grown used to the fact that in Venice you often had to go the wrong way to get to your destination. It was just the way of things. Like how to get from the Atlantic to the Pacific through the Panama Canal you had to go east, not west.

This particular afternoon, for no reason at all, I was following a black and tan shepherd mix mutt. He looked well fed but had no collar and I was curious whether or not he was a stray and had determined to follow him home, or to wherever he might call home.

I was somewhere deep in the bowels of the Dorsoduro and away from the steady stream of tourists en route to St. Mark's or the Guggenheim and there was no one else about, just me and the stray shepherd. The dog had noticed me following him and seemed to be leading me. I guess that was his job, after all, what he'd been bred for. If he had been bred.

At one point, he trotted decisively across a little ponte over a small canal whose name I didn't know and when I got to the arch of the bridge, I had lost him. I stood there for a second, and not knowing which calle he had gone down, lit a cigarette and gave up. While I was crushing out the ember of my cigarette in the stones, I couldn't bring myself to toss it into the canal waters like the Venetians did, he came trotting back quickly, looking for me, and ran right up to my feet.

"Ciao, doggie," I said, feeling stupid standing on a bridge alone, talking to a dog, moreover, a dog whose language I didn't speak, a dog who probably knew more Italian words than me.

I reached down and let him smell my hand and he arched up his head to be pet and I said, "Do you have a home, little doggie?"

I scratched behind his ears and he let out a little bark and made a small gesture off in the direction he'd come and looked back at me to follow. A dog that smart, a dog who spoke more Italian than me, even if he didn't speak, a dog like that needed a name. I couldn't think of a good Italian name but a noble beast like that couldn't just be called doggie. Smart foreign shepherd strays deserve a measure of respect.

In dire need of a good and true companion, I christened him Sancho, probably the best companion in the history of literature. I tried it out on him.

"Sancho, here boy, Sancho," and snapped my fingers and wished I had something to feed him, but he came anyway—is there anything truer than a dog?

He trotted back to me and then nudged me along with him and we wandered almost purposefully to a bar with a dark wood exterior and a long Italian name in words I didn't understand, but he stopped at the door and the place was thereafter Sancho's to me, and Sancho and I went in. He cavalierly let me go in first and I wondered if maybe he was the café owner's dog or if perhaps they would say something about him, but he wasn't and they didn't. There were five long wooden tables along the wall and an old mahogany bar and a glass case filled with elegant Italian sandwiches. Sancho went and threw himself down comfortably in the corner and I went to the bar and ordered an Amaro, senza ghiaccio, and took it over to the corner table in front.

It was still early, but for some reason the bar was closing, you never knew why and I didn't, but I paid for my brandy and me and Sancho left. I gave him half of a cappicola sandwich I'd smuggled out in my jacket pocket and he gobbled it down in one bite and licked my hand.

I scratched his head and we went on towards my apartment and he followed along with me, and I wondered if I would be doing a good deed or breaking someone's heart if I took him home with me. There was a fine line, it seemed, between helping and hurting.

Sancho matched me stride for stride through the little calle all the way to the Zattere and we both looked over across the water to the island of Giudecca and turned left towards my apartment and home. The Zattere was busy with people hopping on and off the vaporetti, heading to and fro, like Michelangelo, or was it talking of

Michelangelo? I didn't remember, but I knew it was J. Alfred Prufrock and I was glad to at least know that. I quoted a little to Sancho and I guess he grew weary of poetry, who didn't really, and who wanted to measure out their life in coffee spoons, but that was the whole point wasn't it? At least it rhymed. I thought about telling Sancho about how Frost had said writing poetry that didn't rhyme was like playing tennis without a net, but I didn't know if he liked Frost.

At the last vaporetto stop before I got to my canal, the Rio San Trovaso, just a few hundred yards from the church of the same name and my apartment, a water bus stopped, the express to the Lido, and some well-dressed Veneziani rushed on and Sancho bolted off full speed onto the bustling boat. I guess Sancho had somewhere to go, and evidently, smart as he was, he didn't even know or care that dogs had to be leashed on the vaporetto. Old Sancho didn't even think of stopping to buy a ticket. He was, like his namesake, a cynical old bastard.

I watched Sancho's boat head off towards the Lido until I lost it in the low-lying mists of the Lagoon. Sancho was my first Venetian friend and I was going to miss him. There were plenty of Quixotic quests in this world and lots of windmills to tilt at, but if you didn't have a Sancho Panza by your side, you were just a crazy old man all alone.

I went home and made some pasta. Alone.

I spent the next weekend wandering around the Lido hoping to run into Sancho, but I never saw him again. Probably he had a nice place on the coast with a warm bed, and maybe he went duck hunting in the spring, or whatever it is the dogs of the Lido did in the springtime. It was winter in Venice still and I didn't know then.

FIVE

WHAT NEWS ON THE RIALTO

I KEPT GOING TO WORK, and though I didn't make any friends in the Ufficio Turismo, my emailed reports to the EU were well received and must have been seen by the right people since they even sometimes came back to me as forwarded emails from other bureaucratic drones.

There was no water cooler to gather around for gossip in the old palazzo confines of the Ufficio Turismo, but the hallway talk was all of America starting another war. Of course there was the already waging and unwinnable war on terrorism, but then we Americans found out that there was an Axis of Evil and yet still other wars to fight. Though Iraq hadn't done anything to the U.S. since the last time we waged war to save Kuwait, evidently it had to be stopped before it kept not doing anything to the U.S. any further. Who knew what they might not do to us?

You wouldn't have peace, the argument went, as far as I followed it, until you fought a war, which sounded more than vaguely Orwellian to me, but you were meant to go along with it, both in 1984 and in 2002. The crisis of confidence at home, the talk of unwinnable new wars, and the multi-billion dollar bookkeeping "errors" that plagued American business weakened the dollar for the first time in years and my salary, paid in euros, grew, so I even got a raise of sorts.

There was a girl in the office, there's always a girl, maybe her name is Tracy or Inge or Genevieve, it doesn't matter. This one's name was Alessandra and she worked hard—and successfully—at being both beautiful and scornful in that way Italian women have mastered through the ages.

She was determined to make a reformed American of me, a new and improved version of the Americanness she found so distasteful.

I'd heard that her family had been Doges, had been listed in the Libro d'Oro, the coveted gold book that meant theirs was, or had been, one of the most powerful families in the world, and though no one called her Contessa or anything, she acted like they should. She was stunning but well-steeped in a fog of expensive perfume and lost nobility.

She stopped in my office regularly to complain to me about the previous days international events.

With little enthusiasm and less conviction, I found myself again doing something I'd done before: defending an indefensible position. I was sitting at my desk staring out a small window at the graffiti on the British Consulate across the Grand Canal. I'd been there, Venice, not my desk, for months and expected most every morning to arrive and see that the graffiti was gone. Only so far it hadn't been. Gone, that is. Every morning, it was still there, and so was I. It seemed both I and the graffiti were stuck in places we shouldn't have been.

Alessandra sat on my desk hovering over me like she did with the typical Italian disdain for personal space and work. Actually, I wasn't sure if she did it so she could look down at me, so she could annoy me, or so that I could see the long, lean lines of her thighs. Perhaps a little of each. I complied by looking up at her, being slightly annoyed, and staring at her legs. She spoke English pretty well, albeit with a strong accent, but it was kind of captivating.

She was crossing her legs and talking about a Palestinian Rights Protest that afternoon in Campo Santa Margherita.

"As an American, Mark, it is, I think, very important that you go. Don't you think it so?"

When discussing work matters with me she fell into calling me Marco, but when disdaining my Americanness, I was again relegated to Mark.

I stared at the graffiti some more then back at Alessandra. She was wearing a leopard-spotted blouse that did little to hide her cleavage. Neither did she, for that matter.

"I'm not really a protest kind of guy," I said.

"That's the problem with you Americani. All the same. You think to do whatever you want and think nothing about it. Not even to think," she said.

I thought about it while she went on.

"For you Americani, the rest of the world is a place to drop the bombs, to drill for the oil, and to build the McDonald's."

Alessandra had a somewhat exaggerated sense of how productive I was. She had used the accursed McDonald's gambit before. This was the point I was supposed to apologize for all the evils of American society that I, as the only American in the office, was personally responsible for. Only I was getting a little tired of being apologetic.

Lately it seemed like every time the son of Bush Sr. stuck his head out of the political foliage and opened his mouth, I had to apologize to someone. It didn't matter to them, not at all, that I hadn't voted for him or his father. Nor that I didn't want my country to bomb innocent Iraqis any more than Sixties flower children, with all their radical peace and love ideas, had wanted the Army to napalm entire Vietnamese villages. I wasn't sure exactly when it was that peace and love became radical ideas. Perhaps they always had been and I had not been made privy to the knowledge.

Consigned to that faraway office, I had tried agreeing: Yes, Bush was an idiot, a warmonger, the dumbest world leader ever. I agreed to this and more, which was easy to do since it was true. Still, for them I was America and much of this was my personal fault. The sins of my country were my sins, and in a way I think I knew she was right. Like the country I lived in, I was sinful.

"Alessandra, I have a lot of work to do," I said, which we both knew to be a lie as little of importance sat on my tiny desk and my screen saver blinked on and off, unmolested.

She stood up in a huff and glared at me with undisguised contempt, which was a good look for her and I rather enjoyed it. The look, not the contempt.

"Ciao, Contessa," I said.

I turned toward my computer, then looked back when a crumpled up piece of paper hit me in the back of the head, only she was gone. If there had been a door to my little office, I'm sure she would have slammed it.

While I unfolded the yellow paper projectile, I could hear her in the hall, "…tipico Americano bruto…porco imperialisto…tutto pazzo…"

I may well have been a typical American, I hadn't voted for Bush, but neither had most Americans. I might well have been totally crazy. I was pretty sure that I wasn't an imperialist pig, though. I didn't feel like one at the time. A sovereign state of Israel, that seemed right. A Palestinian homeland, well, that sounded about right, too. Limited withdrawal from the West Bank, I didn't even know what it meant, but maybe that was right, too. Hell, maybe, just maybe, everyone was right. Or they were all terribly wrong.

One thing I knew was that a religious zealot—no matter which god he prayed to, whether he banged on your door shoving forward a Book of Mormon, or was a witness of Jehovah, or glared at you from a television pulpit on Sunday TV asking you to send money, or was huddled in a cave in the mountains—seemed to cause a lot more pain in the world than good. Also that it was pretty hard to understand the disdaining of ancient heathen cultures and their human sacrifices as barbaric when killing in God's name seemed as rampant as ever, despite love thy neighbor being a common precept to all religions, however deeply they managed to bury it. I wasn't sure exactly what it was about divinity and an afterlife that translated into life having to be bad. But then I wasn't an interpreter.

Likewise, I couldn't make out all the Italian on the protest poster Alessandra had fired at me, but enough to get the gist that as an American I might not have been the guest of honor had I attended, no matter what my convictions were. Since I didn't actually know what they were anyway, I crumpled it back up and tossed it in my garbage can, making a silent bet with myself that if I made it, there would be no war in the Middle East. It was a perfect shot, nice arc and straight in. For a fleeting instant, I was Jordan in the play-offs...until it bounced off the rolled up pages of my morning Herald Tribune and landed unceremoniously on the hardwood floor.

There are days it doesn't pay to read the paper, it was all bad news, and then you threw it away and it stuck out of the little garbage can in your office and blocked your shot with the silent ferocity of Shaquille O'Neal, and there was going to be another war in the Middle East and it was all your fault somehow and you couldn't do a damned thing about it. Or you thought you couldn't, so you didn't. There was always going to be another war.

It seemed too early in the day and too late in the week to be responsible for the sins of the world. 11:00 am on a gray Friday, also too late for the second Italian coffee break but too early for the long Italian lunch. I wasn't Italian though. I'd answered all my emails and read several not very funny forwarded ones that were supposed to have sent me into howls of delight, and across the little ripples of the gray-green waters of the Grand Canal, the British Consulate and the graffiti were still there, so I got up and left.

∞ ∞ ∞

I went to Campo Santa Lucia and had a macchiato and a cigarette and pondered my place in the world. I didn't figure it out, but the coffee, as always in Venice, was excellent. If you ordered a caffè corretto, you got a little espresso with a splash of Amaro. It seemed like a good thing to do, so I did. Sometimes a little brandy in your late morning coffee is just the thing to quench the strong thirst of imperialism, though I guess tea or gin and tonics would have sufficed as well.

I finished my coffee just as it started to drizzle outside, driving the window shoppers and businessmen inside, and I started to feel crowded, so I buttoned up my new coat, grabbed my packet of Stuyvesant's and left some small euro coinage on the marble bar and walked out in the rain.

Most of the shops were beginning to close for lunch and the myriad purveyors of souvenirs were bringing in their postcard racks and pulling out their umbrella displays. The Venetians have been merchants for 1500 years and they were nobody's fools. I had two umbrellas already, one at my apartment in the Dorsoduro and one at my office, but neither with me. Living in San Francisco, I'd long ago learned umbrellas had an impertinent attitude about rain. If you were at home and it was raining, your umbrella would be at the office. If you were at work and Mother Nature started spitting out of the sky, your umbrella would be safely ensconced at home. It had long ago become apparent to me umbrellas just didn't like the rain.

I stood near the statue of some Venetian hero in the rain wondering if it would stain the soft leather of my new winter coat. It was looking pretty blotchy, but it was leather, so surely it had been rained on when the original owner of the pelt wore it. I remembered Seinfeld making the case very clearly: leather comes from cows and cows do spend most of their time outdoors.

People rushed by me fleeing the rain while I appreciated the warm feeling a little brandy gave you on an empty stomach. I held out my hands and looked up at the sky, blinking a little, but letting some of the more determined drops land on my face and felt the brandy and the wind and the rain fight it out inside me. It seemed like a pretty good contest at first, but it had only been a small brandy and the sky was spitting with a bit more determination. I had the feeling that people were watching me, questioning why I just stood there in the rain, but I looked all around the campo and no one was.

I wished I'd been smart enough to bring one of my umbrellas with me or at least to get out of the rain, but I hadn't been. Funny too, because both of them, my umbrellas, were small and compact and one of them even had a nice little clasp that attached itself perfectly to the belt on my jacket, like I envisioned a dagger would have felt. The ever-practical Venetians rarely went anywhere in January without an umbrella, but it had always struck me as a bit pessimistic to bring one along all the time, no matter what the weather. Was it realism or pessimism? Pessimists always said they were realists, but I rarely believed them. Did that make me a cynic? Was there a line, however blurry, between cynicism and pessimism? Anyway, I was old and smart enough to know a lot of people deluded themselves. I smiled. Deluded. I was getting diluted by the rain. Not deluded, though. Standing around in an anonymous Venetian downpour, there's no one else to pretend to be amused by your own feeble jokes. I thought for a second that it would be a fine thing to stand there in the campo and shout out:

"I'm not diluted!" but I couldn't decide whether diluted or deluded was more droll or even which was more true, so I didn't say anything. I might have though, but I had grown used to leaving things unsaid.

I turned away from my small delusions of grandeur and decided the thing I needed was a long, full-size umbrella, more like a cane. That would be a fine thing to have. Next to the Café Rosa Salva was a stand with a beautiful wood handled umbrella for 20 euros, and in a simple trade of a bland blue 20 euro bill, it was mine. The fabric was dark brown and sort of kelly green, or maybe hunter green, I wasn't sure which was which, but it was stylish and just the right height for me. It reached from my hand right down to the ground.

I walked back out into the campo and it was now really raining, but I was already soaked and I was curious whether or not the leather could weather the weather. I thought that was kind of punny too, at the time. If you're lonely enough your amusement standards can become quite low.

My new umbrella was just the right height for a walking stick, so I walked. Left foot, umbrella, right foot. Perfect. I headed toward the Rialto and on the way there convinced myself that if I opened up the umbrella, it would definitely stop raining, and then I'd just have to close it up. So I determined not to give in and neither I nor Mother Nature did, all the way to the Rialto. I wanted to cross the bridge, but then I'd be on the wrong side of the canal from my office and figured that I might not go back, so I turned around, and then I had a sudden strong taste for McDonald's.

I went in and ordered one of the Menu Due and two ketchups, which cost extra. When I saw the price I understood that the young kid at the counter had given me two, due, of the menu one: the Big Mac menu, rather than one of the number two: the Quarter Pounder menu. It seemed like it was mainly my own fault so I paid up and grabbed both the bags. There were no open tables downstairs and I thought that it would be a fine thing to have a Big Mac on the Rialto in the rain. So off me, my two Big Macs, and my new umbrella went. For some reason, everyone else was going the other way and I had to keep ducking my head to avoid the pointed umbrella tips.

Usually the Rialto was busy during the day, but the rain and the lunch hour had driven everyone away. I got to the top of the bridge and was faced with the weighty decision of which side to face; up canal, to the right, looking towards the colorful stalls of the Pescheria and the imposing Ufficio Postale; or downriver, left, where there was the Palazzo Dandolo and the distant invisible dome of the Salute. I went to my left, like Jordan.

The Canal was unusually tranquil, no gondolas out in the rain, just the little ripples of the raindrops and the wake of a crowded vaporetto. I set down my brown McDonald's bag on the wide, centuries old marble railing of the bridge and leaned my umbrella against one of the pillars and lit a cigarette. There was a small sense of poetry borne of standing on the Rialto in the rain and I felt proud that I had been right. I had not opened my umbrella and it had not stopped raining.

I reached into the bag and grabbed one of my Cokes and took a sip. I considered myself a connoisseur of cola and something about the European McDonald's Coke was different than the American. It was less fizzy, and I wondered if there was a different recipe or if America was just less effervescent the further you were from it. Probably both. And less ice here, of course, and I was pretty sure the straws weren't as big in diameter as back home. Still, it was a watered-down taste of home even if Heraclitus was right and you could never drink the same cola twice. Different, but good. I took a long pull of the Coke and flicked the straw wrapper into the Canal. I felt a bit guilty about adding to the litter, but it was a big canal and a small piece of paper and there was already a lot of debris drifting along in it anyway, so maybe I was just seeking comfort in crass conformity.

I'd read Byron used to swim in the Canal every day when he'd lived in Venice. That would have been a display of Byronic heroism to witness, even if it wasn't where the term came from. They never taught you the good parts of the stories in school.

I finished my smoke and ground it out on the marble balustrade of the bridge and held on to the crushed remnant in an effort towards nonconformity to the local lowest common denominator. Another vaporetto came by heading up the canal and I counted the people who got off but lost track at seven as the umbrellas opened and shielded them from the rain and from my vaunted view. As the vaporetto took off, I pondered what would happen if I sort of elbowed my Big Macs right on top of it, but it never quite came in my target range, so I was spared being faced with the impudence or bravery or impetuousness that it took to do something purely banal and stupid. I was glad to be spared the choice, only I had long held the conviction that silly senseless acts were some of man's most glorious opportunities, even if they weren't mine.

A man in a battered black coat and a furry cap like Russians wore came up and asked me for a cigarette, at least I thought he did, but what he wanted was a light, so I handed him my lighter, even though I knew the Europeans always lit the cigarettes of others, I always felt awkward lighting a smoke for a guy. I mean you never saw Bogart or Gable doing that. I wasn't sure if he was hungry or homeless, it was pretty hard to tell, but I called back to him.

"Signor, desidero Big Mac?"

He looked at me strangely and just walked off. I wasn't hungry anymore, but I didn't know what to do and didn't feel obliged to get out of the rain. I grabbed what remained of my Big Macs and my umbrella and tossed the Cokes into the trash can and, lacking any other destination, headed back to the office. By the time I got there, I was drenched and the bag was dripping, just barely containing its contents. I went into Alessandra's empty office and left the McDonald's bag in a little puddle on her desk. I was going to leave a clever note but couldn't think of anything very clever.

Then I didn't know what to do. Didn't feel like eating, didn't feel like working and I was cold and wet. I began to wish I was back in San Francisco and it was Friday afternoon and we were taking off for happy hour down at Rocky Sullivan's. Only in San Francisco it wasn't even Friday morning yet and everyone was still asleep. There was nothing to do at the apartment either, no cable TV, no one waiting for me to get home. I should get a dog, that's what I should do. Then I'd have someone to go home to. A Venetian dog and we could learn Italian together. Oh, Sancho, wherefore art thou?

Instead, lacking a local Rocky Sullivan's or a dog or cable TV, I decided to go out and get drunk. I'd found action could often substitute for progress. I felt a strong urge to be back on the same side of the canal as my apartment, for no reason at all, maybe it was just the urge to be on the other side of something, or the urge to be somewhere else. Or maybe I was just a neighborhood kind of guy, whether it was the Inner Richmond in San Francisco or the Dorsoduro. So I crossed the wooden Accademia Bridge and walked past the graffiti of the British Consulate, again very surprised that neither the Brits nor the Venetians had done anything about it. On the way, I pretended I'd been shot in the leg back in the war and needed the umbrella to walk, and it kept raining. It was the kind of thing you would only do if you were all alone, thousands of miles from home and didn't know hardly anyone, hence it was just the kind of thing for me to do just then. I was pleased with my pointless personal charade.

I limped into the Campo Santa Margherita, which was close to home and had some good bars, but they were unusually crowded, so I passed them by and headed to Sancho's, the bar that was not called that and where the dog who I had named never was anymore, but which nonetheless had become sort of a center of gravity for me. I had some Averna, senza ghiaccio, and proceeded to get busy getting drunk. Good to have a goal. A lesson learned from my grandfather, a barber and a deacon, "Without a vision, the people perish."

∞ ∞ ∞

I was thinking about how I'd been drinking brandy, cognac specifically, with Jack Bindman's wife the night before I found out I was getting transferred to Venice. We'd been sleeping together for some time—did it count as an affair if you weren't the one married? Really, she'd been sleeping with me more than me with her, and though I secretly felt it should have been otherwise, the betrayal seemed to bother me more than her. Anyway, having an affair with another man's wife had seemed pretty grown up even if it was wrong and you knew you shouldn't be doing it, but that's how it was with all the good things: drinking, smoking, sleeping in, staying up too late, sneaking into the wrong bed. You knew they were wrong and maybe that's why you did them.

To me, it had seemed illicit and more than a little stupid and risqué to have a tryst with your boss' wife. Even though I knew no good would come of it, I didn't expect any, so there was little doubt of being disappointed in that regard, and there certainly was an added element of excitement right up until that night at Enrico's in North Beach, where we sat sipping Courvoisier after finishing an elegant secret supper when Jack walked in. My boss and her husband.

He strode purposefully over to our table and I wondered for a minute if he was going to hit me, if I should stand up in case he wanted to, which I guess I deserved. I stayed seated and so did she and he loomed over the table quietly as the three of us shared a silent moment of ponderous awkwardness.

He ignored me and glared at his wife and I had no idea what I was supposed to do, having already done so much that I hadn't been supposed to. I didn't know who to look at so I focused on the small shadow the amber colored cognac cast on the white linen tablecloth.

"Karen. Let's go. Now."

What I thought was very sophisticated was the way she didn't look at him or at me and drained her cognac, set down the glass and got up and walked out. Insouciant. That was the word. He turned and followed her out the restaurant and it was a damned graceful exit.

It's pretty tough to look cool when your boss has just intruded and absconded with your dinner date who happened to be his wife and you're left sitting alone at a table. Try it some time. It's like sitting at the wrong cafeteria table in school when you know everyone's looking at you and your wrongness and it shows.

I saw the tuxedoed waiter staring at me and I made the little writing signature in the air for the check and he smirked. He had one of those too-perfectly trimmed moustaches but it didn't hide the sneer at all and I guess that wasn't its job. That look would certainly be reflected in his tip. I'd get him.

The dinner bill was $245, mainly due to some vintage Chateauneuf du Pape that Karen insisted I try, and I didn't have enough cash. While I was thumbing through my credit cards trying to remember which I owed the least on, I reflected briefly that I was likely to be out of work the morrow and decided to put it on the company card. My boss had been there, however briefly, after all. That was business, in its sordid way. And damn it, they were his wife's expensive taste buds and illicit instincts.

When the check came, I thought about stiffing the waiter and then decided a grand gesture was more appropriate. I filled in the tip box with $255. You only live once. Bet he wouldn't sneer at that, more than a 100% tip. My last supper for $500 on the corporate Amex. Funny thing is I hadn't eaten much at all and I realized I was pretty hungry as I signed my name and took back my silver colored platinum card made of plastic. That guy at the pool party in The Graduate had been right, the future was all plastics.

While I stood up, the sneering waiter glanced at the bill and then toward me, raising one eyebrow. I'd always wished I could do that.

"Has there been some mistake?" he said.

"Lots of them," I said, and went home into the murkiness of the night, which well matched my mood and future.

My message machine blinked at me but I had little faith in it sharing any good news and less fortitude to respond to anyone anyway, so I decided to have a beer and go to sleep and think about it all tomorrow. When the alarm went off at 6:30, I wasn't that excited to get up and face the day, so I turned it off instead of hitting the snooze alarm per usual and rolled over and went back to sleep with my dread of the day to come and my guilt from the ones that had passed, blanketed in a down comforter that offered little solace.

I was kind of proud that I slept so late and so soundly, even if I didn't deserve the sleep of the just. I finally got up at a little after ten, showered and shaved and then debated if I should even go in or not, or call, or perhaps just quit before I got fired.

I decided to face up to my mistakes and put on my best suit, a new olive green double breasted and a gold and green checked Hermes tie, and hopped on the Geary Bus and went to work. I spent a long time in front of the building on Front Street thinking about not going in, but in the end I was just too curious about what would happen and truthfully, if Jack wanted to punch me in the mouth, well, I figured I kind of owed it to him to give him the chance.

It was strange how everyone said hello to me like it was any other day, though it wasn't at all. It felt somehow like the day after tomorrow.

On my computer screen there was a Luddite paste-it note from "The Desk of Susan," Jack's secretary, that said simply:

"Jack's office first thing in the A.M."

It was already 11:30, and with little A.M. left in the day and even less enthusiasm, I went to face the music whose score I had started and left for Jack to finish.

As I walked in, I'd wondered if the new suit was a sartorial slip-up since I might have to bleed on it, but as I'd noted there'd been lots of those so I was getting kind of used to them. Besides, the Asian dry cleaners in San Francisco could get anything out. Out damned spot.

I waited. He looked intently at a memo on his desk, or at least pretended to, and then finally spoke:

"I'm giving the Convention and Visitor's account to Sherman."

It wasn't what I'd expected, for a number of reasons, since it was my account and the agency's biggest and because my wall was plastered with the Addys I'd won for my work on it in the past four years.

But you expect some spills when you dip your pen in the company ink. Damned spot had set.

I stood there waiting to be hit, or at least offered to sit down. It seemed kind of ridiculous to defend myself verbally and I knew it wouldn't work anyway. He just stared at me for the longest time and I figured apologizing would be too trite and demeaning for both of us, but then the seconds and the stillness stretched out and the silence filled the space between us and I started to wish he'd say something—yell, or fire me, or just do something, goddamn it. It was like waiting for a bus you knew was scheduled to arrive at a certain moment and you were fine until that moment, just waiting, taking in the scenery, serving your time. But after awhile, you started to wonder when the hell the damned thing was ever going to get there and what the devil was taking so long. It was just this kind of attitude of his that had driven Karen to screw around with me. Infuriating.

Finally he spoke some more. He wasn't a large man but his voice was thick and gravelly and authoritative.

"Susan has some file folders for you. Read them, make your decision, and get back to her by 5:00. That is all."

So there was a choice: a one month severance package, which wasn't the six months I'd been promised with my previous promotion; or a small, insignificant part in a newly acquired shared account, the Venetian Tourism Council, which surprisingly had been landed by a big presentation they'd made in Italy last year and with which I was thoroughly unfamiliar, not to mention some 10,000 miles from home and everyone I knew. I felt pretty young to be put out to pasture, but went willingly anyway, though I knew there were, strictly speaking, no pastures in Venice.

I'd expected to end up fired, fighting, or quitting, but next thing I knew I was on a plane to Venice and in a suite at the Hotel Danieli on the long, lower sweep of the Grand Canal. Still using, for a time, the company Amex. I'd been meaning to make it back to Europe ever since a two-month post-graduate jaunt anyway and it seemed like a better time than most to go. Away. From home.

There had been some complicated bureaucratic finagling since my arrival. I ceased to be employed by my old company which was just and right and really didn't matter but which didn't have the ring of finality that sleeping with the boss' wife should have had, but had got me away from there and over here, which I guess was the purpose.

I was officially an outside consultant of the EU Tourism and Economic Development Council in Strasbourg. I had never met nor spoken with anyone on the council, though they paid my check and reimbursed me for the furnished apartment I rented in the Dorsoduro neighborhood.

They also sent me vast amounts of gratuitous paperwork, all that was entailed in being a small cog in a large and overflowing bureaucracy, which we all are in some way a part. Whether we wish to be or not. No matter who signs our paychecks or whose wife we might or might not have slept with. My company Amex disappeared and was replaced with a nice expense account and a corporate Visa.

It was at first a strange and rather astonishing adventure, like being kicked out, but also kicked upstairs, and it was not altogether unpleasant. Most of it was actually more than damn pleasant. Though sometimes not, but I had learned that such was life. You were kicked or pushed up or down or out, and you went or fell or moved, and there you were. And here I was, deserving of the self-disdain I felt, yet perhaps undeserving of having been able to trade my small and sordid San Francisco sins for surroundings of such somber beauty.

Guilty memories of the mistakes that had gotten me to this place, Venice, floated around in my head while I sat drinking that afternoon in the small bar, while outside, low-lying Adriatic winter clouds rained unenthusiastically on a quiet dark day in the Sestiere Dorsoduro, and though I was a little lonely, and pretty drunk, they weren't entirely unpleasant feelings. Gave me something to do, anyway.

SIX

COLORS OF THE CAMPO

I WOKE UP TO THE clanging of the bells of the Chiesa San Trovaso, which were just beyond my balcony and altogether the wrong thing for a hangover. It was overcast and dreary outside my windows, and from experience born of months of weekend Venetian hangovers, I knew I couldn't win the fight with the bells, so I got up.

I looked through the raindrop-splattered window glass tritely, and could not help observing that Donne was right and the bells did indeed toll for me. When and why they did was a complete mystery. I'd given up trying to work out the system of the bells, which strangely didn't coordinate with any hour or time on the clock or any kind of mass schedule I could figure out. They just pealed and clanged and sounded through the square beneath my balcony and broke the heavy silence of my solitude and my hangover. Though they did nothing to relieve either.

The best thing about the church, besides the sprawling Tintoretto inside, was the fact that it had two separate large entryways since it sat on what had been the border of Venice's ancient feuding clans, the Nicoletti and the Castellani, who would share the same church but not the same door. It was just a short walk from the church to the Ponte dei Pugni, the Bridge of Fists, where you could still see the footholds in the marble where they used to stand and fight each other. Maybe after church. Usually when I went in to look at the Tintoretto, just because it seemed like if you lived next door to a great master's work you should, I went in the Nicoletti door and out the Castellani, but sometimes I did it the other way, just because. Sometimes it was hard to pick a side.

I grabbed my bathrobe and stood there impotently staring out at the steeple until the pealing of the bells stopped, and then shot God and the church the finger, which was part of this little contest I'd been having with the church in Venice. So far, God and the church bells had been winning, but I had concluded that he was intrigued by my irreverence and had vowed to eventually get drunk enough to sleep through a whole Sunday of bell ringing some time soon, a feat that I had decided would be quite an accomplishment and which I looked forward to with relish. I thought God must have gotten pretty tired of the boring piety of people and the trivial prayers and thanks for winning football games or passing math tests.

If God was up there and had made the whole damned crazy world; the giraffes and geraniums, turtles and tulips, sunflowers and sea anemones, zebras and zucchini, red feathered parrots, blue veins of turquoise and lapis lazuli, rainforests and deserts, jungles and meadows, swamplands and highlands, butterflies and butterscotch, flies and scotch; well he clearly had eclectic tastes and an infinite appreciation for all the forms he'd created, so he must have also had an infinite sense of humor and probably drew great amusement from the follies of man. I know I did. Who didn't appreciate a little irreverence now and then? I liked to think I had at least my share of human folly. Whether or not God or Allah or Jehovah or Thor or Zeus took responsibility for it or even noted it or appreciated it, was far beyond my limited horizons.

Having shot God and his bells my middle finger, I had my typical Venetian breakfast: coffee, a smoke, and several expensive Italian aspirin that you could only get by the dozen and only from the Farmacia.

I had another new Saturday tradition, I didn't allow myself to hop in the shower until the ferry to Greece passed by my window, which was generally sometime about eleven, give or take. I couldn't actually see the water from my perch, but the ferry ships were huge, six or seven stories, and I lived on the fourth floor and my windows faced out onto the Giudecca Canal and the ship's bridge was just about eye level with me while I sat at my dining table. It wasn't quite SportsCenter, but it helped mark the time and I'd always been a big believer in tradition. Perhaps because the grand scheme of my life lacked them so profoundly, I sought them out everywhere in the small things. If you were bored and lonely enough, even the trivial could become sacred, the simple, sublime.

The ferry was late that morning, might have been the rain, but I waited and it came finally, slowly creeping along as it was pulled by a little tugboat I knew was there but couldn't see.

Maybe that was what faith was.

The large white ship dragged by and looked looming and out of place behind the buildings across from my balcony, just a few hundred yards beyond my window. It was strange when you could see the ship but not the water. If I'd been a Nicoletti sniper equipped with a high-powered rifle and confident the passengers were all Castellani, I could've gotten some good shots off. But who even knew if there were any Castellani left? Maybe the families and the ancient animosities had all become extinct. The ship crept by me and my window and then finally came the blue and white stripes of the Greek flag, which I had decided, on purely aesthetic reasons, was one of the top three flags in the world, an accolade I knew no one but me would ever hear or care about, but I give credit where credit's due.

As the ship and its blue and white flag fluttered out beyond my vantage point, I was thinking about Greece and how when I was young and trying to please my father by reading military history, I'd fought my way through a heavy history of the Peloponnesian War. I'd been disappointed to find out the Spartans won when they were so clearly the bad guys. Dad had great respect for the Spartans and all winners in general. He was always annoyed with my instincts to root for the underdog, not understanding at all my natural affinity for them.

Another Saturday in paradise. I was living it up in Venice and was starting to get hungry. The proper prescription for my predicament would have been a Pier 23 Bloody Mary laced with shrimp and bacon, followed by huevos rancheros or even a greasy cheeseburger, but alas, I was on the wrong side of the Atlantic to be pacified by San Francisco's pedestrian Pacific pleasures. The grass is always greener on the other side of the Atlantic, I thought, and then wished I had someone to say that to. No doubt some maritime-minded Venetian had thought it and said it long before, even if he pined for other pleasures or sought simpler salves.

With a glance at my lonely fully furnished apartment, none of which belonged to me except the loneliness I had brought myself, I went out into the small world of Venice in search of succor. And a newspaper.

The grayness of the day was lifting, the rain had stopped and the sun fought valiantly to break through the low blanket of clouds, but still I took my new umbrella. There was a kiosk just around the corner from my house, but for some reason I hadn't taken to it and had gotten in the habit of walking past it, through little Campo San Barnaba with its old deconsecrated church, across the small Ponte dei Pugni, where the guy who sold fresh produce from his boat carried out his trade, on past Franco's Bar and into what I considered my campo, sprawling Santa Margherita.

Church bells pealed harmoniously but out of sequence from one another from old stone churches at both ends of the campo and a noisy group of Venetian boys kicked around a dirty soccer ball while a little black dog chased after it barking frantically. The dog was much quicker than the boys but not as skilled in soccer and he ran up and down, back and forth, and I had the sense that they were aiming for him more than any goal, but he was quick and you couldn't tell for sure.

I carefully skirted the edges of their makeshift field on the paving stones of the campo and went to the kiosk in the center to deliberate over the choice of an International Herald Tribune or a USA Today. I knew I'd get more of the news of the world in the Tribune, but the news was never good, and the USA Today was a guilty pleasure and the crossword was much easier, and I wasn't feeling too interested in the machinations of the war-mongers in DC, so colorful simplistic headlines were just the thing. I didn't feel like doing the crossword, anyway. That was two decisions already, which if you've ever been very hungover far from home, you know is not bad at all.

It was around the mid-forties Farenheit, which didn't mean anything to the Celsius society I was in. I'd never figured out the conversion but I knew it was cold. You could add and divide and do the complicated computation, but in the end, you didn't feel any different. Everyone talks about the weather, right? Still, the Venetians loved the chance to be outdoors and all the cafes in the campo had tables set up outside. Musing on the temperature set me to thinking about learning the conversion, then about Farenheit 451, the temperature Mr. Bradbury told you books would burn at. Did they convert it to Celsius when they translated it? If so, what was the title? If not, did they get the significance, even as they burned different books in conflagrations measured by other classifications?

I sat down and thought about ordering a cappuccino. Local protocol dictated that it was a bit late in the morning for steamed milk, but there was no denying it tasted better. When the waitress came over, I tried anxiously to remember if cappuccino was masculine, uno, or feminine, una, or one of the many other cases I hadn't yet figured out. She was quicker than my hungover mind and placed herself before me before I finished recalling what I didn't know or had forgotten. Strategically, I omitted the article.

"Cappuccino, per favore."

She went off to do my bidding. I had a way with women, it was undeniable. While she did, I stared at the colorful little bar graph on the bottom right corner of the USA Today that told me Rotterdam had the world's largest total shipping tonnage. Rotterdam?

My cappuccino pulled into the port of my table, while I digested the usefulness of this information in case I ever decided to become a Greek shipping tycoon. The gravity-defying foam arched above the edges of the cup and sported an elegant sprinkling of cocoa powder, which was a nice touch. Probably the cocoa powder had been unloaded from a ship in Rotterdam. I was feeling pretty savvy just then, for a hungover guy in foreign territory. The cappuccino foam made a meniscus. Or did that just count for liquid? Was steamed milk still a liquid? The answer was not diagrammed anywhere in the paper.

Glancing through the front pages told me the White House was fully engaged in the war on terror, that there was an Axis of Evil, that the world community didn't want the US to bomb Iraq. There wasn't much mention of what the Iraqis thought of being bombed, but I figured it was safe to assume they weren't too thrilled at the idea either. A couple of eggs over easy and corned beef hash would've been good but like many of the good things, was unavailable to me. So I got another cappuccino and a brioche, slyly omitting the article again. The waitress managed to hide her obvious deep appreciation of my mastery of the nuances of Italian, but she was undoubtedly impressed. I could almost feel my pheromones floating around above me like the airy foam on my second coffee.

Next to me sat a well-dressed young French couple, probably on a weekend getaway to Venice, and I avoided them while they cooed lovemaking sounds in guttural French to one another and focused instead on the clarity of the crumbled-empire cadences of a loud group of Brits sitting near the door of the café complaining about how cold it was outside. I laughed at the idea of English people complaining about the weather anywhere, but it was good to hear English. There will always be an England, indeed. Other than the whining of the Brits, the sounds of French and Italian around me went on indecipherable to my ears.

It was pleasant to ignore the English in a Gandhi sort of way. Very passive civil disobedience. It was easy to get lost in yourself when you were surrounded by sounds you didn't understand. It was a comfortable cloud of anonymity, and I wasn't sure if it was more the presence of things I didn't understand or the absence of things I did, but probably they were one and the same. The same difference, whatever that meant. If I'd been sitting next to a beautiful woman who was sharing this slow Saturday with me, I'd have asked that.

"What does that mean, the same difference?"

She'd smile at me and her perfect teeth would show, white as cappuccino foam, and it wouldn't matter what she answered or if she did, but it'd be something to say. Then she would probably want to do something, and so we would. She wouldn't be anyone's wife or no one else's true love. I wondered what color hair she would have and if she painted her toenails or not and how many other people would have known about the mole—beauty mark, I corrected myself, never mole on a woman—on her backside. Probably only me.

But she wasn't there, or maybe she was and I didn't know it, didn't know her and someone else loved her. It was pretty depressing having an unrequited affair with someone you didn't even know over cappuccino all alone in the campo that morning. I decided that probably she snored and nagged and stole all the covers and only read Cosmo and drank carrot juice smoothies and did pilates too early in the morning, watched The View and got all her opinions from Oprah and didn't care about anything important anyway.

Probably I was better off without her. Much. I was one lucky guy. Once I'd finished my coffee and confidently put my love life to rest, I paid my bill and left.

∞ ∞ ∞

Other than the girl I didn't have and no longer wanted because she was superficial and nagging and didn't love me, I could have found anything else, almost, that I could have wanted, right there in Campo Santa Margherita. In this, Venice's second largest campo, one could have and do almost all the things necessary for living. It was that sort of campo and a good place. There was, as in most campos, no glimpse of water, the canals being hidden away behind the houses and shops. Off to one side of the campo stood a lonely little square building, rather like a town hall, which had once been the Guild for the Furriers but was now the office of the local Communist Party.

You could see that campo meant field as the space was long and irregularly shaped, with the broader end dominated by the stony sentinel of an ancient decapitated campanile, once a church and now a college cinema, while just beyond the edge of the long-paved field stood the stern imposing facade of the Carmini church, where there was a Carpaccio and a Veronese, but never any tourists because it wasn't in all the guidebooks and was closed during the frequent daily masses, preferring the age-old business of worship to the admiration of great masters of art and touting of tourist dollars.

Between these looming stone presences, the campo was a small self-contained town. In the middle stood three bare old trees whose buds impatiently awaited the coming of spring, and they were surrounded on all sides by green benches which were the domain of the old men and women who gazed imperiously at the goings on around them every day and always had and always would. Maybe someday they'd be replaced, but it would be pretty easy to do in Venice, replace old people, because there were a lot more old people than young. They were very worried about the declining birth rate and all the young adults moving away. So there was no shortage of old people.

Within the comfortable confines of this long enclosed campo, you could feel the beating pulse of the real life of Venetians. While not as illustrious or grand as Piazza San Marco, it had an authenticity the tourist-dominated Piazza did not. Here life was lived in its simple and stately way, an island within an island that harbored the everyday needs of the locals, and it felt good to bear witness to the marvelous mundanity of it. The wonders of workaday Venice also called for fulfillment of prosaic pursuits and most any and all of them could be accommodated by Santa Margherita.

While the pace and the needs may have been pedestrian, they were all there in these small and insular surroundings. There were two banks, one in a fine old thick timbered house with a security gate and a sign advising you in Italian, French, German and English, to take off hats and sunglasses upon entering; four cafes; three restaurants; two produce sellers at either end; a toy store; a tobacco shop where they sold cigarettes, Snickers, lottery tickets, stationery, and stamps; a sort of drugstore where they sold tape and scissors and art supplies and blankets and coffee makers and computers; a full art supply store with brushes, canvases, easels, and watercolor sets; two gelaterias, one run by a young man and his wife and her sister, even though you couldn't tell which was the wife and which was the sister; a swarthy wine shop beneath the church tower to which you brought your empty plastic 1.5 liter water bottles to be filled from barrels for only three euros, frequented by winos and tough old Venetian ladies and well-dressed businessmen and women, and where the purveyors spoke no English but would let you taste from any barrel before making the important decision of which wine to purchase; a beauty shop; Punta, one of Venice's most crowded and busy grocery stores where the old women tied up their little Venetian dogs in the small entrance alcove so they could bark at each other and passers-by while their owners shopped; a pharmacy where the owner spoke English and had been to New

York and would sell you a package of 12 ibuprofen for 13 Euros and if you told him you had been drinking too much would open an old wooden drawer and get you the 400 mg strength he said you were supposed to have a prescription for and reluctantly sell it to you for 15 Euros and laugh at you and call you his pazzo Americano and where you'd found out that the Italians didn't even have a good word for hangover, they just used mal di testa, the same as headache, which didn't even necessarily imply that you'd been drinking. It made me wonder if Arabic nations had words for hangover, but I'd probably never know.

Center stage of the campo sat a brightly colored kiosk with magazines and newspapers in Italian, French, German, English, Spanish, and several Arabic languages, and lots of pictures of scantily clad women, and comic books for kids all strewn together, and everyday the same old man peering out at you from behind the lurid pictures of the world's film stars and the sordid news of the day.

There was all this and yet the place was never too crowded, people came and passed their time with business or pleasure and left to be replaced by others. There were other things in the campo that came and went too.

If you got there before noon, there was a fish market where they wheeled up the day's catch from the nearby canal behind the church. The still squirming fish, and eels, and other things you didn't know the names of and that didn't look like they wanted to be eaten lay there, living out the final moments of their lives as castaways in colorful displays on the chipped ice. If you stammered, "uh, per favore," and then used your hands and a dumb look because you didn't know the right words for the procedure and also didn't know or want to know how to fillet a fish, the smiling fishmonger turned executioner and chopped off their heads and filleted them for you. And though you had not caught them or gutted them, you'd been complicit in the death so that you might kill an appetite. The Italians, who presumably knew the right words, either preferred the fish heads on or knew how to fillet a fish.

And always, even in this most Venetian of campos, in this real square of Venice, there were random holidaymakers strolling by looking lost with their faces stuck down deep in their Frommer's or their Fodor's or their Routard, reading about the sites they could have been looking up and seeing, generally on their way to grander places and looking for things that somehow weren't there, and almost always preferring the printed page to the reality, but stopping every now and then to take a picture to send home to prove to all their friends they'd really been here, wherever it was, and indeed it was a wonderful place, and now that they had been and had their photos they could go home and cross Venice off their list and brag about it to instill envy and boredom in their friends.

The Venetians came to the campo to live their daily lives, the young boys kicked around a soccer ball, and grandparents bought their grandchildren ice cream and confetti, and much of the detritus ended up on the stones of the campo: colorful confetti, and red and green and yellow smears of gelato licked off cones by too-eager young tongues, and smashed cigarette butts. And the tourists were all heading somewhere else, and there were few better places to sit and sip a drink and watch the world of Venice float by, even though you couldn't see the water.

When Venice's fickle winter sunshine decided to break through the gray blanket of clouds that covered the city in off-season, the path of the light dictated which side of the campo was more popular. As the precious winter rays shone down on one side, they acted like a force of gravity and children playing ball and eating ice cream and adults sipping wine, coffee, or Campari were drawn to the light like moths on a backyard porch light.

Observing the drift of light and people was like watching the movement of the tides, it was natural and inevitable and still astounding. The sunshine seemed an unfair advantage. When there was little or no sun, each café drew its own devotees who sat cozily ensconced looking as if they would never leave, and you wondered if they wouldn't sometimes and made up little stories about their lives in your head and how these people, unlike Americans, had so much time to sit in cafes.

But when the sun broke through, people paid their bills at the shaded tables and naturally went to sit wherever the sun dictated, café owners temporarily blessed by the light set out additional tables and the pace quickened for a moment while everyone drifted over, and then as the sun was dragged across the sky, the people naturally ebbed back to where they started to get the last remnants of sunrays.

When there was no sun, everyplace was equal. The sun, it seemed, was not impartial, but like the others, I followed the drift and became part of it, feeling the innate and simple human urge to be a part of something, some movement, some grander scheme of things, even if I did not understand the scheme or had little confidence in the existence of a Grand Design nor too much appreciation for the sun, having spent winters in Illinois, New Jersey, and of course, summers in San Francisco.

∞ ∞ ∞

One afternoon such as this, when the drift was beginning and the tiles of the campo's intricate mosaic were rearranging themselves, I watched a group of artists pack up their easels and move on to the sunnier climes of the far side of the campo, I guess to touch up the new revelations the light had revealed on the campanile from a better and brighter vantage point across the way. I wondered briefly if they would have to rework everything they had done with these changes, or if they were making up sunlight on their canvases and placing it where they wanted to with all the power of the gods.

I had stopped to watch them several times before and enjoyed the intrusiveness of peeking over someone's shoulder and watching their work, surprised this didn't bother them, though I guess you had to become accustomed to such things if you were going to paint a place like Venice where the world's eyes were always on you and your subject, always judging. I was glad I didn't have to write press releases with anyone looking over my shoulder. I had seen some beautiful art there on the paving stones of Venice and had marveled at one artist rendering a colorful impressionist view of a canal with a gondola that wasn't there, all yellows and oranges and light pastels floating across the canvas, while another would be painting a somber looking portrait of an old man sipping a coffee, and you couldn't see what either artist saw exactly, but they were both good, nonetheless. You wondered who would decide how much they were worth, these paintings, and which tourists or galleries would pay money for them, and where they would hang. You wondered, but you didn't know. Art was elusive.

I watched this group of artists pack up their stuff and drift along in the sun and set up again and grew particularly intrigued by one of them, a girl, who stayed, admiring her determination not to be drawn away by the sun like the others. She seemed resolute and content right where she was, which I appreciated even if I had not often managed it.

When you looked at the artists, you wanted to see them all dressed like Renoir with a little beret and an artist's smock and one of those big, rounded wooden palettes, but they never were. No matter what they painted, they were modern artists after all.

This girl wore simple clothes, artistically distressed jeans tucked into her tall, snug-fitting suede boots, and she had on a black velvet hat, and I could see her chestnut colored hair pulled up under the edges of it, and I sat and watched as she worked diligently on her painting, switching between the brushes she held like chopsticks in her left hand as she created a small world of her own on her canvas. I should buy some art, I thought. Or perhaps I should call over the waitress and send a drink and a sandwich to the girl who might have been a starving artist from Rome or Paris, or wherever starving artists were from nowadays before they came to paint Venice. I decided to go and ask her or at least invite her for a drink. It took more courage than I had, but being bored and alone, I couldn't help feeling I had nothing to lose, which was something like feeling brave.

I wandered over to her very nonchalantly. I was brave and nonchalant, all at the same time, pretending I just happened to find myself standing there where I put myself.

"Scusa, dispiace, uh, forse desidero un café?"

She looked over at me as if I was a bothersome stranger, and I guess I was, so I didn't take umbrage, but in the way of annoying strangers, pretended not to notice her observation. A lesser man would have been daunted, but I wasn't. Never be daunted in public.

"No, grazie," and went back to work.

"Sta bene, dispiace." I said, having nearly exhausted my small repertoire of Italian excuse mes and I'm sorrys, ums, ers, and maybes and feeling pretty daunted, pretty easily thwarted.

Thus humbled and foolish, I went back to my table, which had lost real estate value with the shift of the sun, and sat down, glad at least not to have been seen by anyone else or not to have noticed anyone noticing me, anyway, which was just the same in the end.

The cloud cover had thickened and thwarted the other artists across the campo, who I noted had put away their things, though still the girl kept painting, and she never even looked over to see where I had gone or catch me watching her, so I continued.

As I sat there staring and feeling cowardly and daunted, Mother Nature turned brave or angry and it started raining. Pouring. In a flurry of activity, the clouds unleashed a quick and heavy arsenal of raindrops, Mother Nature having fully committed to her decision to soak the campo.

I watched the girl in the black hat with the reddish-colored hair quickly tilting her canvas away from the rain and trying to hold onto it and her brushes and the painting all at the same time. I could see where the rain made Jackson Pollock-like splashes on her painting that weren't where they were supposed to be at all, and it seemed a terrible intrusion as the colors flowed together and one section that had been all grays and whites and blues turned all murky brown, which was not the color of the painting nor the rain, but was there on the canvas all the same. Thankful I had my trusty new umbrella with me, I dashed over and opened it up and held it over her work, feeling like Sir Walter Raleigh laying down his cloak for the Queen in another place and another time. Chivalry had not died with me. No sir. A coward dies many deaths.

She paid little attention to me and quickly opened her large satchel and placed her painting inside it and closed up her box of paints, and in a moment, the crisis was over and she was packed up, the painting saved, what was left of it, anyway, and I felt again like an intrusion and she looked up at me, folded her little tripod seat and smiled gently. It was a pretty smile, accented on one side by a short and small dimple missing its twin, which somehow made it a better dimple than it might have been otherwise.

Rarity, I knew, was valuable and if there were less of things, they were worth more. Simple economics from Macro-Econ 101 at Princeton. Taught by the TA of some prize-winning economist, so it was true. Had to be.

"Grazie mille, Signor," she said.

"Niente," I said, rather gallantly, I thought, while struggling to find the right Italian words to query her about a drink again. It was tough enough to meet women in your own language, much less one you weren't privy to.

I was still holding the umbrella over her and her things rather than myself, even though she was all packed up, and the raindrops were cold and I was getting drenched, but I kept the umbrella slanted over her, a true patron and shielder of the arts and the artists, and I stood there patron-like getting doused by the rain. The weather. What was the goddamned word for rain? For cold, for wet? You needed so many inanities to communicate in another tongue and I didn't have them. Oh, I had plenty of inane things, of course, just not in Italian. However personal my inanities were, they were foreign where I found myself.

I stuck out my hand.

"Piacere," pleased to meet you, was the best I could do.

She shook my hand and said across light laughter, "I hope your English is better than your Italian."

The comfortable home field advantage of my own language opened up before me while I stood there in the rain, all the thousands of English words I knew, how many thousands of words comprised a healthy vocabulary? I could say anything, I could be clever and witty and charming. Almost anything. All I had to do was overcome a bit of surprise and stupidity and embarrassment. And be clever and witty and charming.

"It's raining," I said.

"How wonderfully observant of you to point that out. Are you going to just stand there getting soaked or should we go inside for a hot chocolate?"

"Hot chocolate," I said.

"You do speak English?" she said.

"Usually, uh, yes."

"I'll take your word for it."

She picked up her satchel and left her other bag of supplies and tripod there, so I grabbed them and struggled with the umbrella and the supplies and felt clumsy and not so much anymore like Sir Walter Raleigh as I followed her inside the café, where in what seemed elegantly simple Italian, she spoke to the waitress.

"Avete cioccolata calda?"

"Certo," the waitress said.

"Due, per favore."

This was a woman who knew her tastes and mine as well.

The waitress brought over two large cups of thick and steaming hot chocolate, syrupy sweet and viscous, nothing like the thinner and blander varieties back home, and I quickly took a drink and burned my tongue but pretended I hadn't. I knew I wouldn't be able to taste anything there tomorrow.

She took out a yellow, paint-splattered chemise cloth from her satchel and handed it to me.

"I thought you might like to dry off."

"Sure, right. Thanks a lot, really," I said, as if I'd never wanted anything so much as to be dry.

I remembered how silly I must look with my wet hair plastered around my skull and ran the soft cloth over my face and across my hair and then brushed it back, hoping it would look sleek and cool like Clark Gable's or Cary Grant's and that perhaps a strand would fall out of place and hang down my forehead and she'd lean over like Myrna Loy or Carole Lombard, or whoever it was that was always leaning over and kissing Clark Gable, and brush it back on my forehead and we'd fall in love and live happily ever after. I'd read once that Cary Grant, when asked what it was like to actually be Cary Grant, had said: "Sometimes I wish I was Cary Grant."

Instead of leaning over toward me, she looked at me with her head cocked like the world's most endearing red-haired cocker spaniel and laughed.

"Just my luck. A girl can't catch a break. Leave it to me to flee America and all things American and land at a café table next to an American. What brings you to this fair city in this foul weather?" she said.

"I'm sort of getting away, too. But working, too. Well, I'm here to get more Americans to come here, part of a long, boring story of an EU tourism committee, call it a job transfer program of sorts."

"Sounds like you're not any better at fleeing than I am. I find life is too short for long boring stories, don't you? But since we're stuck here in the rain, I guess we might as well do something."

I looked outside.

"It is raining pretty hard."

"You absolutely sure you're not some wayward weatherman?"

"Sorry."

"You're apologizing for not being a weatherman?"

"Well, for being foolish."

"Foolish is good. Besides, you're not nearly fat enough to be a good weatherman. Weathermen have to be very fat, don't they? Fat or bald, don't you think? So do share with me the long, boring story of how you didn't become a weatherman. I'm all ears."

She picked up her cioccolata calda and pursed her lips and blew on it before taking a sip and I could see the little ripples her breath made on the surface and she made a small sigh of pleasure when she took her first big sip and looked up at me with those eyes, right at me.

And we shared our stories and it kept raining, and I found out that she had recently quit her job as a graphic artist in L.A. and come to Venice to paint like she'd always dreamed—to be any kind of artist, she said, you had to go to Paris or Italy. It was as simple and clear as that in her mind. And then perhaps to meet her father. So maybe not so simple.

"So, you're Italian, then?"

"No, no, no. I'm American. Born and raised. But my real dad… well, really, I only just found this out myself and haven't told a soul."

"I'm practically soulless."

"Okay, I may as well tell a complete stranger I just met in the rain."

I angled myself toward her conspiratorially and whispered.

"Sometimes complete strangers you meet in the rain are the absolute best ones to tell secrets to."

"Of course, there's always the chance they're axe murderers, too."

"So you're some kind of bigot, prejudiced against strangers and axe murderers, huh?"

"No, just men. Maybe it's just a phase, who knows? Sometimes my inner bitch acts up in the rain." she said and I could tell in the way she said it she didn't paint her toenails or drink carrot juice in the mornings.

"Do you paint your toenails?" I asked, because I was curious, very curious all of a sudden, and of course couldn't see through the suede boots.

She laughed.

"A failed weatherman, foot fetishist, axe murderer."

"But pure of heart," I said.

"Do you paint yours?" she asked.

"No. Your turn."

"Okay, sometimes. Eight of them at least. When I'm going out and wearing open toed shoes."

"Uh, you have eight toes?" I said, trying to sound like it was no big deal, in the way you would if you had lots of friends who were artists and short a couple of toes. Were toes digits? Would eight toes be mementoes of having ten toes? Could women's toes be me-men-toes? Oh, I had so many inanities and none of them served me well.

"No silly," she said, holding up her booted feet and leaving a little puddle under the table, "I have a full set, ten, but I always forget until the last minute and then I put on my sandals and I'm running late, I look down and see my naked toes. So I just grab whatever nail polish is handy and just slap it on and the pinky toe, it's almost impossible to get to and if you're already wearing shoes, you know how it is."

"Ah ha," I said.

"You're familiar with that experience?"

"No, but I like to say ah-ha."

"Are you doing some kind of study, toenails and tourism?"

"I might, I just might. These kind of things can be very important in travel marketing. This might represent an entire un-targeted demographic."

"I'll bet. And you get paid for this?"

"Oh, yes, I'm ridiculously overpaid. That's why I do it, I guess. Well, there were other reasons, like getting to run away from a few problems at home, but, again, long, boring story."

"You seem to have a lot of those."

"Man's got to have a hobby."

"And you like this, the travel marketing thing?" she asked.

I thought about it.

"Well, I can't say as I love it, or that it's terribly fulfilling, but, well, travel doesn't hurt anyone and I thought it would be just sort of a pastime until I, well, found my true calling. I kind of thought I'd move on to something else, but by then I was pretty good at it."

"And being overpaid and getting to move to Venice doesn't sound too bad…"

"And there's that. And well, here I am."

"And your true calling?"

"Ah-ha," I said, "that remains an elusive mystery."

"Elusive ones are the best kind. I know the feeling," she said, "art school was filled with these very earnest people who had a true calling. Everyone wanted to be a great artist and knew they'd never be able to do anything else. There was nothing else. Instead we all sold out and got jobs in graphic design or at dot coms. Then you had lots of talented artists making logos or designing high tech corporate identities for these companies no one seemed sure what they even did. I wished I had a true calling, like a great artist. Only I didn't. I just wanted to do more things I liked doing and I like painting more than making graphics for silly advertisements."

"Sounds like it makes good sense," I said. I don't often have deep thoughts, but I recognize them in others. Sometimes.

"I keep trying to tell myself that, only I'm never very convincing."

"I'm convinced," I said.

"So," she said, "tell me a short, interesting story, why don't you?"

"Okay," I said, "there's this guy, a little lonely maybe, but really very nice and he's sitting in a café staring outside at a beautiful woman painting."

"I think I've heard this one. Is he an axe murderer, a paid assassin? Some soulless, perverted foot fetishist who asks strange women very personal questions."

"No, this is a whole different story. See, this guy, well, this guy is-"

"Cute," she said.

"Right. Cute." Ah ha, I said to myself. I was cute.

"And humble, is he ever so humble?"

"Oh, yes, this guy, well, humility is just one of his many outstanding characteristics."

"I'll bet," she said, and finished her hot chocolate.

The chocolate left a dark smear on the inside of the cup in an intricate lace pattern that seemed like it could have told a fortune, perhaps mine, if one could tell fortunes from such things.

"And he has all these terrific things to do, all these things he wants to do with someone else, and just then he meets the beautiful young artist."

"And her? What about her? Is she any good? Maybe I know her work."

"Well, that's the thing, he doesn't know if she's any good, he doesn't know anything about her, only that he thinks she's stunning and she has this beautiful hair."

"So he's pretty superficial, this guy, huh?"

"Oh, no, he's really not at all, he just, well, has an eye for beauty."

"I see. A sensitive type. What color?" she said.

"Color?"

"The hair?"

I knew enough about women, even in my ill-fortuned experiences, to know that calling the hair color wrong early on could be disastrous and I struggled for the right hue and word that would sound and seem right to a beautiful artistic temperament.

"Let's say, for the purposes of the story, that it's chestnut."

"She probably dyes it."

Actually, her hair looked much like the color of the chocolate residue in the glass, only I knew chocolate was brown or black and her hair wasn't, so I didn't say it, but thought maybe I should have.

"Maybe, but this guy, see, besides being humble, well, he's far too gentlemanly to ever ask such a thing."

"I should imagine so, a humble and polite guy like that."

"And he asks this artist girl-"

"Wait, wait, wait. Wait one minute. This artist girl? What happened to the beautiful artist, the stunning creature?"

Oops.

"That's implied."

"I see, I get it. Got it. It's implied, just not spoken outright anymore, so that's how it is?"

"So this divine artist, this gorgeous woman of the arts, he figures maybe she's a starving artist and he should buy her dinner, so they leave this little café and off they go and have dinner in the world's most romantic city and they have a marvelous time."

"Do they kiss, walk off into the sunset and live happily ever after?"

"It's a mystery."

"Ah, a mystery. I like mysteries."

"Yes, me too."

"What do they eat?"

"Well, this guy, see, besides being humble, happens to know a great little bar, and first, see, they stop and have an aperitivo."

"Uh-oh. Maybe he's got some sort of drinking problem?"

"No, no. He's got other problems. Just he's away from home and he maybe drinks too much sometimes. He's got vices, there's no denying that. But they're all a part of his charm."

"Vices, sure. Vices can be good. Charming can be good."

"Yeah, vices because, well not only because, but one time he happened to read, this guy, he reads a lot and he read where Lincoln said that men with no vices have very few virtues."

"So he's one of those," she said.

"Those?"

"Those guys who's always quoting dead presidents."

Uh-oh. Presidential quotes floated through my head: Ask not what your country can do for you. We have nothing to fear but fear itself. It depends on what your definition of the word is, is. And even more recently: That guy's a major league asshole. Presidents were always saying stuff.

"Only when the situation absolutely calls for it."

"Oh, good, if it's called for. Then that's all right. Maybe he does it to show he's not as superficial as he sounds, I mean, at first," she said.

"Maybe. I think part of it is that he gets kind of nervous when he meets a beautiful woman."

"He sounds kind of sweet when you look at it that way," she said.

"Yes, he's very sweet. He really is. I mean this is the kind of guy, if you gave him a chance, you'd find out just how sweet he was and you almost couldn't believe it."

"Sounds too good to be true. God knows where they make that stuff up."

"So finally, he looks at her, and he says, why don't you let me take you out to dinner-"

"Does she go? Just like that, with some complete stranger? Maybe she's not too bright? I mean if she colors her hair, paints pictures, knowing only dead artists ever sell, you never know. You can't be too sure."

"Oh, she seems very bright, very intelligent, I think that's one of the things he likes about her."

"How could he tell? If he only just met her?"

"He's intuitive, like that."

"Humble and intuitive."

"And cute, don't forget."

"So how does it end?"

"Well, they have this aperitivo, they go to this outstanding restaurant," I said.

"Maybe he knows some quaint little Italian place?"

"Oh, yeah, he's just that type of guy, and then he walks her home—"

"And then the rest is a mystery, right? Some sort of big bang surprise ending?"

"Oh, yes, it's a real cliff hanger, very romantic, but in this story, you can tell right away that good things are going to happen."

"Sounds to me like they're just trying to hook you for the sequel."

"Oh, yes, it's definitely that kind of vehicle. Huge blockbuster potential, sequels, rave reviews, the whole works."

"That sounds like a good story, why don't you tell me the rest over dinner?" she said, and we walked out into the rain.

∞ ∞ ∞

First we had spritzes, the omnipresent libation of the Venetians—white wine, Campari and soda—at Franco's, and then we went to the Café San Trovaso, which was conveniently located right near my house, and it was the most marvelous first date I ever had and I felt totally and completely open and alive in her presence, almost as if I was seeing Venice for the first time. Though strangely married with that sensation of appreciating the feeling and beauty of Venice was the awareness that I was paying no attention to Venice and all to the girl.

We had red wine in a carafe, a green bottle of Pellegrino, and shared appetizers of asparagus wrapped in prosciutto and marinated squid and then, because you had to order a pasta course so as not to disappoint the Italians and seem uncouth, we compromised on sharing a cream sauced vermicelli entangled with an eclectic assortment of seafood that I had no idea what most of it was, but it was fun to share, and when it came time for us to order secondi, we had finished our wine and were like old friends, except for the irritating little quirk that she wouldn't tell me her name.

In that regard, she was very specific: "No questions," she said.

And so there were none. In place of history and interrogative, I got mystery and divinity. I just did not know what to do with them, having long been convinced the way to make a person like you was to make them talk about themselves.

In place of knowledge, I got us another carafe of wine, grasping that crucial moment when you know you have to either savor the last remnants of the first bottle or promptly order a second. For our secondi, she had the scampi grigliatti and I had the sea bass in butter and garlic. They were pretty good sized scampi but still I thought it was neat that she managed to make them several bites each. She left two crimson skinned scampi on her plate that, if I had known her better, I might have liked to have, but didn't, and they were taken away. He who hesitates.

We finished it all up with caffè macchiati and Averna, which I was pleased to find she hadn't tried yet, and finally, sometime late at night, I lost track as we'd been there for many hours, I looked around and we were the only customers. After I gestured, the waiter brought us our check and I liked that she didn't fight me for it and that in Italy they would never bring it to you until you asked. There's something, I think, so alluring about a woman comfortably letting you buy her dinner and it suited the civility of people who won't bring you a bill until you want it, and we went off into the night and I hoped she was as drunk as I was, or at least drunk enough to tell me her name, which so far she had coyly refused to share.

Somehow it seemed like everything else had gone so perfect, I didn't want to sully the idyllic nature of the evening by admitting I had maneuvered us to a restaurant near my house, so when we left I turned away from my apartment and offered to carry her things and walk her home. Only she wouldn't tell me where that was, either.

It had stopped raining and the streets were very quiet. As she wouldn't let me walk her all the way home, my border was the far edge of the Campo Santa Margherita. We walked by the site where we'd just met some hours ago and it seemed to have a looming importance to me now, and I reached out for her hand, and she wrapped her fingers in mine and we walked through the still damp, silent stones of the campo and everything seemed perfect, strolling hand in hand with a red-haired artist whose name I didn't know in the thick stillness of a chill Venice winter night.

We stopped on the little bridge over the Rio Foscari just beyond Santa Margherita and before Campo San Pantalon and I wanted the moment to last longer and I leaned over and kissed her, touching her lips tenderly at first, testing, exploring, until she opened her mouth and we kissed and we kissed, our lips, mouths, tongues, all intertwined, and it seemed like this moment might actually last forever for a second and then like it was over before it began and I just held her there in my arms and she turned around to look down the canal and I held my chin on top of her head and slid off her hat and her hair fell down onto her shoulders and over my arms and I kissed the top of her head and we stood there for several beautiful, quiet moments, me caught up in the fragrance of her hair, which somehow smelled like a freshly-sharpened pencil.

"Who are you?" I said, disturbing the stillness of Rio Foscari and leaving the agreed upon confines of no questions.

"Don't confuse me," was all she said.

Then she turned back to me and thanked me for an excellent evening, and before I even knew what was happening, she had gathered up all her things, gave me a moist peck on the lips and strode off. I was stunned and more than a little surprised and dismayed if perhaps the divinity of the moment I thought we'd shared had shown itself only to me and not to her at all. I watched her walk down the steps of the little bridge and head off toward the Chiesa San Pantalon and thought about following her, but I didn't want to ruin anything, to do anything else wrong, so I stood where I was on the stone arch of the small bridge and broke the stillness of the night as I shouted:

"Wait, tell me your name, please!"

She stopped and turned around.

"Then it wouldn't be a mystery. No one would ever buy tickets for the sequel."

I smiled and felt sort of sad at the same time as I watched her walk away, happy that Venice in winter was a quiet place and a small town. I would find her again, soon enough.

I walked home in the heavy air and looming silence of Venice, and it was the most beautiful and captivating city to be walking through having just had an almost perfect night with a woman whose name I didn't know. I even skipped part of the way down a dark calle when I was sure no one was around, and I thought that I was far too old to be skipping like a teenager after his first kiss, far too old to be skipping at all, but it felt pretty damned good and I thought it might well be the last time I ever skipped in my life, and that was pretty good too, to be aware of it.

Life does not often always offer enough intuition for awareness of those important moments that are the last pure ones before they're desecrated: the final Christmas you truly believed in Santa Claus, the last moment you believed your parents knew everything, the exact time in your life you still truly believed anything at all was possible for you, your final fleeting feelings as a virgin, all things one would and could never feel again, never as pure as they were before knowledge and life sullied them and changed you forever. I knew this was the last time I would skip and it felt good to know it as it happened and I was damned pleased with myself.

SEVEN

THE MOUTH OF THE LION

IN THE DAYS THAT FOLLOWED her disappearance on the little bridge, I started looking at myself and the things around me more closely. I don't know why she instilled such a sense of self-awareness in me, but I felt as if my self and my present surroundings stood out in bas-relief against the pale and plainer background of my past. While my mind thought about her and hoped to see her again, my gaze grew more intently focused on where I found myself. I began to question again what I was really doing here. The sharper focus did little to lend clarity to this mystery.

I became more aware of how lonely I was, but not homesick. I didn't particularly miss home at all any longer, as a matter of fact, I started to feel almost guilty, as if I should have been homesick and couldn't catch it, but I couldn't find anything to instill the sickness. Was it possible, perhaps, to be homesick but not able to say for where?

I read in the Herald Tribune about Ashcroft's Operation TIPS and his recruitment of postmen and cable workers and neighbors to spy on one another. I remembered the useless spy in Stratego, the little plastic piece of red or blue that was weaker than every single other piece on the board, save one: the lordly Field Marshal. Though technically speaking, the United States did not have a Field Marshal, rendering the spy useless, though evidently many more were needed.

Being in Venice amidst the beauty and treachery bequeathed by its ruthless power, I couldn't help but think of the Bocche dei Leoni that were still perched amongst the old stones of the city. The open-mouthed roar of a lion's stony face that allowed one, anyone, so un-lion like, to secretly denounce any person they chose, friend, foe, jilted lover, hated neighbor. Charges of the time included blasphemy, foul language, or the ever-present Venetian sin of giving away any state secrets, consorting with foreigners. One lion's face near the Campo dei Mori bore an inscription: *Bestemmiate non piu, e date Gloria a Dio*, Swear no more and give glory to God. The ferocity of the lion's faces, their foreboding open-mouthed roar that looked like a scowl or sneer when worked into stone, let the Veneziani drop secret accusations in the lion's mouth to denounce whomever they pleased. Like the trinket sellers in today's Piazza, the lions never wanted for customers.

In the gory and glorious time of The Venetian Empire, when the Doges were among Europe's biggest power brokers, nothing was more important to them than their ability to get their citizenry to spy on one another and self-police and an anonymous accusation in a lion's mouth generally meant a conviction without the trouble of a trial, much like what was happening to—was it 100, 700, 1,000— Arabs being held without charges or hearings or trials in Guantanamo Bay. Liberty and justice are much harder to build than they are to take away. Ashcroft busily pilfered from McCarthy's playbook only now the bad guys were brown instead of red. Maybe someday REM would write a song about him too, since he seemed to have no sense of decency either. No sense of decency at all.

I saw with disgust that back home in America the citizenry were eager to give up any amount of privacy and civil liberties for the hope of security. A security which seemed impossible in the modern world, an elusive one, that meant little without the nobility of liberty. I wondered what ideals were worth protecting if liberty was not inherent in them. I read about two foreign diplomats, a Canadian and a German, who lost their government positions because they noted that President Bush happened to be an idiot. Being too observant was perhaps a thorn in a political career.

Of course, you got used to Canada complaining about the U.S. because they lived upstairs from one of the world's noisiest neighbors. But when Germans were complaining about war-mongering Americans, you had to pause and appreciate the irony. Even in countries where they still had monarchies and primogeniture, which as Prince Charles was finding didn't count for much if your mom lived forever, they seemed to be noting that America might not be the great light of liberty it had purported itself to be. Though the U.S. wasn't saddled with the burden of hereditary monarchy, the idiot in the White House did happen to be the son of the former president who'd started the whole thing in the Persian Gulf to begin with.

Then there was the National Security Agency and Tom Ridge directing the new Department of Homeland Security, which begged the question of what the Department of Defense was doing if not looking after such matters, but coaches were always saying the best defense was a good offense and it was hard to imagine a leader who needed more coaching than G.W. Bush.

It seemed pretty clear, both before and after the eleventh of September, that the world was not a safe place but I didn't think that in itself was a new discovery. I remember thinking how kind it was of people the world over to assist those in the taking away of their own power and dignity. Where would the Doges, the Hitlers, the Husseins, the Mussolinis, the Stalins, and the Ashcrofts of this world be without the helpful assistance of a concerned and frightened citizenry? Why was hatred such a sturdy pillar of politics?

Hate and love and war had all happened in Venice before even though all the news reporters kept saying the world had changed forever. I was not convinced, there on her shores, that it had. It seemed to me, as I studied the intricate history of Venice, that the world was as much or more like it had been than ever before.

Venice had broken other paths that had been well-trodden in the wake she left on the world; the Venetians invented the income tax, the powers of the great Venetian navy, the scourge of the Mediterranean, were built in the city's Arsenale, hence our word: Arsenal. During Venice's dominion of the seas, a ship fully outfitted for plundering sailed away from the Arsenale each and every hour. Her secrets at shipcraft and naval warfare were as closely protected as nuclear knowledge today. Perhaps more so.

Venice, in her long history, navigated other unexplored waters as well. Long before anyone else, Venice opened herself to Jews of the Diaspora, but put them in the world's first ghetto, which originally was a Venetian word meaning foundry, but was of course now just a place where people who could go nowhere else had to stay, whether it was Cabrini Green, Tirana, Havana, or Soweto, it little mattered to those who couldn't leave. The name makes little difference, and of course it must be called something, so ghetto might as well be as good—or as bad—as any other word. I wasn't convinced there was any substantial difference between keeping people out or keeping people in. The East Germans had always maintained the Berlin Wall was to keep people out, not in.

Nevertheless, America had embraced the love it or leave it jingoism and someone had to be at the till, and while I watched the passing of the gondolas and the vaporetti, the ships of the modern states sailed on, and I, not at the helm of anything, sallied forth, as you do.

I studied more on Venice and kept discovering distressing synchronicities as I read the news in the Herald Tribune and the worries over germ warfare and smallpox.

In 1649, after Venice had been ravaged worse than any other European city by the Plague of Black Death, a shrewd Venetian doctor had offered the Doges an essence of the Plague, which he recommended could be spread among the infidel Turks by infusing it into Venetian textiles sold to the enemy infidels, who of course thought the Christian Venetians were themselves infidels. But both were faithful believers in making money. The power brokers in the Doges Palace in San Marco chose not to use it but just in case, to keep anyone else from doing so, they locked this patriotic Venetian doctor away in the prison of the palace. The same prison that Casanova had escaped from.

Today germ and biological warfare was much in the news again. Christianity and Islam, too. People looked to God for understanding but religion was very confusing as far as I could tell and I grew tired of religion and politics and the fact that the church was so much more political than it should have been and politics was so much more religious than it should have been. I was not a big fan of either, whether shaken or stirred.

Yes, Venice was a champion of Christianity, but didn't let this interfere with her greater goal of empire building and money making trade with the Middle East. Early in the 1600s, a Pope in Rome told Venice not to trade with infidels. Much to the chagrin of the Papacy, the Venetians asserted their right to trade with any one they wanted, of any faith or none, and so became the first champion of secular state's rights.

Meanwhile back in America in the twenty-first century, people pondered if war in the Middle East was a possible thing or a necessary thing for peace or if indeed it might just all have been about oil. And secularity was questioned, and the Circuit Court in San Francisco ruled people couldn't be compelled to say one nation under God in the Pledge of Allegiance, but everyone still swore on the bible in the courtrooms and read In God We Trust on American money. I did not know what was printed on currencies that passed through hands in various Muslim nations, but did know that much of the actual wealth of theirs came from the U.S. need for oil.

Earlier, in 1202, Frankish Knights on the Fourth Crusade had approached Venice as only her ships and masters were able to take them to the Holy Land and liberate it from the infidels.

"No other power on earth can aid us as you can; therefore we implore you, in God's name, to have compassion on the Holy Land and to join us in avenging the contempt of Jesus Christ by furnishing us with ships that we may pass the seas," their emissaries said to Doge Enrico Dandolo.

The Doge was a Venetian, hence a businessman. It is not recorded when the moment in history was that being the leader of a people became a business, nonetheless, the thing had happened at some previous point. The tradition thrives today around the world, even a mediocre C student like G.W. had managed to get his MBA before becoming CEO of the USA. His degree must have well prepared him, even if it didn't seem so initially when his early endeavors included not being able to find oil in Texas and trading Sammy Sosa. Probably the MBA helps you overlook the little things in big business or great empires.

"On what terms?" the savvy Doge had replied, getting to the heart of the affair.

A price was agreed upon without too much worry about charity and church and Christian scruples. The price of Christian charity had gone up since the night before Jesus was nailed to the cross and his life traded for thirty pieces of silver to line the pocket of the apostle Judas so the King of the Jews could be nailed to the cross by the Romans, which made you wonder why there were anti-Semites but not anti-Romans.

Back to business, the Doge and the Crusaders came to terms: 85,000 silver marks, plus half of all booty and plunder. For this sum, Dandolo the old Doge, who was all of 88 when they arrived, agreed to transport a Crusader army of over 30,000 soldiers and keep them in provisions for the year. Though there's not much recorded as to how they doled out the contracts.

The deal was done and the Crusaders arrived and were consigned to wait on the island of the Lido while the fleets of Venice were prepared, where today they had the Venice film festival and all the waves and beaches and stars and the summertime casino.

Dandolo even got caught up in the fervor and expressed the idea, though he was going blind, of leading the army himself. Sight is not always crucial, history tells us, for a visionary.

However, when it came time for the Crusaders to pay up, they didn't have the funds. The Venetians were rigorous, always, as they are today, about such details. When you agree to let them perform a service, whether it's to feed you in an overpriced trattoria or transport your troops overseas, they expect, when they bring the bill, that you will pay it.

The Crusader army was put under surveillance on the Lido so it did not sneak away in the dead of night. Though there was little chance of that since no one but the Venetians could successfully sail the shallow marshy waters of the Lagoon, the tidal plain barriers that so well protected them from both armies of men and ships.

The funds did not arrive and the Venetians made a deal of their own, brought forth another bill of lading. The Crusaders could still be shipped to the Holy Land, they said, if instead of payment the army would agree to make some unscheduled stops along the way to subdue some troublesome colonies abroad and secure Venice's trading routes. The terms were accepted and the army sailed for the Dalmatian Coast, people were subdued, trade routes secured.

Having indeed decided to lead the fleet, the old Doge Dandolo then made another proposal to the earnest Crusaders. They agreed to delay the humiliation of the infidel and go along with Dandolo and capture the Greek Christian bastion at Constantinople, whom the Venetians were at odds with over something else. Led by the old blind Doge himself and his wisdom of 88 years, they stormed the towers of Constantinople long before it became Istanbul and deposed the Emperor and divided the loot and the Empire, bringing back some of what are now Venice's most cherished treasures.

Interestingly enough, these particular Crusaders never did reach the Holy Land or get to fight the infidels, and the fall of Constantinople, the last lingering shreds of the Roman Empire, only served to widen the vacuum for Islam. Nature, I had been told more than once in more than one classroom, hates a vacuum and you could see it in our untidy world.

Victorious in his scheme, Doge Dandolo sent his ships and bounty home to Venice after having thoroughly exploited everyone, Christian, Crusader, and Infidel. Venice and the Doges became "Lords and Masters of a Quarter and a Half-Quarter of the Roman Empire."

I thought it interesting that Venice was a she, La Serenissima, but also a Lord and Master. But perhaps gender did not count for much in these things. It seemed strange that it counted for so many other things, like the fact that women could be saints but not priests, the Church having effectively managed to exclude a full fifty percent of the inhabitants of the world successfully, which was quite a feat when you stopped to think about it.

The Venetians acquired control of distant foreign lands in the Balkans and the Greek islands of Crete, Rhodes, and Cyprus and happily secured their trading routes and took home ships laden with gold, precious gems, and sacred relics and installed them all for visitors to Venice to marvel at, which they did. These relics made their way occasionally into my press releases even today. Though I couldn't fit in Dandolo, I did stop and visit his former palazzo whenever I was in the neighborhood, which still stood near the Rialto Bridge.

Rialto, I learned, came from the Latin, *Rivus Altus*, high river. It did me no good knowing this, but I liked it all the same, especially when I stood there on the bridge and looked down at the high river. There's a certain small delight in acquiring and saving useless bits of knowledge that do you no good at all, and I'd always prided myself on my capacity for them, which was almost limitless.

Of course, the Venetians, at the time, had no use for oil. Perhaps President Bush had some slightly different goals but they have never been well-shared by those whose job it evidently is to keep such things secret rather than share, whatever their title, and as the Republicans enlarged the already barely functioning U.S. bureaucracy, there were always going to be more secrets to keep and more people to toil at keeping them.

While Byron was in Venice he wrote the words: "Oh, for an hour of old blind Dandolo, the octogenarian chief, Byzantium's conquering foe."

I wondered what words would be written about Mr. President W. Bush if he failed or succeeded, but was pretty sure it would not be those since Byron lay long dead somewhere in Greece, having also wanted a chance to fight the occupying Turks. The Old World had no wish to accommodate the Young Turks.

Things were not simple or safe, and I wondered if the status quo could be in a state of flux and could change be constant, even as mankind repeated the same mistakes and when faced with the same trials, repeated the same errors?

It seemed to me as I toiled at tourism marketing in Venice, that one could find anything and everything there in the history of Venice, somewhere buried in some book or in the Archives of State over near the Campo dei Frari, which I had been made privy to on several occasions. Where I was supposed to uncover some interesting tidbits for travel marketing press releases, but didn't usually, but went all the same whenever I could.

If you left the office late enough on some errand for trivial knowledge, you could skip the Archives of State and just sit in a café near the Frari, where the sport of drinking was more entertaining than working, and then you didn't even have to cross the Grand Canal again and go back to work at all and you never hardly missed it. I guess it's like that with most drinks and sports and jobs.

About the time I lost my pass to the Venetian Archives of State, I noticed that the international newspapers complained much about access for covering the possible impending war in Iraq and worried that they weren't told enough. Bombs were dropped and it seemed like it was indeed war, in all but name, anyway. I even read that Bush said we were indeed at war, but it was hard to tell for sure and no one seemed to know. War, despite the teachings of my father, was a rather ambiguous thing nowadays.

You couldn't help but notice that governments of all types in all times tended to always veer in the direction of wanting to know more about their citizens and wanting their citizens to know less of their government. It had been thus in Venice and was becoming so in the U.S. And the world turned, kept spinning on its axis. And possibly the axis was evil.

I didn't have any secrets to keep but would have liked to keep them to myself if I did find some good ones.

Only the secret I most wanted to know was the name of the red-haired artist who I somehow never managed to find, though I kept looking whenever I could, having little else to do with my leisure time.

The only useful thing I did early that week was to stop and put a handwritten note in a lion's mouth on the Zattere near the Gesuati church, "Ashcroft sucks ass." Of course no one collected the notes anymore, the Doges had long since seen their last days, deposed by Napoleon, and my little note would be, well, little noted. It made me feel better all the same. Even if the only useful thing I did was utterly useless.

I thought it strange that I couldn't find any mention of Napoleon in the Archives of State, but one thing, something about a statue of him that was to have been erected in the Piazza San Marco but wasn't there now and I couldn't find out for sure if it ever had been. One never knew and no one else seemed to care. The absence of things like statues and weapons of mass destruction was very hard to investigate, no matter how hard you tried. Like the absence of goodness or a certain girl.

I spent the next days going to work and thinking of her, the unnamed artist, and took all my coffee and lunch breaks and afternoon walks to the spot on the campo where we'd met, always expecting to see her there, but she never was. I enlarged my circle and found the many hidden places that the painters of Venice congregated and even scoured the many art supply stores and still I didn't see her.

So I just kept working and kept searching and kept thinking about her. And somehow started to feel like I was falling in love with a woman whose name I didn't know, whom I'd only spent one delicious evening with.

If I looked at my feelings closely, which I had been doing more than was good for me, it seemed hopeless and sophomoric and romantic and more than a little bit ridiculous. But I didn't mind that much. I had found a lot of time and space for those feelings.

EIGHT

SPRINGTIME IN VENICE

FINALLY, I STARTED TALKING some sense into myself. I gave up on missing the girl. I missed the pursuit, missed the feeling of missing her, even. But knew that dreams of what might have been have a limited lifespan in man. I worked and wandered aimlessly. Even when I stared at the back of every red-headed crop of female hair in any crowd, I reminded myself that I was only wandering aimlessly.

One day the gravity of nice weather and Venice's early springtime crowds drew me to the Piazza San Marco, Europe's sitting room, as Napoleon had called it before he took it for himself and then traded it to the Austro-Hungarians as easily as you might trade Marvin Gardens for Park Place.

In Venice, if you didn't know where you were going, you usually ended up in the Piazza and since that was always true, maybe it was always where you were going.

That was when I came across her sitting down on the stones in front of the Basilica San Marco, leaning against the brick foundation of the campanile. It was a Thursday, I think, it must have been the week before Easter.

She was wearing the same black velvet hat and clutching an empty sketch pad, just staring off into space and she didn't see me walk up. I circled behind her and put my hands over her eyes and said: "Guess who," and when I did, I could feel she was crying, just quietly sitting there with tears pooling in her eyes and I got her teardrops on my fingers and suddenly felt horribly invasive.

I thought maybe it was some somber stirring of the artistic soul, perhaps the beauty of the place, the Piazza and the people and the setting, had all overcome her and I felt bad for ruining an aesthetic moment. The inscrutable inner-being of an elusive woman is beguiling enough and added with a dose of artistic leanings and sensitivity I was not indoctrinated in, I was all too aware of my unsuitability for the moment I faced. I was not informed or enlightened enough about art or beauty and the shapeliness of her soul. No matter how badly I wished for the key that would unlock all these things, I remained an outsider. I didn't know what I was dealing with, really. I navigated unfamiliar terrain, though I had been here before.

She sniffled and just said, "I was wondering when you'd find me."

"I was beginning to think never," I added, wistfully as I could.

"What's wrong?" I asked

She didn't say anything, so I went with my instincts, which seemed feeble and wrong, but alas, were all I had.

"Is it just that it's all too beautiful, too hard to put on paper?" I asked.

"No, it's not that. Not that at all. It's just the opposite. Just that the world's so awful, so terribly sad, that sometimes I can't stand it."

I sat down next to her.

"It can't be that bad," I said, not knowing if it was, or what to say at all.

"You have no idea."

"Listen, why don't we go over to Harry's Bar and you can tell me all about it. Your name and the whole story. They say you can get everything at Harry's. Even happiness."

At Harry's there was always an interesting mélange of people that was at least diverting. The Bellinis were highly overpriced but the bar always well-populated with a heady mix of tourist trap day-trippers, the aristocratic social set of Venice, and the occasional international jet-setter, all equally treated by the aloof tuxedoed waiters.

Seemed everyone hoped for a slice of happiness to be served up, though technically speaking it was not listed on the menu.

Rumor had it that Tom and Nicole had recently had a rousing argument there before their divorce. I didn't believe the rumors but it set me to thinking about how many famous couples of today and yesteryear had ended badly. In modern myth-making Hollywood it was no surprise, nor in history and literature. Romeo and Juliet. Antony and Cleopatra. Samson and Delilah. Bogart and Bacall. Gatsby and Daisy Buchanan. Heathcliff and Catherine. Were there any famous couples to draw on who had been blessed with happy endings? Was the risk of delving deeply into another person's soul worth the odds?

What good was a place like Harry's, wherever it was, if you could get anything in the world there, even happiness, but if things never worked out in the end? What kind of happiness was that? What good were endings at all? Maybe, I thought, it's a matter of deciding to end things before they get bad, before you mess them up, of making life stop so you could hold onto the goodness before the real world reached down and plucked it out of your hands like a capricious conjurer performing the same old trick. Everything ends badly, otherwise it wouldn't end, right? Maybe the trick was just not to have an ending at all. Or wiser still, to never even begin and neutralize the whole dangerous process before it started, to stay forever far from the show. By forgoing the magic, you might insulate yourself from injury.

"I don't feel like being around people," she said.

"Do you want me to leave?" I asked, hoping with all my being that the answer would be no, thinking that maybe this incomprehensible magic was all there was.

She started crying more and I watched her shoulders tremble with the effort.

"No, no. No, it's all right. Just let me sit here. Sit here with me, Mark," she said through small soundless sobs.

Eager for access, I sat down, getting as close to her as I could, pining for proximity. We sat there silently on the cold stones of the Piazza.

"Perhaps we should introduce ourselves again," I said, not wanting to let more moments in her presence pass without being privy to at least her name. It seemed cruelly unfair that she knew mine and I didn't know hers.

For some reason, I had started to call her Monet in my mind, it seeming a good name for an artist even if Claude had been a man, but I wasn't sure if she would like that. They were a mysterious sort, women and artists. Would have been nice if I'd been right with my guess, but I doubted it. Though I had every confidence that I could have learned wonderful things from a girl who might have been named Monet.

She wasn't taking the bait and I guess it was a pretty meager offering, but I stood there patiently waiting for some sort of bite or sign, alert lest my red and white bobber dip underwater.

A flock—were they flocks, I knew crows were a murder—of noisy pigeons scuttled ferociously across the stones in the middle of the piazza.

In the center of the Piazza, two kids stood holding clumps of pigeon feed in their hands and the ugly, dirty birds, all gray and white and black, swooshed down from the sky and lighted just long enough to peck some food out of their hands and make the kids giggle gleefully and run off screaming, scaring the pigeons, until the kids and the pigeons got brave enough to try it again. Proud parents stood by snapping pictures of their adorable brats feeding the foul fowl. A larger and lovelier lone white seagull without a flock or a name circled the square slice of the sky above the Piazza, floating above everything, arrogantly disinterested in the goings on below. Perhaps like Jonathan Livingston Seagull, he was honing his soaring skills or maybe working on his target acquisition ability.

In previous and perhaps crueler centuries, corpses had been hung or buried head first in the stones of the Piazza. Now orchestra music wafted, waves lapped from the shortened shore over by the Piazzetta and everyone had video cameras for their Aunt Marjorie back home to be bored by their trip, so painstakingly chronicled on digital tape technology. How did they turn numbers into pictures anyway? How indeed did the intricately chiseled facets of the crystal clear scene before me get reduced to a banal series of binary numbers?

"Look, no offense. I'm sorry. I'm so sorry. But I don't feel like talking, okay? Let's just sit, can we do that?" she said.

She put down the empty sketchpad and I moved closer to her on the ground and leaned up against the clock tower campanile and feebly put my arm around her.

What do you do when a beautiful woman is crying and you like her so much, maybe you could love her, but you don't know her name, probably it isn't Monet, you don't know anything about her, except the first time you saw her she was stunning and smiling and happy and it was raining and your heart had skipped a beat when your lips touched, and the next time you saw her she was sitting there crying her eyes out in the afternoon sun of the Piazza in the spring and, well, you just have no idea what to do, and I didn't.

Many people had cried in the Piazza, that I knew, even though I didn't know her or their names. The stones of that Piazza had before been well soaked with tears, of that there was no doubt, salty water of any kind was no stranger to those stones.

So we sat there and she leaned her head on my shoulder and she cried and I would have done anything in the world for her right then, just about anything, only there was nothing to do for her. I could have been wrong. Perhaps there was everything I could have done for her, perhaps I could have somehow reached into her soul and stirred forth the beauty and the grace I'd seen before in her single-dimpled smile, perhaps I could have dragged her out of her depression and offered her a life preserver. Perhaps the right words or deeds would have made all the difference in both our lives. Only I did not know what they were, those mysterious right words and deeds, that again, as they had before, remained elusive to me.

I felt as if I'd been woefully miscast in a badly written, unfinished melodrama and it was opening night, only I did not know my lines, nor did the writer. I didn't even have the goddamned cast of characters right. And there was no director, only me and the teary eyes of the sad, beautiful girl with no name, sitting there on the sprawling stone stage of the Piazza San Marco.

That's the thing with life, there's no dress rehearsal, no preparation to ready you for the performance, no time to fix the things you're not good at, no director in the wings to guide you, no Cyrano in the bushes whispering perfect phrases to you. By the time you discover you don't know the right lines, the right words, the performance is coming to a close and there's only this, this one long performance that ends so quickly, where everyone strolls through it striving to learn or pretend to know how to act. And before you know it, you're afraid the play is going to end and you don't know how or don't understand but all of it probably must mean something. So you wait for Godot. Or you speak in prose. Or, not knowing your lines, sit and say nothing, stifled by an inadequate preparation for all that life might have given you.

So I sat there some more and shared an unknown sadness in the beautiful Piazza with a girl whose name I didn't know and whose sadness I didn't understand and not understanding made it all the more melancholy. I put my arm tighter around her shoulders, feeling only that she possessed more gravity than me, that her sadness possessed more weight than my happiness, but perhaps it is always so. I knew only that I was more drawn down to her level of mood and feeling than her up to mine. And it was sad and beautiful, all at the same time, and the pigeons strutted and cawed, and I thought for a bit about all the people who had shared moments of such despair amidst the old stones and shining basilica that made it one of the world's most beautiful places.

If you were going to be sad, there were few better places to do it. What I remember most is that we were sad there together with our heavy hearts almost touching yet still so far away and I could feel the coldness of the stones through my pants and the warm wetness of her tears on my neck.

I don't know how long we sat there, time ticked away irretrievably until finally the sun left the Piazza, the children and their parents went on their way, back to hotels and apartments or the train station, and the lovely, winsome couples at the Cafés Florian and Quadri moved inside and the waiters, in white shirts and black vests, brought in the white tables from the square.

I tried to think of a way to stop time's ineluctable passing and to leave the place and the sadness. I thought of whisking her off in a gondola but it seemed to funereal given the mood and it was not a good time for riding in gondolas. The early evening was busy and commercial and the gondoliers at the Piazzetta were the worst sort, hunting the easiest prey. Leaving the place and the sadness was a journey that demanded to be made on foot, if a man and an unknown woman could make it at all.

I stood up and reached my arm down to her and she put her hand in mine and I pulled her up off the stones. She left her sketchpad sitting there beside the tower, haphazardly leaning askew against the campanile and we walked, hand in hand and without saying anything, underneath the portico of the Doges Palace, past Harry's Bar where you could have gotten anything, past the blue lights of the American Express office, in between the chic windows of the designer shops on the Merceria, past La Fenice, where I had never seen an opera but where I expected all the songs inside were sad and most all the stories ended in death or despair. Too many operas seemed that way, like too many lives.

We made our way towards the Accademia bridge and the other side of the canal, passing slowly together through the Campo San Stefano, where there were heat lamps outside to fight the chill of the nighttime air and everyone was dressed up and drinking red spritzes and bubbly prosecco, and we walked by the Chiesa San Stefano, where we passed three old women coming out of the church dressed in the ubiquitous Italian widow's costume of old fashioned, timeless black of mourning, only I noticed they were all laughing, and I thought if they could find laughter there, that maybe anyone could.

There was a large green banner near my office heralding the Canaletto Art Show that month, and I wondered if she'd been, but I didn't ask. We kept walking through to the small Campo San Vidal that lined the Grand Canal and led to the wooden beams of the Accademia Bridge. We crossed the bridge and I noticed the graffiti, as always, still sat there in ugly, spray painted red letters on the side of the palazzo that was the British Consulate.

We walked on down the Rio Terra Foscarini, the wide paved road that had once been a canal and had been filled in to make a street, having evolved from still lagoon water to busy canal to pedestrian thoroughfare, where we stopped for awhile and she looked up at me and said only, "Thank you, Mark," and I smiled a little, but carefully, so as not to make it too big for the sadness. She pursed her lips and looked away and we kept walking and cut through the small, dark Calle Nani that led to the Rio San Trovaso and the little bridge we had to cross to get to my apartment by the church.

∞ ∞ ∞

When we got to the gate of my building, I had to stop and unlock it with an old skeleton key. I wondered briefly if we might go inside and make love, that maybe it would be some salve to her sadness, but I looked at her eyes and felt so guilty for even thinking it, that I just said:

"Let's go inside and we'll just sit together and if you want to talk to me, you can. No pressure."

"I don't think I'm very good company tonight."

"Well, I don't want good company. I just want to be with you."

I don't think it sounded right to either of us, but we walked up the stairs, there was an elevator but I never took it, and went inside my apartment.

I took off my coat and laid it on the small table in the foyer and pulled my tie off, and I wanted to change from the suit that I'd put on so long ago it seemed, only this morning, but I didn't want her to get the wrong idea, so I didn't. I opened a bottle of wine, an inexpensive bottle of Valpolicella that I had sitting by the sink, and she went and sat on the couch in the living room. I poured the crimson colored wine into two thick water glasses, feeling wine glasses weren't proper for the heaviness of the moment, and carried the glasses and the rest of the bottle into the living room and sat down on the corner of the couch facing her.

"I'm not usually so tragic, you know. I used to be very simple."

"I know, I mean, I believe you. Life isn't always simple though. Talk to me."

"You don't deserve to have to listen to all my problems."

"Maybe I do. Anyway, I want to."

"It's…it's just that they're not fixable. They're just problems, like everyone's problems, I guess. Only they're mine so they seem more important to me."

"Because they're yours, they seem important to me, too," I said, "truly."

She looked up at me, she looked right into me and brought her eyebrows together and I noticed she had very arching fine eyebrows, that the space above her sad green eyes to her eyebrows was large and higher than usual, and I wondered if all women's eyebrows and the space above their green eyes were that beautiful only I'd never noticed before. If I had been oblivious and such expansiveness had somehow always been there waiting for me to find.

"Why?" she said and it seemed very serious and to demand just the exact answer, no trite or clever response would have sufficed, and to tell the truth, I don't know exactly why I seemed to care so much, right then, but I did, more than anything.

Sure, I had had my own problems before, but they had never struck me like hers did, and for a moment I wondered if it was nothing more than curiosity on my part, the fact that there were no obligations between us, the comfortable shield that we weren't yet connected and I could listen to and hear her problems and handle them and accept them because they couldn't demand anything from me the way my own conundrums could.

"I'm not sure, to tell the truth. I just feel like you need to talk and I want to listen. I feel like I'd like to know you," I said.

"You may regret it."

"I've regretted things before."

As she told me, we sipped our wine. It wasn't a very good wine but it seemed right for the setting and I was glad that I had brought out the thick water glasses instead of the flimsy, celebratory wine glasses and, I thought, having wine in water glasses next to a disconsolate woman with a heavy heart was just the thing I was meant to be doing right then, even though I could have been doing anything else.

"Okay, my real dad was Greek. Only I never knew this growing up. I never found out until just recently. When my mom died. She was all I had, really. I was an only child and the man who I thought was my dad my whole life, the fantastic father who raised me, died without ever telling me anything...and if my mom had been taken quicker and more peacefully maybe she wouldn't have told me either. Maybe I should never have known, maybe there's things we're not supposed to know."

It didn't seem the time to tell her that I too was an only child of sorts and didn't seem to mean much that both of us were alone, together, and seemed even to quietly dispute my simple economics lessons of rarity and value, this loneliness.

Of course, you never know the right thing to say when someone talks to you about death in the family. If you were a cop I guess you said, "I'm sorry for your loss," and went out to find some perps, if you were a priest you talked about going to a better place, if you were an old friend, you just listened and lent your ear for as long as it was wanted. Most times though, you just don't know what to say. Even though people died and always had and always would, the unavoidable remained difficult to deal with.

If you were sitting next to a girl with auburn, no, chestnut hair, I remembered that was the color I had decided to call it, yet someone you barely knew, someone who'd just briefly passed your path in a campo in Venice where you'd never even expected to be, an artist you'd just met one day in the rain, that you'd kissed on a dark night on a bridge over a small canal and who hadn't told you her name, who wouldn't tell you her name, you absolutely didn't know what to say and I didn't. I sat there and looked as compassionate as I could.

"I'm so sor-"

"No offense but when you lose your mom you get tired of hearing people tell you they're sorry. Everyone's sorry. I'm sorry. You're sorry. She's still gone. Death is like the opposite of love. You know, never having to say you're sorry. Death is always everyone, 'I'm sorry, I'm so sorry.' She lived a good life and she was ready. It was me who wasn't. I'm trying so very hard to accept it. But there's nothing you or anyone can do for me and I'm sorry enough for myself. I have to do it for myself. I just can't seem to remember how," she said.

"I guess that's about all you can do, one foot in front of the other," I said, feeling entirely helpless and feeble.

"Listen, I don't mean to be rude, really I don't, but I just don't feel like talking anymore, not now," she said.

"Could you eat something? I could make some pasta, I have more wine, we could just sit and not talk or we could talk about anything or nothing or not at all."

"Maybe. But after falling apart in the piazza, I feel like I have to get myself together. I feel all grungy."

"Well, you don't look grungy," I said, and she didn't, she looked wondrous and proud, somehow, as if her sadness and her grief made her more noble to me and I knew so much about her, or felt I did, and I even stopped obsessing on the fact that I didn't know her name. I knew other things more important than that.

"Why don't we do this? I'll get you some fresh clothes, you can take a shower and I'll make us something to eat and then we can just do nothing, for as long as you want. No strings attached, nothing up my sleeve, just pasta and wine and a shoulder to lean on," I said.

Even sad girls with no name have to eat and drink and if I could slake some smaller needs perhaps I could lighten some small slice of grief.

I went and got her two shirts to choose from, a plain old comfortable blue oxford that I should have thrown away but hadn't, and a newer, smart green pullover that seemed warm and cozy and innocent, and somehow I hoped she'd choose the oxford, and I agonized over giving her jeans or khakis or sweats, all of which I knew would be too big for her anyway. I knew the sweats would seem innocent and devoid of any predatory feeling of being in a man's apartment, but they didn't seem right, so I grabbed a pair of Levi's and was glad that I had clean towels and I put them all down on the bidet in the bathroom and turned on the water because it took a long time to heat up, and I quickly threw all my shaving stuff in the cabinet next to the sink and hastily cleaned up as best I could, running some dampened toilet paper over the whiskers I'd allowed to accumulate in the sink and expected no one to see.

"The water's on, I put some clothes down in there for you, in the bathroom. I'm going to cook us some pasta. You shower."

She smiled at me and it was good to see her smile, and I felt like I could perhaps be more than but a bit player in this little drama, and while the water waited to boil, I chopped some onions and some zucchini and some tomatoes and opened a jar of puttanesca sauce and wished I had some bread, but I didn't.

She was in the shower for a long time and I hoped it was doing her good and washing away some sadness, and I wondered what the night would bring, but reminded myself again, for some reason I didn't fully understand, not to want it to bring anything. That this sad woman deserved to have no expectations placed on her.

She came out of the bathroom with her long hair all shiny and wet and brushed straight back and all her makeup washed off and looking completely purified with my blue oxford hanging down to her thighs and asking for a belt for the Levis she was holding up and in other circumstances it could have been extraordinarily alluring, I couldn't help feeling that it was terribly, unbelievably enticing, but I went and got her a brown leather belt and she thanked me and I told her to sit down at the dining table where you could look out onto the lights of the church.

I wondered if she believed in God or if she hated him or didn't believe or if she'd ever given him the finger, but still I thought it was good you could see the lights of the steeple across the tops of the trees in the yard, some of which had started to sprout greenery. I knew springtime threatened to take away the view of the church and exchange it for new leaves and another season's panorama, and I wondered which was more godlike, the leaves of the trees or the church that had been there since the 14th century. I thought it was the leaves but I didn't know and I wasn't really crazy about trees or churches but they were both good to look at and enjoyable in their own way.

I dropped a hearty handful of linguini into the boiling water and put the colander in the sink and when I brought out the plates she was staring out the window and I wondered what she was thinking. I wanted to know, but I didn't ask.

We didn't talk some more while we ate and drank and then I took the dishes into the kitchen and brought out another bottle of wine. We went and sat on the couch where you could look out onto the lights of the church across the trees beyond my balcony and it started to drizzle, I could hear the drops on my balcony and see the reflection of the church lights in the small puddles on the tiles. She fell asleep nestled in my arms and her hair was all dry now, it had taken a long time, and it hung down over both of our shoulders and I felt closer to her than I had to anyone in many years, maybe ever, and first my arm fell asleep from the heavy weight of her head, and then I fell asleep.

∞ ∞ ∞

When I woke up, she was gone. Next to me was a charcoal drawing of myself sleeping in an awkward position on the couch, and where there should have been a signature at the bottom, she had written simply, "Thank You." It was a skillful drawing and then I noticed that instead of my shirt, she had sketched in a suit of armor which made me more than a little proud.

I was looking at the drawing and thinking how I should never sleep with my mouth open, but glad that she had made me look perhaps more handsome than I was, when Sunday's church bells went off and I forgot to give God the finger and simply said a little prayer to him asking her to be happy, wherever she was. I knew people had prayed for less consequential things.

In those lonely morning hours, abandoned and empty feeling in my fully furnished apartment, outside the sun shone down and the rain clouds had wandered out to sea en route to other appointments.

I went to work. I came home from work, to my apartment.

When I wasn't at work and didn't want to go home, I strolled around the small streets of Venice, went often back to the café where I'd met her thinking I might see her again, only she was nowhere to be found. I went and asked several other painters in the campo if they knew her, but met only a Frenchman who offered to paint my portrait and someone who spoke no English but painted red gondolas and a German couple who were painting very different pictures of the same scene and looked at me like I was kind of crazy, and none of them knew her.

I lost myself in the minutiae of the rest of the days and stopped in several churches, took in some Tintorettos and Tiepolos, strolled by some Canalettos and Caravaggios, even bought some fancy stationery I knew I'd never use, wandered in some small galleries near the Accademia, skimmed the English newspapers and one day completed the crossword, except for 32 across. I celebrated my success and solitude with some pasta and a carafe of Valpolicella at a ristorante near the Campo Santa Margherita, wandered home and slept soundly until the church bells woke me up. I gave God the finger again, and got ready for the world.

Several days later, I was digging through the bathroom cabinet to replace the blade in my razor after nicking my chin when I found a note from her. Another tangible reminder of her absence.

It was carefully written out in red felt tip and she had lovely, graceful cursive, almost like calligraphy.

My dear sweet Mark,

I sit here in the quiet of the night while you sleep on the couch with only the sounds of your snoring and my thoughts to keep me company. I feel warm for the first time in a long while after being cold and alone so long. Thank you for finding me and giving me your shoulder to cry on when I needed one so much. I've been so alone lately I'd nearly forgotten what it's like to feel this way. You made me think you understood me a little bit or at least cared.

I realize it's too much to ask of anyone else to try to understand me when I'm having so much trouble understanding myself. I thought I could run away from the grief and sadness that had trapped me back home after losing my mom. I tried to leave everything behind. I even thought it might be good to go to Greece and find out what my real dad was like. But I know now that I'm not looking for someone else. I'm looking for myself and the way back to my own heart. I need to find the person I was. The happy woman who wanted to paint and who looked forward to the future. The one who laughed easier than she cried. The woman I used to be, that I liked. I miss her. I think you would've liked her, too. There was something karmic between us, something more than I was ready for now when I have so little of myself left to give. If only things were different. But they never are.

I tried running away from everything, the grief, the loss, and even a very nice guy back home in L.A. and all I did was get farther from my self. Talking to you made me remember how much I missed being happy. I'm going back home to find that person and pick up her pieces and try and put her back together again.

I drew you a portrait. I hope you'll think of me when you look at it and remember that you helped a heavy hearted girl just when she needed it. And she was grateful to you. I'll hang the memory of this night in my mind when I remember Venice and a nice man who cooked for me and listened to me and gave me a glimpse of the person I used to be. If I understood myself and all this better I might have been able to explain it to you in the daylight. Only I'm still trying to explain it all to myself.

So I'm slinking off into the night. And in exchange for your portrait, I'm taking your shirt to remember you by. I hope you think of me fondly and know that you helped a girl when she needed it most. Thank you for being a sweet and gentle man and giving me the strength to go home and find myself.

Some lucky woman who knows herself better will be very fortunate to find you.

Sleep softly, my sleeping knight in shining armor,

Ciao and all the millions of grazies there are,

The painter who left in the night

So there it was. I had meant something to her and perhaps I should have, could have, done something, everything different. But maybe she was right and maybe I did mean something or did help, at least. Maybe some woman would be lucky to find me. I was more than a little disappointed that I'd driven a woman, again, back to another man. It was not a good habit to get into. But as is the way with so many habits, the bad ones are so much easier to fall into than the good ones. Who was it who said the unheard song is sweeter far? I tried to listen for her sad song in my head and couldn't quite catch the melody.

NINE

THE BUREAUCRACY OF EDEN

MONDAY CAME AGAIN. Even Venice had them.

I thought about all the ways I might try and hunt down a graphic artist in L.A. whose name I didn't know, the internet, a detective, hopping on a plane to seek her out, but I only played with the idea for awhile before deciding it was ludicrous, and well, I just didn't want to be that guy. There was little solace in not being the guy I actually yearned to be, but it was all I had.

For a time after I found the note, I fancied myself to be a hardened Bogart à la Casablanca, a guy whose insides had been kicked out waiting at a train station, but there was no war to fight, not for me, not one I cared about anyway, and it didn't seem a good time to move to the desert and open a café. At least I could say to myself, "We'll always have Venice," and I thought if you couldn't always have Paris, Venice was not a bad substitute. In the geography of places to have and lose, Venice was prominent on the list. You probably couldn't say, "We'll always have Milwaukee." Maybe no one had tried.

Up until then, there hadn't been much to do at work and I hadn't decided if I wasn't being ambitious enough or just hadn't acclimated to the Italian way of doing things, which was different and much more laid back than I was used to, but refreshingly so. It had often occurred to me that the Protestant work ethic was the bane of Americana, though I was not a Protestant.

Nevertheless, I did feel a sense of appreciation when the next weeks found me unusually and refreshingly busy.

Being busy was as good a way as any to forget about being lonely and was, I guess, what most people did for it. It was a nice change of pace from my serial and slothful self indulgence and feeling of exile. Until then, I'd been giving serious thought to quitting, but had

been at a loss for what else I should do or where else I would go if
I did. So I hadn't. My life grew a momentum of sorts.

I'd wondered what I had been doing in this city and not my home,
or any other, why was I in my two bedroom furnished apartment with
two large beds in the Dorsoduro sleeping alone and not in another
sleeping with the girl of my dreams, why was I alone here instead
of in a crowd back home, why did I walk across the thousand year
old stones and bridges of this town to work and not take the bus
or drive in my own town? Why was everything like it was? What
had led me to make this journey and not another, prompted me to
board a plane to Marco Polo International and not a car across the
byways of America? What friends, enemies, successes, failures, lies,
truths, calculations of time and circumstance and geography, what
reading of maps, what myriad assortment of fickle fate had fed me
to where I found myself, which frankly, was lost? Could you even
find yourself lost?

Had any one thing been different, would every other thing? It
was the philosopher's everlasting cud and being alone and abroad had
left me too much time to chew on it and without the self-awareness
or wisdom to know. There was a certain maturity that came with the
realization I was ill-prepared to know the answers, a certain wisdom
in self-admitted ignorance. I was very wise and very alone and a little
miserable, but without company.

Lacking the answers to the larger questions made the smaller
issues of work more appealing and I committed myself to them with
an enthusiasm that thankfully distracted my mind and kept me busy
enough not to worry too much about my place in the world or where
else I might have or could or should have been, what else I might
have been doing, and who else I might have been with.

I beat on, as we all do, boats against the current.

While I worked here, wars were waged elsewhere, battles that
were not my own went on without me, and Venice, the inimitable
Serenissima, kept sinking a little bit at a time and the waters kept rising
and kept lapping against her shores and the ferries to Greece kept
passing by my window. God and his minions kept playing with the
church bells beneath my balcony but I kept giving him the finger and
grew more confident that he was amused by my folly and I started to
feel pretty chummy with God, even though I didn't feel too confident
he was up there, he became like the imaginary friend I'd never had.

While I blissfully enjoyed my ignorance about my presence in
the grand scheme of things, for some reason I accidentally became
important.

September 11th had wreaked havoc on the tourism industry and Europe, if not the Europeans, missed the American dollars. I was an American and had toiled in tourism advertising and PR successfully for some years at home and the same things that made me an ill-fitting cog to the routine of life in Italy made me a commodity with the avaricious Venetian Tourism Council. Lacking the right lures for American tourism in the dangerous new world that to America had changed forever, they assumed that as an American I knew how to tie the right fly to attract the tourism dollars that sustained Venice since her empire had crumbled.

Venice's desire to beckon the diffident American dollars meant that I was the fortunate son enlisted to receive, read, and review reams of paperwork and tourism studies, a bevy of Brussels bureaucracy that seemed to exist solely for the purpose of minions like myself to skim and sort.

No matter where you sit, even in an office overlooking a Venetian canal, bureaucracy can make you feel very far from everywhere.

I busied myself stacking them up into piles of presumed priority. There was a plethora of plenitudes from other faraway cogs that comprised the vast machinery dedicated to the task of snaring tourists and their sundry currencies. There was no shortage of listless lackeys and I had mounds of their monotonous paperwork to prove it. My desk was a tangled mosaic of tourism tedium. Feeling that the mosaic needed some design, I had decided to pile them by proximity.

I started with the files from the Venetian Tourism Board, then the Regional Promotional Association of the Veneto, meandering up to the various national Italian organizations.

Even if you could have been anywhere, it was good to have a sense of direction.

This was the simple part, where notionally you were nationally beholden to ENIT, the *Agenzia Nazionale del Turismo*, known in English as The Italian Government Tourist Board, but which of course was formerly the *Ente Nazionale Italiano per il Turismo*. Most all things Italian were formally something and in this regard, at least, the boundaries were clear. This was only the beginning, as despite toiling locally for Venice, the Veneto, then Italy, we were all but a blip of the grander and larger corporate conglomerate that was the European Union. If you went to Venice, you went necessarily to the Veneto, to Italy, and thus to the EU. If you came here, you went there and that's how it was.

There I sat rearranging reams of papers, the living embodiment of thinking globally while acting locally.

Being a part of the EU was where it got interesting, if you were the type of person who liked such things, and as inexplicable as it seemed, there must have been those types of people, somewhere. The papers piled on my desk were testament to this.

For one could be besieged by studies and proposals of the ETOA, the European Tourism Association, from two different ETCs, the European Tourism Commission and, not to be forgotten, the ETC that was the European Travel Commission—the body set up by the National Tourism Organizations of the eager and optimistic nations that had embraced the union of Europe. At least one of the ETCs had been newly mandated by the European Commission to play a central role in cooperative marketing campaigns. Besides all looking out for our own interests, and the interests of our assigned little far-flung fiefdoms, we were, all of us, cooperating. That was the thing, merging your self-interests with the cooperative outlook. It was simple, really. As long as everyone in Europe could subsume their own self-interests within the larger union, all would be well. For everyone.

Of course, no one could read them all and you sat there stupefied that anyone anywhere had written them all. There was so much damned cooperation that it generated a maelstrom of paperwork vying for someone's attention. Cooperation was a hard and competitive craft in these modern days.

Deep in the bowels of this bureaucratic excreta, I discovered EDEN—European Destinations of Excellence. This was a new cooperative commission that was a competition to select "Destinations of Excellence" based on a commitment to social, cultural, and environmental sustainability. EDEN was not open to everyone. There was a competition. What better way, I thought, to enter Eden than by winning a competition? And upon winning the competition and entering the Elysian fields of Eden, if you were Abel, then you could commence full cooperation. If you weren't killed. Both Eden and brothers could be lost, as I well knew. It was a timeless tragic trope of humanity long before Milton put it into verse.

Eden, I thought, is where I wanted to be, and no matter how cutthroat the competition, I would elbow my way in there one way or another, if that's what it took. Getting into EDEN was largely about sustainable tourism, which was a newly nascent hot-topic in the Venice tourism circles in which I toiled. Once you proved you were fully focused on sustainability, you could be in EDEN for a whole year and bask in its bounty. Right up until you were cast out to make way for EDEN'S new inhabitants. There were only so many places, and sustainability got you in, if only for a time. No one could sustain Eden forever but as the poets had said, perhaps its very evanescence was what made it Eden.

I was engrossed in studying the machinations of how to get into EDEN when Signor Contarini stuck his well-coiffed head into my office.

"Ah, there you are," he said, as if he'd not expected me to be in my small office perched behind piles of papers.

"Have you plans for lunch?" he asked.

I did not and I said as much, with what I hoped was only moderately evident anticipation.

It was no secret that Contarini and his expense account were habitues of some of Venice's finest restaurants and long, lingering lunches.

"Benissimo. Why don't you come by my office. I need to talk to you for a few minutes before I go to eat."

Eden and expense account lunches, it seemed, remained just out of reach.

∞ ∞ ∞

Contarini was pleased, he said, with the small presentation on "Attracting American Tourism in the New World" I had given the previous week at the association meeting at the Doge's Palace. It had been brief and straightforward but everything I said had been simultaneously translated into Italian, which had lent it an element of significance it likely did not deserve.

The illustrious Signor Contarini had determined that my native tongue was an asset and could allow him to spend more time at home and also away at his villa in the country in the foothills of the Dolomites. It was odd but for those who lived their everyday lives in the midst of the grandeur of one of the world's most dreamed of destinations, having a place to get away from it all was of paramount importance. Perhaps too much beauty is hard on the soul, as the exceptional fades into the unremarkable.

Now that I'd evidenced an acceptable level of foreign competence at being American, Contarini had decided that he required an emissary for the sundry trips throughout the EU. This suited us both as he had reasons to remain ensconced in Venice and I did not.

I kept toiling in tourism and traveled as I did it.

It seemed fitting and proper because Venice was no more home for me than anywhere else had been. Elsewhere was where I lived.

The travel was well-funded and often times effortless.

Flying in Europe was easy because everything was accessible, everyplace was just an hour or two away from anywhere, like Los Angeles, but in a good way. If I didn't want to fly, I had an array of choices of first class trains from Venezia's Stazione Centrale that carried me away during the night and deposited me in the morning in Rome, Salzburg, Nice, Geneva, or Ljubljana or some other elsewhere. Alessandra of the office made all the travel arrangements for me and seemed pleased to do so and thus get rid of me for awhile, having failed at converting me into a better version of America or an American.

People began acting like I was relevant, and I tried to feel like I was, despite my own skepticism. I applied myself to focusing on what lie ahead rather than the inaccessible things that lay behind, forever out of reach.

On a business trip in Geneva, I attended a tourism conference at the UN building and stayed in a suite overlooking Lac Leman and the misty spray of its tall fountain. Geneva was properly international, pristine, well-ordered, and redolent with the insipid air of bland neutrality.

Perhaps feeling insipid myself by virtue of my surroundings and my ineffectiveness at overcoming an obsession with a woman I would never see again, I spent an entire Saturday and most of Sunday in bed with a charming dark Dutch woman on an Erasmus exchange program from the Sorbonne, who besides being stunning and the color of mouth-watering caramel, distinguished herself by having used the word vapid more than three times. Though she herself was not vapid, speaking with fluency six languages, plus just a little of two more. I noted how differently the similar experiences of empires built on the sea had marked Holland and Venice; while the Dutch had turned tolerance into convention and vigorously embraced the world, Venice had narcissistically turned in on itself and become insular and even boastful of their singularity. People, canals, empires on the sea, students at the Sorbonne, though similar on the surface, handled things differently.

One of our conversations turned from Erasmus to other famous Dutch people, a topic which I was superbly under-informed for her taste. Steering to what I thought was safe terrain, we talked of Van Gogh. She thought Van Gogh overrated, a "peasant with a paintbrush," she called him and said those who were not Dutch could never properly pronounce his name. I was indeed kind of Dutch, but still couldn't. To properly pronounce it you had to sound, Dutch-like, as if you were choking on a large amount of phlegm, so I wasn't particularly eager to prove her wrong and apply myself. Being with her and being away helped to pass the time, but not to forget that it was not where I wanted to be nor who I wanted to be with.

In Salzburg, the lovely Austrian town that had built its fortune on the white gold of the salt mines but traded them for tourism and hawking favorite son Mozart with a Disneyesque fervor, I lost almost a week's pay at the quiet blackjack tables atop the fortress-cum-casino, but in doing so befriended an Australian who was on a one year walkabout and tried to get me to accompany her on her mandated pilgrimage to Gallipoli, someplace she couldn't of course go home without seeing, and then on to Thailand or Korea to teach English, or even just, wherever. Her moral attitude shared a similar flexibility to her travel planning: she'd recounted a busy travel tour of casual sex all over Europe, though we didn't indulge. In effort to get away from the pushers of Mozart memorabilia and because Australians seem to always need to be doing something, we went outside of the town and visited a salt mine and its underground lake together, but walking through the salt-walled caverns besides the simple girl who was not whom I wished to be with felt very much like pouring salt on the wound I was trying to mend in my ego and my heart. I remembered hearing how scar tissue is supposed to be even stronger when it heals, but didn't feel convinced of its veracity.

I left Salzburg and returned to my ersatz home in Venice thinking about how the standard Austrian greeting there was Gruss Gott, greetings with God, and remembering that goodbye was supposed to have been shortened from the Old English salutation God-be-with-you. No matter which one you prayed to or whether you believed at all, people were still going to give you gods' greetings and their goodbyes. Looking around at the world, it was hard to believe he could have been with us all, easy to even question if he was indeed with anyone.

Another trip, another hotel, another city, another little aimless adventure.

Beckoned by business to Budapest, I let two young American backpackers who'd just graduated from Bryn Mawr stay in my suite at the Royal Kempinski, and we ordered club sandwiches and wiener schnitzel and a bottle of Apfel Schnapps from room service and they slept on the bed, me on the couch and I never figured out which one was Samantha and which one was Sarah or if they were perhaps a couple or if I was supposed to try anything, and I didn't much feel like it anyway, despite having conjured up similar situations in countless illicit late-night dreams. So I didn't. Feeling full of schnitzel and schnapps, thus expansive and wanting to share something, I told them about the mysterious artist haunting my libido and mind and thought they would think it was a terrifically sad romantic story. But they only reacted by saying she must have been pretty mixed up, a real head-case, and I wished I hadn't said anything about her at all and felt the strange tugging of remorse at sharing things I wished I hadn't, as if I'd betrayed a confidence.

I remembered again something I kept learning over and over yet seemed doomed to repeat: that you could never count on how women were going to react, no matter how hard you tried. Not if you were a man, and a pretty stupid one at that, in a faraway place. And Budapest is pretty far from everyplace. Sure, on a regular map you can find Budapest right there in the heart of Europe. Only when you're there in your hotel room late at night with two girls, feeling so forlorn and alone you can tell, you can actually palpably feel, that the place doesn't know where it is. Partly a result of not being sure what it wants to be, in the way that adolescents after a growth spurt are uncomfortable with their new bodies.

∞∞∞∞

Attending a conference in Milan, I shared a taxi to the Jolly Hotel with a Senegalese businessman who looked like he should have been playing power forward for the Warriors but instead was carrying perhaps the largest briefcase I'd ever seen, a heavy battered old satchel, and we stared out the cab window at the snow blanketing the Dolomites, which hovered rather surprisingly right on the upper fringe of the staid gray environs of the city of industry and fashion, and I found out that the Senegalese have no word for snow. He got out of the taxi before me, stretching out his lanky frame to its full height, grabbing his case, politely nodding his head at me before walking away, but somehow it was clear he had already traveled much farther than me to get there.

It set me to thinking about Huck and Jim rafting up the Mississippi and how their trip was geographically the same distance but how people could travel further than others on the same trip. Maybe it had something to do with relativity. Anyhow, I remembered how proud I was when Huck tore up that letter near the end and hoped I would have done the same thing. It had always seemed strange that people complained and banned the book for its racist epithets, especially when you could see that Jim was the only purely good man, the only noble man, in the whole damned beautiful book filled with colorful collages of white child abusers, con artists, cutthroats, and liars. Jim was a fucking hero. Of course you weren't supposed to say fuck, either. Hero, you could say. If you could find one. But then I'd never been black and never rafted a river, so maybe I didn't know what to say at all. But I thought I could tell a hero when I read about him and was pretty sure that Twain could when he wrote about one.

Places, events, people, days, and trips slipped by, things, as they do, continued to happen and I added them all to the mental diary that was my present slipping into past. I saw some fascinating places and had some amusing experiences but still felt that my life's structure was, well, lacking a structure. Or perhaps the foundations of my life, like Venice's palazzos, were built on marshy ground that could not support the weight it was meant to bear.

The more other places I went, the further from home I felt and I found my already infrequent calls and letters became even less so, and moreover, that I didn't miss them. There had been a time in those halcyon years after college, when we had all been so terrifically naive and optimistic and when all the big experiences were new, that it had been very important to keep in near-constant contact with my small group of friends. New paths had been explored together and horizons and possibilities opened up for all of us and we enjoyed catching up and sharing them together. In recent years, the horizons and scale of my group had shrunk. They all led thoroughly comfortable lives, owned homes and had good jobs and most of them were very busy procreating. They had clearly marked maps and none of them ever strayed off course. I missed the unguided wandering journeys of our youth, straying down the wrongs roads, often and lengthily, had seemed to me to be the very idea of youth, and was one I clung to as long as I could. I noticed that I seemed to be alone in this as they all were so pleased at finding their paths so well trodden.

There had been a certain youthful excitement to having friends on the edge and to being right there on the edge with them, to being privy to their mistakes, whether they were drugs, cheating on girlfriends, illicit one night stands, paying for abortions, or simply and necessarily lying to parents. The pastimes that had made youth and all its folly so indescribably exhilarating and gloriously gut-wrenching all at the same time.

Youth: the illusion of infinite choice and marvelous multiple mistakes. Adulthood: babies, mortgages, IRA's, stock portfolios, nannies, package vacations, cruises. Far as I could see, adulthood was pretty disappointing, though I was oft encouraged to join these ranks in the same way a Mormon on a bicycle wants to convert everyone he meets. There is no zealot like a convert, though I remained unconverted. No one cherished mistakes anymore, nor, it seemed, got any pleasure from remembering with fondness the follies of youth.

I had grown tired of being the token single friend at the dinner parties and had little enthusiasm or interest in cooing over each and every baby or home redesign or family scrapbook, or going for a ride in each new gas guzzling SUV and BMW. To me, the babies, houses, and cars and trucks all looked alike, but not in a Platonic ideal way. Tired of all that pretending and doing everything friendship necessitated you had to do even if you didn't want to do it. "Once you have kids everything changes, you wouldn't believe how you never sleep again, what hard work it is, how it completely takes over your life. It's great, you should do it. It's so much harder than you'd think. You never have time again." The philosophy seemed to me as simple and as admittedly time-tested as "you should be more like us," but I thought it noteworthy they all found time to share their observation nevertheless.

Friends who had cut lines of cocaine in the Eighties, people who'd filmed their more perverted exploits, now filmed their wives giving birth, and of course you couldn't talk about the former and you had to talk endlessly about the latter. Guys that encouraged you to keep drinking after you'd just puked for the second time after another too many tequilas now coached their boys in t-ball or diligently drove their daughters to soccer practice.

And they all started planning for early retirement, all were certain, no matter how cautious and careful they lived, that you could never be too careful. Hell, I had friends younger than me, and thirty-five didn't feel old, didn't seem old, but I had friends younger, who already had retirement plans and lawyers and stockbrokers, and just "guys"—they always had a pool guy or a lawn guy or a laser eye surgery guy, and their guy, of course, was always the best guy, being that he was "their guy." You should try "my guy," I kept being told. I came to find that I kept being told the same things over and over. I seemed to be the only one who grew weary of the eternal carousel and its rounded repetitions.

In the impressionable and fleeting times of youth, friends had been the yardstick by which everything had been calibrated, but then we started measuring different things. I don't remember looking away, just that at some point I looked back and everything had changed. The potentiality of youth had given way to the predictability of adult conformity and I had become detached from what defined everyone. It was as if there was a secret club and I didn't know the password. Uninitiated in the proscribed rites of passage, I had become but an onlooker to rituals beyond my understanding.

As for me, I fell into the bed of another man's wife, got exiled to Venice for my sins and acquired a few gray hairs along the way, a merit badge of maturity I felt unworthy of displaying. And back at my former home, everyone had grown adept at the rituals of raising families, swinging short irons, and forging happy homes. My old sleep-deprived friends were awakened from restless slumbers by crying infants or buzzing alarms heralding long-ago scheduled tee times. They had things to do, places to go. It seemed that picking up a nine-iron was the culmination of the course of youth. It was just a theory, but outsiders seek explanation for things they do not understand. I had a lot of theories since I had a lot of time on my clubless hands, no one having taken over my time or my life yet. They didn't do me a damned bit of good, but they were what I had instead of routine. I even had a theory that if you lacked theories you weren't looking close enough at life, though no one agreed with me or bothered to disagree since I didn't have anyone to try and explain myself to. I was the proverbial tree falling in an unpopulated forest, without witness to my sounds. A forest of one.

My friends, the stalwart companions of my youth, the irreplaceable battered baggage of my earlier life, still left a presence, or a noted absence, more like, in my life. At home, they had all kept telling me to settle down and catch the boat with them, and somehow I'd missed it, the maturity boat or train or SUV, whatever the mode of transport was, it seemed to me an unappealing one. Instead of feeling like I'd missed a scheduled important trip, I felt more that I'd dodged the bullet of utter boredom and being like everyone else. I knew I was supposed to worry about it more, and I had tried to for quite awhile just to be more like everyone else, but in the end, I had grown tired of pretending. I envied what I was supposed to have, what they all had, and we all grew a bit awkward that I hadn't been converted to the modern American family man like I was supposed to be.

I found I had little interest and less inclination to go to the trouble of keeping up with things back home and made do with working at enjoying my new life in Venice, reading great books I'd never had time for, eating and drinking well, too much and too often, and even trying to do pretty good work, if more out of habit than inspiration. All of which was pretty fulfilling and surprisingly easy. With no one

to worry about but myself, I stopped remembering to worry at all.
I couldn't have grown an ulcer if I'd tried. I wanted to say that to
someone, but you had to be careful of talking about stomachs or
livers or kidneys with the Italians, as they had a remarkable and rather
voodoo-like sensibility still about the inner workings of the body
and just the word liver could launch long, little understood diatribes.

Left with little to really worry about, there was but one thing I
kept agonizing over: where was the beautiful chestnut-haired artist?
And why had she decided to go back to L.A.? In the Chronicle, Herb
Caen had once written how nice it was that people who preferred
Los Angeles to San Francisco lived there. Was she happy in the sun
and smog of Southern California? Did she ever remember crying
in the Piazza and eating my pasta and her warm tears landing on my
neck, and ponder what might have been? Was she home and making
a second act in her young life, despite what Fitzgerald had said? Did
that guy there appreciate her and admire her and think about her as
much as I did, or did she hold no mystery for him for his having had
her? My father had been fond of saying, in the days after my mother
had left the two of us alone and he thought it wise to share sexual
wisdom unasked and unwanted by me, "Show me a beautiful woman
and I'll show you a man who's tired of fucking her."

He was a coarse and candid man, but he did the best he could
with me and with everything he did, and maintained a simple outlook
on life, which he had all figured out to suit him in a masterful and
confident way I had never acquired. He wore a uniform to work and
thought he was a Prince of the Sea, Lt. Colonel Vandermar, and I
never told him otherwise. He told me once he missed the Russians
and I believe he did, and he was damned sad at being retired and
too old for new wars and at having bred a son ill-prepared for any
war, new or old. One of the things I missed most about him was
his confidence in knowing who his enemies were. Something I was
never quite sure of, though having been a military kid and a fairly
educated individual, I knew there was always an enemy of something,
somewhere. Only to his disappointment, I had never picked up the
desire to kill strangers because I was ordered to do so.

I liked to think of ignorance as an enemy but it didn't make
things much clearer to me or me much wiser. Loneliness became a
mild, token enemy of sorts while so far from any home shore, but
it was one I'd grown accustomed to, so I didn't wage any successful
campaigns against it. The casualties I'd left behind in my little battles
thus far were a boss' wife who went back to his bed and an artist who
went back to her boyfriend. The battle raged on, quietly circling my

flanks there on the shores of Venice. The Lt. Colonel would have been very disappointed at my poor tactical ability. I knew better, you should always protect your flanks. I just hadn't managed it. Or had mismanaged it.

∞∞∞

More and more, I went back to the café where I'd met her and drank hot chocolate if it wasn't too warm outside. No matter what I drank, I never saw her there again, but I hoped wherever she was, that she thought about me, as I did her.

Maybe, even though she'd adorned her anonymous note only with that minute word, fondly, she thought of me more than fondly. It had been a pretty nice note, which I reread far too often for my own good, it sitting there on my kitchen table most mornings to remind me of all that was not. I was a poor tactician, indeed. I wondered why there wasn't a good word between like and love. What languages had better? Probably most of them. Like is a small, a terribly small word and love encompasses such vast territory and seems so banal from overuse. At least that's what I'd thought, but still hadn't come up with anything else. I'd have to look into inventing a theory on that myself since Dr. Phil and Oprah weren't on in Italy.

At a tourism conference in Sweden, I'd learned that with their use of formal and informal words for you, there was no proper way to say cheers formally, and there were many jokes about trying to avoid having to toast with people whom you didn't want to be on an intimate, informal basis with. That was fascinating to me. The Swedes, though, not so much. Oh, they were all nice and polite and earnest and hearty and good-looking besides, but maybe they were just too earnest. They were delightfully convinced that Sweden was the best country in the world, and that was a lovely thing and an educational experience for an American, finding out that most people, indeed, preferred their own home. I hadn't had the occasion yet to go places where home was unbearable and which no one would prefer, but thought it still a thing of beauty for everyone to prefer their own place.

In Budapest for the third time, I'd learned you weren't supposed to toast with beer because the Nazis had done so after hanging Hungarian patriots in the square. Both sides of the Danube, the towns of Buda and Pest, resonated with the feel that old Europe seemed like it should have. Though the economy there struggled along and there were many people living in inconvenient conditions, suffering the shaky trajectory of transition from Communist satellite to burgeoning democracy, they were still a proud and patriotic people. And the paprika, they had entire stores of it, hundreds of different kinds and varieties and strengths of it, entire stores devoted to this national spice. Which seemed good somehow, whole stores devoted to a single spice, a tasteful unanimity about seasoning, but perhaps it was just the remnants of having lived under so many totalitarian regimes so long.

The beautiful spires and ivory colored lights of the large Parliament building lit up the Danube at night. You could see them from the square on the other side of the river where all the barely dressed whores stood around in little groups and mingled amongst themselves until they were approached by an admirer, a possible customer. In the square by the Royal Kempenski hotel, they sold papers in every language you could imagine and you couldn't help noticing that all the people: the whores, the drinkers, the bums, the tourists, looked like they were from someplace else. If they were Huns, maybe they were. It seemed there was, according to the travel guides, some dispute about the origins of the Huns. And some mystery about Finnish-Hungarian language similarities, though I didn't learn either and didn't know for sure.

I watched several deals being brokered there between the oldest profession and its customers, as the police wandered by unfazed, stopping only to rush along some Gypsies selling counterfeit watches and handbags, that being more serious or bothersome to those who got bothered by such things. The Gypsies moved along, as they always did, being Gypsies. Though you weren't supposed to call them that. Romany was the nomenclature for those who cared about propriety, when you could find them.

Nearby at the Parliament building, the other old profession of ruling a people would begin in the morning and I wondered how many of them engaged in or were customers of both professions, but would never know. Which only made you wonder more, as it did with all things. I tried to formulate a theory about who compromised themselves more, the prostitutes or the politicians, but in the end I couldn't decide conclusively and lacked enough hard evidence or stern convictions. Much like many of the politicians in America I read about. Lacking knowledge and conviction.

On the way back to my large and sadly sleek suite at the Kempenski, I stopped before an otherwise unoccupied prostitute looking eager to ply her trade. Just out of curiosity I asked if she might like a drink. It might have been a fine and good thing to be in a strange city and buy a drink or a meal for a bleached blonde prostitute and how many chances would you have to do such a thing? She was wearing black, thigh high leather boots and fishnet stockings and a small red leather skirt and just a bra and purple fur boa, which seemed kind of strange and sad, that boa that should have been at a costume party or movie premier or somewhere else, instead of where it was.

"Are you looking for company?" she said, in thick English of indeterminate origin.

"No, just someone to have a drink with."

She and her boa peered over at me.

"No, thank you, I'm working."

I reached into my wallet to give her what I thought was a healthy and charitable amount of money and she just looked at me strangely. For some reason, I wanted to give money to a whore if I couldn't have a drink with her and didn't want to be with her.

"Do you want someone to love? You like date?"

"No, I just thought, for you," I said, holding the bills forward.

I had large, colorful zlotys because the Hungarians had not yet earned the bland and boring bureaucratic euros. I'd heard they were going to join the EU, so they might and probably would if they could. Everyone wanted to sit at the popular table no matter how boring it was. The law of nature that ruled high school cafeterias as well as global politics dictated that there was always one popular table and more people who wanted to sit there than there were seats, a never ending game of musical chairs. Of course the most popular were rarely the nicest, but most everyone wanted to be more popular. It seemed nowadays as if few wanted to be nicer.

"I am working. I am no beggar," she said, disdaining the money, arrogantly flipping her boa and turning away to go off toward a group of other comrades and talk about the stupid and insulting foreigner in dire straits who'd offered her money for nothing. I was the wrong sort of commerce and I guess we both knew it.

I was pretty sure that politicians took money from anyone, so I decided that was enough evidence and finished my work in Budapest and made sure to make a visit to the Hungarian National Museum before leaving, not knowing if I'd ever come back because no one makes a fourth trip to Budapest. Living in Venice and missing the absent artistic woman who had slipped away had left me with a strong new interest in art. I wished at least if the prostitute hadn't taken my money, that I could have gotten her name.

There were a lot of women in Europe doing all manner of things whose names were unknown to me then, and the space between what was right and what was wrong and what I understood and what I did not grew larger and more mysterious.

The Danube flowed by notoriously not blue despite its waltz, and the city itself very gray, but the colors of the paintings in the National Museum were bright and vivid and modern and I didn't understand them but liked their craving for color. Even the paintings that were abstract made me think unsettled concrete thoughts about the chestnut-haired girl off in the Southern California sun so far from me. Thinking of her made me feel I was seeing more of the paintings and I was seeing more of them, both literally and figuratively. I went to more museums and maybe I appreciated the art more or maybe I knew I missed an artist, it little mattered as what counted was having something you wanted to do and I guess I wanted to miss her.

There were other trips on the same business to other cities in Europe where I always meant to go to a museum and didn't. But still meant to. I remembered reading some of Steinbeck's travels where he'd written about being abroad and the importance of having a goal, like going to a museum, and how once you'd chosen the goal you could somehow be freed from having to achieve it. Even if you didn't do it, it made the other things you did better because you meant to do it. I think he'd written there was a word for the feeling in Spanish, but I didn't remember it, no matter how hard I tried. I'd lost that data in my mind and perhaps could have offered up a prayer to find it to the Saint of Lost Things we'd been told to pray to at Catechism, but I couldn't remember his name, either.

There was irony everywhere. It was pitiful.

TEN

A MINOR REFORMATION

BACK IN MY LITTLE OFFICE IN VENICE, that damned graffiti on the British Consulate was still sitting there and I was starting to have more piles of work stacked on my desk, but they were mostly just reports to read and easy email questions to answer and I did.

The graffiti across the Grand Canal from my office spoke to me loudly: "Stop War," it said, every day in red spray paint. No one would cover it up, not the Venetians and not the British.

I decided that it probably would have gone away if I crept over some night and spelled out "Stop tourism. Leave Venice." I was sure then that someone would cover that up, but I never did go over and make that grand meaningless gesture. I always meant to, though. I had grown rather attached to the idea and the spray painted letters. I bet if someone told Tony Blair about it, it'd be repainted. No one did, I guess.

I'd convinced myself that you had to be pretty irresponsible and maybe even a bit unrealistic to be an artist, whether your medium was graphic design, graffiti, or oil and that seemed to me a hell of a wonderful thing. Irresponsibility. Painting consulates and canvases, making beauty, saying things that needed to be said but were not.

Lacking any other strong motivator and any peers around to counsel or constrain me, it seemed that more irresponsibility was just what my life needed. I threw myself into it with reckless abandon. Well, not utterly reckless, but I drank a lot and very artistically.

I started keeping later hours and longer times at more bars and cafes. I even wrote bad poetry on the flimsy, ever present cocktail napkins, which I always ended up taking with me to crumple up and throw in the nearest canal, an act which evinced more poetry than the poetry itself, a solitary performance art. I set the Guinness world

record for weepy haikus about a girl with an unknown name thrown
into Venetian canals. It was good to excel at something.

Bored with my solitudinal longings, I began to acquire a new
social self, which was nobody really, in that my Italian was not good
enough yet to have any lengthy meaningful conversation with the
locals, and their English not good enough for mine, so when strewn
together, I spoke bad Italian and they bad English, which in itself
was a rather pointless but satisfying charade.

I became an expert at ordering drinks, all manner of drinks, the
Italians being lovers of the right drink at the right time. Every bar and
café, no matter how small, was always lined up with colorful bottles
of distilled herbs and secret ingredients, all manner of yellows, reds,
blacks, and greens. There was a delightful palette to the bar shelves in
Venice and there were perhaps more kinds of liquor than there were
of pasta, but it was a close contest. People had been fermenting things
ever since they had been growing things and I was more interested
in the imbibing side of the equation.

One evening I was out again, later than I should have been,
and for some reason, perhaps because it was there, though it always
had been, I was drinking Cynar on ice, a foul artichoke liqueur that
the locals were fond of after dinner. It was not good, in fact it was
heinous, but was thus an accomplishment in and of itself, though
I didn't know exactly why except that I'd developed a taste for the
distasteful.

There was a young American couple near me in the bar, loudly and
confusedly trying to figure out their change in euros and discussing
the inconvenience of the night trains and the prices of everything.
Generally doing all the things Americans do abroad that when you're
not with them, make you embarrassed of them. Then you felt guilty,
like being embarrassed of your parents at a PTA meeting. But in that
same manner, you were a helpless victim of these feelings. Even
though you knew better or knew at least you should have been better
than you really were.

They politely came up to me and said slowly, "Scuzi, scuzi, can
you give us directions to the train station?"

I looked at them for a second.

"Train station!" he shouted, as if I was deaf and stupid.

The station wasn't far, just a ten minute walk, and I was about
to speak in English and relieve them of their confusion when the
guy looked over to the woman he was with and said, "None of these
dudes speak any English. It's crazy."

So I spoke to them in bad Italian and gave them thoroughly

wrong directions, even threw in some heavily accented English words, and they continued to act like it was utter irresponsibility to be sitting in a bar in Northern Italy after midnight and not speak fluent English. So I felt little guilt for leading them astray and actually rather pleased with myself as they continued to trade inside jokes at my expense between them.

The barman listened to the whole exchange and nodded his head sagely at my wrong directions. When they left, he gave me another Cynar and smiled and poured one for himself, and I felt a part of something, a co-conspirator against the evils of tourism. I went to the office during the day and sent emails and then people like that came to bother you in a bar and you couldn't help feeling responsible, even if you weren't. There were people like that everywhere. Only some of them were your countrymen.

I wondered if being embarrassed of your countrymen and giving them wrong directions was a traitorous act, and would have bet that it was in Ashcroft's mind. I would have been no good at Operation TIPS, but then unlike Ashcroft, I'd read the Constitution a few times.

When they left and the barman and I were the last ones there in the dark little Bar Postale, he took out an old bottle of something syrupy and homemade from under the bar, a sort of grappa, that he said his uncle made. At least he said something about home and his uncle, I recognized only that much with my limited Italian. Deductive reasoning can only take you so far when you don't have the vocabulary knowledge.

"Mi dispiace, molto dispiace. Non parlo bene Italiano," I said, apologizing at being still in his bar and not speaking his language well enough to cement our friendship, just as guilty as the stupid couple who'd just departed, but at least knowing I was guilty helped.

"No," he said, with a trace of English accent, "your Italian is not good at all, this is true."

I laughed.

"So, you speak English."

"I should hope so, I lived in London almost 15 years. I'm Bruno," he said.

"Mark Vandermar," I said and shook his hand. That was one of the good things the Colonel had taught me, always shake the bartender's hand.

"Vandermar? You are Dutch?" he asked.

"Not really, American."

"But Dutch name?"

"Right," I said.

He looked at his watch, then glanced at the empty drink glasses on the tables and then at the door and I thought it was time to finish up and get out of there. Despite the crowds during the day, Venice is not a late night town, not at all, and for most neighborhoods midnight was very late, even during high season. If you wanted late nights and crowded bars or discos you went to places other than Venice for them. It had not always been so. For several hundred years, Venice had been the liveliest and most decadent spot in Europe with parties, balls, courtesans, casinos, lovers, and nightspots of international renown.

At one time, the Café Florian in Piazza San Marco had boasted that their doors had never closed for two centuries. Now they closed around midnight. Venice took her money during the day and slept soundly at night or went home to the mainland, to terra firma in Mestre.

He walked over to the door.

I finished off my drink and reached for my wallet.

"Leaving, or drinking?" he said.

I stood there pondering the politeness of leaving him to his ministrations of closing the bar, conflicted with the desire for some conversation with an interesting new ally who spoke my language. There weren't many Venetians that did, even though you thought there would be. And it was easy to grow weary of banal conversations with tourists, so I avoided them nowadays. Both banalities and tourists. Perhaps they were the same. I grew to think it so anyway, but it was an occupational hazard of my job and my life.

He made the decision simple for me.

"Do you have someone waiting for you at home?"

"No," I said, which was truer than anything I'd said in the bar up until now and maybe ever.

"Yes, me neither. So, we are drinking, no?"

He closed the door and returned to his place behind the bar. If you've never been in a bar after the doors have closed and locked, you've missed what is one of the greatest pleasures in the drinking world.

It's always nice to be on the right side of the closed doors and most often you aren't. Prohibition was probably what made the twenties roar, all the abandon that went on inside closed and secreted drinking spots, where you could drink illicit liquor and speak easy. Bernice might not have bobbed her hair were it not for the bathtub gin and a Kennedy would never have sat in the White House were it not for desire to thwart the strictures of Prohibition. But the Kennedy's had always been very catholic in their attitudes about laws and morality, despite the fact that their church was not one that ever distinguished itself for its own catholic attitude.

He got us out two new glasses and poured healthy doses of the syrupy drink that was strong and warm and burned all the way down and left a trace along my throat. I could feel it actually sitting in my stomach, and the burning felt pretty damned good in that dark little bar and it seemed like we had put a good one over on some tourists for no reason at all.

It went without saying that both of us would have been out of work without these same tourists. So we did not say it.

I put my cigarettes on the bar and he took one, and we both smoked while he refilled our glasses.

"How about you, Bruno, no one to go home to?"

"Ah, just my wife, but she is already angry with me. If I come home straightaway, she'll still be up to yell at me."

"So we drink?"

He looked around and spread his hands expansively over the bar.

"That's what one does in a bar, no?"

We avoided talk of trivial things, the lubrication of the homemade liquor and serendipitous meeting having relieved us of the necessity of actually getting to know each other. We talked of women we'd had and more of ones we had almost had, also a good thing to do late at night in a bar behind closed doors, the very kind of thing men talked too much of behind closed doors.

I told him things I'd never told anyone, things that were part of my past but had not yet shelved themselves properly into my present. With a certain inevitability, the talk evolved from women into things we'd done wrong, things we had not done and now would never do and knew it, but still wanted to. Things we still did wrong. I told him about Jack Bindman's wife, and being Italian, he was not the least surprised by this admission of marital infidelity, only surprised that I didn't lose a job or a few teeth from it. We both agreed that we would have handled it differently.

"We men, we are all of us very stupid creatures, aren't we?" he said.

"Seems so."

"But the beauty is, I think, that we are each stupid in our own way. There is one way, only one, to be smart, but there are thousands, millions of ways to be stupid. Don't you think?"

I agreed and we toasted to the mysteries and possibilities of stupidity. The little bar practically filled up with them.

As we touched glasses, I remembered something I'd heard or read.

"They say the reason we touch glasses is because during Feudal times when you stayed at someone's castle you would each raise your glass and both pour some of your drink into the others' to make sure it wasn't poisoned," I said, because I'd often thought about it and certainly planned on doing so if ever invited to stay at someone's castle. Or if the Dark Ages come back. Only history shows that no one knows it's the Dark Ages until after they're over.

He smiled and we touched glasses and drank again and the home brew seemed less malevolent.

"That's a good story, but it is not right, not right at all. I'll tell you what it is," he said.

He lifted the glass to his nose and inhaled deeply. Then he held it up against a dim yellow light behind the bar. He dipped a calloused finger in his glass and licked it. Then he took a healthy swig.

"See, we can smell it, we can see it, we can touch it, we can taste it. But we are blessed with five senses, grazie dio. So we must not leave out the poor ear. If we do not clink the glass, the ear, you see, does not hear the drink. So this way we touch all the senses," he said.

Though I was a bit drunk by then, it seemed a perfect piece of pithy commentary on culture. The English were worried about being poisoned, the Italians were worried about leaving out any of the senses.

That night everything on the right side of the closed bar door was easy to understand and all very clear, though much of the substance of the evening remains fuzzy to me, helped by his uncle's brew.

This unassuming man who owned a small bar in the quiet Santa Croce neighborhood of Venice had lived a very interesting life and was pleased with himself for having done so but had given it all up, the interesting stuff, to settle down and give his mother grandchildren. It was very clear, the house was for his wife, the children for his mother, the bar for himself. Each border was clearly demarcated to that man who tended me that night at his bar. Having lived abroad and returned, he had much fondness for remembering other places, the way exiles the world over do upon returning home.

He missed England a bit, but found that when you got older you had to go home, which was Venice.

"The English," he said, "they make the best kind of men, though very different from an Italian man, very interesting, no less. But the worst kind of women. Cold women, no passion. It is a very sad thing, a woman with no passion. Like a crime."

He regretted greatly that he'd never gone to bed with an American woman, not so much as he'd met anyone in particular he'd desired to have, but because he should like to have gone to bed with an American woman, the idea of it.

We decided having the idea of it was perhaps better and I thought again of the note the artist had left me and wondered if she and this man were privy to wisdom I'd not gleaned. Maybe I was guilty of wanting too much to come true. I'd been guilty of other things. Some of them were among the better things I ever did.

We got drunker and continued talking of things of little importance, though they seemed so at the time, and I think what I liked most about him was when I asked him, what if he had millions of dollars, what would he do, where would he go?

He looked around his quiet little bar, surveying his dominion, current population two.

"I would come here, I think, the same way I have done. I have my own bar, not too many problems, there is my wife, but a wife should get mad at a husband to show she loves him, this is part of the marriage. Sometimes there are money problems or the kids are difficult, but that's what kids are, and of course, when you have a business in Italy, this perfectly crazy country, always problems with the government, but in this, I think, too, it is something of necessity. There must be some problems, some hills and bumps on the road, so you can enjoy looking back and seeing where you've been. There is much time to look back and one should enjoy the view."

It took us a couple of hours to finish off the bottle and conclude on agreeing on everything about life. We did both. Then we left the emptied bottle on the bar and walked out into the night, and the darkness of the canal was still and quiet, without even the lapping of little waves, brightened only by the reflection of one shining light of a piano nobile, the only light aglow on the whole street, that danced a quiet little show on a patch of otherwise dark canal water. He gestured meaningfully toward the light of the arched apartment windows.

"My wife, I guess, she is still up waiting to yell at me. What persistence, yes?"

"Admirable."

"Yes, beautiful, in its own way, I think, so many ways of beauty" he said, in his Italian flavored English.

"You live very close to your bar."

"Dangerously close. If you should ever happen to have a bar, I should recommend that you do not live so close to it, I have found in my experience. But in Venice, everything is close. I think I shall blame this all on you. A difficult, wealthy American who came in, got very drunk and we will say that he left without paying his bill and had to be chased down and was never found. Something like that. She will expect a good story from me if she has waited up this long."

"You could make me Dutch, I mean, I am, sort of," I said, with some strange stirring of patriotism or protectiveness, having already once made a small betrayal of my country that evening. There were a lot of slippery slopes, after all.

"American will do the job better. She will believe anything possible from an American. Besides which, it is true, you are American, you are drunk and you did not pay."

There are some truths one can not argue.

"Will she believe it?"

He exhaled a long breath of air from deep behind his lips and teeth and looked over at me with hearty Italian bemusement.

"Of course she will not. She will think it is something much worse, that I am away on some affair with some woman."

He leaned over and spat into the dark waters of the canal, then cleared his throat, wiped his chin and went on.

"It is a terrible thing to get in trouble for sins you did not even commit."

"Not this time," I said.

"Right, but there have been others, other times and others sins, and still she deserves a good story, I think."

"Buona fortuna," I said.

"Cheers," he said.

And we walked off into the night; me heading down the deserted dark fondamenta towards my little empty apartment in the Dorsoduro and him just a few yards up the canal side to where his wife awaited a good story which he would graciously provide. I would rather have liked to have seen the performance and how she handled it and if she believed him or whether or not she even wanted to. Wanting to believe was strong medicine.

∞ ∞ ∞

As I staggered home, even the perennial late night haunts of my neighborhood in Campo Santa Margherita were empty and quiet and dark, but it was nice weather now and the tables had been left outside the closed shutters of the bar.

I wondered what time it was that they were all closed, a few of them generally stayed open very late, the latest bars in all of Venice anyway, but at the same time, I did not want to ruin anything by looking at my watch, pleased as I was that I'd already had too much to drink and I had Venice, all of Venice, to myself this quiet drunken night.

I sat down at one of the tables and put my feet up on it and clasped my hands behind my head, an inebriated king taking stock of his domain. I was Ozymandias, King of Kings. Only I couldn't remember if there really had been a statue and an Ozymandias. You could never find out the important things when you needed them. Like in the dark stillness of a drunken night in a campo in Venice.

There was a darkened restaurant there in the campo that had a chalkboard sign that said: No Pizza, No Lasagna, No Directions. Information, 5 Euros. If it had been open, I might have been able to go inside and ask. It would have been well worth the price but it was closed, like everyplace else in the campo.

I knew that elsewhere in Venice, tourists were asleep in hotels, waiters and dock workers were at home in bed, at the train station there was a young American couple complaining about the stupid Italians they'd met who didn't even speak English and how hard it was to find the train station, that there was a friendly, philosophical bartender making up a story for his wife to cover up sins he had not committed, and there was no beautiful artist sitting next to me appreciating the fineness of the moment. Nevertheless, I was thinking of her and I felt pretty damned irresponsible and good about myself and leaned back a little further in my chair and reached for my cigarettes, which thoroughly unbalanced my precarious position and toppled both me and the chair and then the table, all of us crashing down onto the pavement. Like Ozymandias, a forsaken pile of rubble.

It made a thunderous clanging and I awaited some voice of complaint or authority, police or window lights being turned on, me having so disturbed the stillness of the peace that lay over the usually crowded campo, but as I lay there all akimbo on the cool stones, there was nothing but my own inebriated laughter.

It was all mine, this Venice, that night. If there was a keeper of the peace he wasn't there and I certainly wasn't him, nor going to do his job for him.

I carefully stood the chair back up and righted the table and placed it back where it belonged.

Then it came to me that it would be a worthwhile thing indeed to move all the silver outdoor metal tables of this bar and exchange them for all the green metallic tables of the bar on the other side of the campo. It seemed like a lot of work and a little rude, but it would certainly be amusing, I thought, in the morning when they opened up.

So I started rearranging and it was much more senseless labor than I'd anticipated and took me a good while to drag all the tables across the cobbled stones, but no one came to help or hinder me, so I had to do it myself, and once begun, convinced myself it would be just plain undisciplined and disrespectful not to finish.

Upon finally finishing, I realized that no one but me or the bar owners would have noted the difference, since all the tables and chairs were well organized and arranged, and unless you knew which style and color went with which bar, you wouldn't have known anything was amiss.

I carefully selected a table to sit down and view my perfectly pointless handiwork. It was quite a lot of effort, actually, to be so drunk so late at night, or early in the morning, I guessed, to be rearranging the furniture of the campo, but it looked to me like a job well done. Look on my works, ye Mighty, and despair, indeed.

I walked across the way and sat down where I had started, but this time on a newly arranged green table. If I'd had a clown and an accordion player, I could have been in a Fellini film. Pointless perseverance was its own reward.

I sat there wondering how the opening hours would go, would they arrive and even notice first thing or would they carry on business as usual? Or perhaps they would, eager to serve the first morning cappuccino drinkers, just agree to leave things as they were for the day and take care of it all after closing. I wished they would do that and I would have been happy to come back and put everything back in its right place for them.

Maybe a big feud would break out, except instead of the Hatfield's and McCoy's, it would be the Nicoletti and the Castellani, the ancient feuding families of Venice. Maybe it would linger for years. Probably not, but you never knew with feuds. Not at night when you were drunk and alone and sitting in a self-rearranged campo in Venice. Anything was possible. Nobody knows who the enemy is. Sometimes even the enemy doesn't know. Or maybe, just maybe, I had met the enemy and he was me.

Not ready to go home yet, I decided to wander around my Venice until either the sunlight shone or someone else ruined my solitary surveying of my personal dominion, and I had to pee and had been meaning to pee in a canal, so I headed across the campo, past the closed gelato shop and the tilting campanile, and stood at the bottom of the bridge where I'd kissed the artist, and thought, just for a minute, about jumping in, just to have jumped in a canal.

But the water was damned dirty and I didn't want to get washed up with any of my own bad poetry, and besides, I was wearing new soft leather Italian shoes which I rather liked. The Italians were much better at footwear than I was at poetry or love.

I compromised on my lack of bravery or gallantry, strode purposefully up the few darkened steps of the bridge and raised my fists and spun just like Rocky and then climbed carefully atop the arch of the bridge, standing right there upon the stone rail that we'd leaned against together, thinking, as a connoisseur of fate, that if I was meant to go in the canal, I would fall in my drunken condition and that in and of itself was a good exercise for fate. Fate, I thought, could use a work out.

Perhaps I had flipped God off one too many times and he would nudge me in and let me drift out into the Adriatic so that I could be flotsam along with my bad poetic attempts. Or would that make me jetsam? It seemed like a good test of something and man, I really had to pee and I unzipped my pants and took it out and let forth with a loud, long stream of piss that made a melodious splashing sound in the canal waters and I thought as I was peeing that I was going to get discovered and be embarrassed, but that too was unstoppable now, like the stream of Bruno's uncle's home brew. The sound was lovely, very musical, though I couldn't write my name in the canal waters like you could in the snow, I tried.

I put myself back in my pants and couldn't avoid the passing hedonistic and perverse thought that it would have been a beautiful thing to make myself come and spill my seed into a canal, really let the little guys have a work out, see if they could distinguish between a birth canal and a Venetian canal, but I was so drunk that I had no desire or ability to actually do the thing. So I just stood there on the railing of the bridge watching the little ripples of my pee make indecipherable scribbles in the waters of the canal as they floated away, having succeeded at nothing more than but briefly disturbing Venice's indelible watery shroud.

I looked around and still there was no one else about, just the lights across the way shining on the church at Campo San Pantalon and the ponderous quietude of the night in between the dark buildings that lined the canal, and I was thinking that they would probably have made a great echo chamber, but I didn't want to wake anyone up by testing it, so I didn't. I wasn't utterly uncouth, after all.

So I braced my feet on the marble rail of the little bridge and spread my arms out and said, quietly, just for my own pleasure:

"It's me, Mark Vandermar, Prince of the Sea. Go ahead and push me, God."

I wasn't loud enough to cause an echo, but I thought for that second if I was indeed pushed in by the invisible hand of God, I might have to become a believer or at least more God-fearing. But he didn't push me and I didn't fall, so I smiled and climbed down carefully off the railing, feeling saved from an ordeal but not without some lingering sense of disappointment.

Then I decided to go and say hello to God, having thus introduced myself. Just to have a little quiet conversation, not a prayer really, but some things that needed to be said to God that maybe you didn't have the fortitude to do unless you were well liquored up, and I went to the church and pulled on the door and was surprised it opened right up, having expected it would have been locked as were most Venetian churches in the night.

It let me into a little alcove, which would have been a great place for a homeless street person to sleep. Even Venice had them, though strictly speaking they didn't have streets. I wondered if perhaps they didn't know about it or they knew but weren't allowed or they were allowed but didn't out of respect. It all seemed very mysterious but probably it was just that some parish priest had forgotten to lock the door that night, because the two doors leading to the inner sanctum of the church were indeed held together with a large chain wrapped around their heavy wrought iron handles.

They were tall, maybe eight-foot high wooden doors, and the chain was draped around their handles from the inside, but it was a long chain and the doors opened quite a bit before the links of the chain stopped them. I held them open to see out of curiosity— needing to talk with God as I did, having some things to say, though I didn't know what—if I could slip through them, and I was surprised that I could just shimmy right between the small opening and then suddenly found myself standing in the heavy dark stillness of the church.

I remember thinking it was a good thing I wasn't some vandal or art thief, knowing that this church, like most all of them in Venice, had its share of Titians and Veroneses, as well as heralded religious relics, gold and graves and saintly skeletal remains. They'd had whole empires as a supply house and they were good curators.

I went in and fumbled around till I felt the chill of the holy water in a large marble basin just beyond the door. I may have been drunk and unsure if it was God's house and even unconvinced if there was a God. But I had been raised Catholic, so I dipped my hand in and made the sign of the cross.

I couldn't see any deeper in the church, it was filled with a thick blanket of blackness, and didn't remember if this one had pews or not. Some of them didn't in Venice and if it did I didn't want to trip over them. So I took out my lighter and it gave me just enough light to see the holy candles, where I could read the sign in English and Italian that said candles were one euro. I felt more than a little foolish having broken in and to be digging around in my pocket for a coin, but glad that I had one and wished I had another because I could have used a few candles, but only took one all the same. Protocol was protocol.

It was cold inside the church. The night outside had been room temperature, but inside it was not and the thick marble slabs of the church floor were like air conditioners, and despite what you learned in school about heat rising, you could feel the chill of the stones through your shoes.

From what I could see, it looked like they must have been doing some remodeling or reconstruction. In Venice, the churches were continually under repairs, endlessly waging the battle of being a part of a city where no city belonged. I noticed there were a lot of paint cans and tools and tarps lying about and I didn't want to mess anything up by making my way all the way up to the altar, so I found a pew and sat down.

I couldn't decide exactly what to say to God and kind of hoped he'd make the first move, but he didn't. So I sat there some more and hoped he could read my mind. I wasn't asking for anything for myself, just that there would be more goodness in the world and I was sorry I hadn't contributed more, that I'd allowed the minutiae and triviality of life to overtake me. That I had lost my purpose and hoped to find one.

"Sorry, God," I said, disturbing the stillness, and it sounded loud in the church even though I spoke quietly.

I was sleepy by then and didn't want some devout early morning priest or art restorer to come to work and find me locked in his church, so I decided that it was enough for now with God. We'd all had enough of me. God, if he was there, certainly had better things to do. I even had better things to do, godless and oblivious as I was.

As I was making my way to the door, my dwindling candle dripped hot wax on my hand, but it seemed like well-deserved penance. So I accepted my small punishment, eager to get out before the candle died. Then the little flame flickered and threw a small patch of light at something on the floor.

I saw a painting there near the door that looked very pretty and surprisingly colorful for an Italian church painting, but those Venetians, I'd learned, had been the masters of color, the colorists, after all. I tried to hold the meager remains of the candle up to it so I could get a good look and remember which one it was for coming back in the daytime. Only just when I moved closer, a big drop of wax fell and I dropped the candle and stomped it out so as not to burn down the church. I was left there in the darkness wanting to know the mystery of that painting leaning against the wall.

I thought for a minute about getting another candle, but couldn't remember where they were. So I picked up the painting and took it with me to the front door of the church. It was a pretty big painting, unframed but still heavy. It must have been on wood. I leaned it there against the door and slipped through the chains into the alcove and then reached in after me to get it and pull it outside so I could hold it up where the church lights were brighter and then put it back inside when I was done. It seemed important to see that painting at that moment after being stuck in the darkness of the church, almost as if I had been blind and yearned to see.

I looked to make sure there were no witnesses about and finding none, brought the painting with me into the dim light in front of the church.

It would be just my bad luck to get caught, no policeman in the world would ever believe I was going to just look at the painting and slip it back, but I did it anyway and held it up there under the light. I wondered what Italian artist had painted it, and when, and had it been done for the church. It wasn't a Christ or a Madonna or a chubby cherub or even winged angels floating on a cloud. It was a knight on a rearing horse and beautiful, I thought, and how did the church come to have it? I took it further up to the little bridge, where I had pissed in the water a long time before and kissed a beautiful girl an even longer time before that, and decided to spend a few minutes memorizing my private art show in mine own personal Venice.

It was this great white, rearing horse and this shimmering silvery armored knight with a long cloak of red hanging down his back, rippling over the hindquarters of the stallion. It was even more beautiful there on the bridge than it ever could have been in the church or a museum.

I sat there trying to commit it, the painting and the whole scene, to the drunken miasma of my mind, to save this memory forever, as something special and personal and profound. Somehow, in striving for the poignancy and detail of a nostalgia yet to come, and in having drunk far too much stuff made by some bartender's uncle, I must have dozed off.

I awoke uncomfortably to the light pink and gray complexion

of Venice at dawn, my head tilted up awkwardly against one of the little marble pillars of the bridge. I heard the slow chugging of a motor boat below and looked to follow its wake and then saw the painting and stood up, sad to find myself in the breaking morning light accompanied by an accidentally purloined painting. It was a little like awaking in a strange bed with someone you didn't know in college, when you did such things. Only you still knew that you had to find out where you were and how to get home safely and why you did the things you did. It occurred to me that perhaps Venice had brought forth some heretofore latent kleptomania in me. First a gondola, now a church painting. At least it evidenced upward mobility.

Across the way, the church doors were still closed but the newspaper kiosk in front of it was open and there were three early morning workers going about their business as usual.

I stood there trying to decide what to do. I knew I didn't want to be caught in the light of day taking back the painting, which could only mean trouble. I thought of just leaving it right there where they'd be sure to find it, probably right away as they opened the church, but then I thought, what if someone else less likely came along and took it, what if someone stole it from God and it was all my fault?

It was a real quandary, there on that special little bridge, where I had kissed and peed and slept, and the plum purple grayness of the skies was giving way to brighter and more determined pinks and oranges and the boats passing below the bridge were growing more frequent. Around me the world chugged along, oblivious of my sins.

The only thing to do was to take it home and then sneak it back some other safer time. So I grabbed it and walked purposefully toward my apartment, comforting myself that if that church's Christ had died for my sins, at least I was going to commit some good ones so as not to make his martyrdom useless.

Nobody even gave me a second glance as I made my way through the campo with the painting. Not the baker opening up his doors, not the fishmonger unloading his cart, not anyone.

I was just another person strolling along in Venice's morning hours taking their artwork for a walk. I wanted to stop for coffee, but dared not and just hurried all the way home, me and God's painting, wandering through the aurora. I was glad to have looked up the Italian for dawn, even if I never got to say it and rarely got to see it.

I put the painting down in my bedroom, leaning against the wall, thinking to wait until the right sober night to take it back. All I would have to do was find the right night. And remain sober for it. Simple.

I showered, made two consecutive coffees, gulped them down

and got dressed for work. I put on a red tie to be in quiet communion with the bright red cloak of the knight in my painting and was even a little pleased with myself for the first time in quite awhile. Let Vesuvius spew forth, at least maybe I'd be engaged in some interesting shit when it happens.

ELEVEN

OLD STONES SOMEWHERE ELSE

THAT MORNING AT WORK, before I'd marked the approach of lunchtime by loosening my tie, Signor Contarini told me I had to go to Prague right away. There was a Council conference he couldn't make or didn't want to, so I was delegated to be discharged in his stead.

I went home and hastily packed my things for a short trip: a suit, a jacket, some casual clothes. I paused briefly to admire the painting leaning against my wall, disturbed by what I'd done and distressed that rectifying the situation would have to wait. It had become clear to me that I had grown too accustomed to making mistakes that I lacked the talent to remedy. Perhaps having gotten lost so frequently in Venice and elsewhere had hindered my moral compass.

I walked to the traghetto stop through a low-lying fog that matched my moral ambiguity and then hailed a mahogany motoscafo that whisked me to Marco Polo Airport and left behind a churning transitory wake of transgressions.

Although it was early in the day and the flight was a short one, I quickly fell into an uneasy sleep and woke only when everyone around me was standing up.

I'd been to Prague on my post collegiate jaunt of Europe years before but had arrived by train and without an expense account for my travels. Youth may be wasted on the young but expense accounts were wasted on the old. I was determined not to waste mine, precisely by, well, wasting it.

From the front of the little international airport, I took a taxi straight to my hotel and went to sleep, weary some from travel and more from drinking and stealing from God and feeling rich in regret but also more than a minor measure of pride in the fact that at least

I was doing some interesting things.

I awoke in my small but elegant room at the Tri Ostriche Hotel at the head of the Charles Bridge in Prague. It was a beautiful spring morning and the sun sparkled on the Vltava River and there were several people out on the river in beaten up pedal boats. It was nice to look down on a different ribbon of water even if it wasn't as exalted as the Grand Canal.

There was an EC Tourism Council Meeting in Travel Marketing, it had some much longer and official name than that, but I don't remember exactly what it was, these meetings all being pretty much the same and tending to blend together. I was speaking about Venice on Tuesday.

It was, I thought, the first time I was in Prague for the second time and I whistled as I got dressed and was excited there was just the right amount of mystery and nostalgia—I knew where the big stuff was but didn't know the city enough to have it sullied by familiarity and I didn't have anything important to do until Tuesday. Clearly I was the beneficiary of Contarini having built in some down time for a trip he thought he'd make. Before that, there would be some meetings and cocktail parties to miss if I could find a reason to miss them, which was usually pretty easy to do. I was excited to sate my thirst for beer after having indulged in so many fine Northern Italian red wines for too long. Ale does more than Milton can to justify God's way to man.

Prague was gloriously stunning, a medieval princess perched along a wide green river and adorned with spires and cupolas and buildings that all looked too breathtaking to be real. It should have been a movie set, but then I thought a lot of life should have been more like the movies, even if I hadn't yet properly cast my own role. I wasn't sure if it was the life I led or the movies I saw that made me think that.

I was pleased that my hotel looked over the bridge and the river because in European towns there is always a river and always a bridge and crossing them gives you something good to do.

When I walked across the Charles Bridge, I listened to some would-be Bohemian Beatles sing "Imagine" in thick Teutonic tones and then watched a rotund bearded man in a faded fez swallow a three foot sword, which was both disgusting and riveting. I tossed some coinage into his hat for having provided a spectacle and having the temerity to wear a fez.

In Old Town Square, I remembered having heard the legend of the king blinding the clockmaker after its completion, the legend that was passed around in almost all European towns with a noteworthy old clock, but was probably still true all the same, in all the cases. In the long chronology of Europe, there was no shortage of old public clocks or tyrants.

I watched the sunset alone from an outdoor café at the base of the bridge, Karluv Most, where I could see the spires of the castle, and the sunrays made the copper domes glare such a bright gold-green it hurt my eyes to keep staring at them, though I did. I got chilly and thought long and hard about going back to my room and changing, mostly because I wanted to look alluring and meet a woman to hang out with and buy drinks for and maybe even to dance, if I got drunk enough, and certainly to kiss. That was generally the order, get drunk enough to dance and then dance enough to kiss and kiss enough to forget.

Then I thought that changing would be trying too hard and those elusive elements that so enrich life never happen when you're looking for them, so I tried to feign indifference and didn't go to my room and didn't change and pretended I didn't care.

I tried not to hum "Don't Go Changing," while I waited for my bill and paid for my ridiculously cheap and tremendously tasty Pilsner Urquells, less than three dollars for three of them, and I felt rich, filled with potential, positively reeking with potential, but also all too alone. Of course that made you think of other Billy Joel songs, damn him.

I got up and vowed to stop in the first bar I came to and buy drinks for the house—something I'd always wanted to do, and for which my present setting and economic circumstances seemed well-positioned. I wondered if the gesture was less sublime due to being in one of the cheapest cities in Europe, if somehow that made it less noble. I'd done things lacking in nobility before and was sure to do so again so I didn't get too hung up on that, just thought too long about it in the way you do when you're far from home and alone and don't have anyone to talk to. But it was good to do things. Things were there to be done after all, whether you did them or not.

The first bar I came to had a thick old brown door with a blurred glass window set high up in the wood, so high you couldn't see inside the bar from the window and anyway, what would you have seen or expected to see? Inside it was dark with smoked-soaked walls the dingy color of faded Austro-Hungarian decadence. There was a long zinc bar and several shabby looking linoleum tables and empty chairs. It was a chaotic collection of castaways from Prague's history: the neoclassical baroque architecture of the exterior, the bland and numbing sameness of the ubiquitous mass-produced Commie furniture, the feeble and out of place new and refined metal bar, and the abstract art on the wall that was trying to assert their fresh and invigorated capitalism. More than a declaration of any one thing or system or history or style, it was a diminished testament to many of them, thus not any more successful at creating a new statement than it was at repudiating the old ones. It was like what Stein thought about Oakland, there was no there there.

It was the kind of place where you could forget all about Billy Joel. No piano sounding like a carnival, no microphone smelling of beer. Instead, there was recorded accordion music, some kind of polka, coming from tinny speakers somewhere behind the bar, and I was disappointed to find there were only five people in the place, all dour-looking workmen types, no real estate novelists or anything, but guys who didn't seem so much like they wanted to be bought a drink. Guys who could and would buy their own drinks. Damned if I was going to waste a noble drink-buying first time gesture on just five people lacking the thirst for my generosity. Man, what was I doing here? Damn Billy Joel.

I drained my beer and retreated from that sad place in search of more fertile hunting grounds, hoping to do something exciting besides going out to dinner alone and back to my hotel room. Alone. It was tough to be exciting alone. Maybe if you were ascending the peak of Everest, that might be something, even alone. But even then, I bet you'd stand there and think: this is really amazing, I've done a great thing, if only there was someone here to see me do this terrific thing. If I ever met anyone who'd climbed the world's tallest peak alone, I'd ask them.

I wandered down, or perhaps up, depending on your outlook, a quiet cobblestone street listlessly lit by old-fashioned street lamps in search of a place filled with just the right amount of thirsty people to buy drinks for. Surely there were a number of places just like that, right here in this city, probably in most cities. It was just a matter of putting yourself in the right place at the right time. That was the real challenge in life. You hoped to put yourself in the right framework for fate to take hold, only fate was aloof. Maybe hunting fate was like hunting snipe.

Caught up in the sullen stream of my own consciousness and feeling very Joycean, I walked along aimlessly, seeking some destination that wanted to be sought. As I passed a foreboding Gothic church, all dark stones and sneering gargoyles observing my progress behind the colonnade of a dim loggia, I heard the familiar melody of "American Pie" wafting out from a place called Jo's Bar and I knew that would be the place. I vowed to just walk in and order drinks for everyone and hoped the language barrier wouldn't prevent me from acting out my destiny.

It was perfect, more people than I could count, maybe twenty or thirty, all about my age or younger, which was okay because though I was my age, I wanted to be younger. Though no one stared at me or paid me too much attention when I walked up to the bar, I couldn't help thinking these people would well appreciate me buying them a drink. They were clearly a thirsty and enthusiastic bunch, drinking up their youth with proper abandon. A young woman with eggplant colored hair, two silver hoops encircling her left nostril, and a short t-shirt that didn't quite encircle her torso came over.

"Pivo, prosim," I said, because I knew enough Czech, hell, enough of many European languages by now, to at least order a drink in the native tongue. I had thirsted in many different places. She smirked at me, not as menacingly as the gargoyles of the church out front had, but like them, having seen things I had not, all the same.

"Beer? Large or small. Light or dark?" she asked in flavored English. Maybe it was Australian or Kiwi, I couldn't always tell them apart.

Once I knew she spoke English, and with Don McLean still droning on about the levee being dry, I should have done it right there and then. The moment was ideal but also ephemeral and I lost it while distracted by trying to figure out what the tattoo surrounding her navel was. It was hard not to notice that you had to be pretty rebellious to be a young foreigner in Europe and not have a tattoo. Maybe I was a rebel after all.

"Uh, Large, dark," I said. I hadn't had dark beer in quite some time.

She went off to get my one dark beer while I stood there, disappointed in myself but still optimistic about the setting and all the potential. The unrealized potential. While I acclimatized myself, I noticed that for the first time in many months, I was surrounded by people speaking in my own tongue. It was good to be able to eavesdrop again.

She brought my beer, my sole and cowardly pivo, and made a single little tally mark with a felt tipped pen on my coaster and walked off. I still didn't know what the tattoo was. I wasn't brazen enough to stare any further nor bold enough to ask and anyway it was none of my business. I felt like she was sneering at me with that one mark on my coaster, reminding me I was not audacious enough to buy more like I'd planned.

I took a long pull from my beer, dark and almost syrupy sweet, and it was good and it still wasn't too late to buy one for everyone and I was surreptitiously getting the lay of the land, so I set it down, surprisingly half finished in one go—I really should have gotten some dinner—and lit a cigarette. There were some very enticing things about smoking if you'd grown accustomed to not censoring the little demons of your own bad behavior. To be young or at least want to be, to be far from home, whether you wanted to be or not, to be in a beautiful city more than a little drunk and stand in a bar and light a cigarette, something you couldn't do back home. Back home there were laws to keep you healthy even if you weren't properly inclined. There were still some places in Venice you could smoke but I was no more sure if that beautiful city I then lived in and had just left was any more home to me than America was. In my itinerant life, I'd gotten used to the fact that home was often the place I'd left and there wasn't much I could do about that.

Even if you thought about home while you were away from it, it seemed better in the perception and memory than it had been in the reality. I busied myself trying not to think too much about things I couldn't figure out and left my smokes sitting on the bar next to my beer in case anyone wanted to bum one. You could make a lot of friends while you killed yourself slowly.

While I took a long drag, I listened to the laughter and loud American voices next to me. Don Mclean stopped singing, finally. The levee was still dry. It was still the day he would die, again. The voices of American English around me grew louder and more forceful. Maybe we Americans were louder than the Europeans. Or maybe just there were more of us and we were drunker. Or just maybe it was something borne from being the world's last remaining superpower, holding onto the largest nuclear arsenal in the world and being naive enough to be fearless. I bet during the heydays of the British Empire the Indians in Delhi thought the English were pretty loud, too. Probably the Gauls complained about the rambunctious Romans. Well, the French complained about almost everyone. Galling, really. And everyone complained against every Reich, just not loudly enough.

Next to me a loud voice said, "I'm right, motherfuckers. I've got absolutely no regrets."

It was a good thing to be able to say in a bar, at least I thought so.

Then another voice, "No, you're crazy, is what you are Aaron. Absolutely certifiably insane."

I couldn't help looking over and I tried to figure out who was crazy, ever hopeful that it was not me.

"You American?" the voice who might have been right or might have been crazy said.

"Yes," I said, "How's it going?"

"Okay," the crazy, right guy said, "we'll let a stranger settle it."

"You know anyone here?" he asked me.

"Not a soul."

"Perfect," he said, though it hadn't seemed perfect to me.

"Wait. You don't live in Prague?"

"No," I said, "Venice. For now." I couldn't help feeling a little arrogant. The name of Venice carried with it a lot of cachet and I'd been waiting for some of it to rub off on me.

"You're not Italian," he said, a little too emphatically, I thought.

"No, I'm from San Francisco, I'm in Venice working on—"

"Doesn't matter," he said. "here's the deal. Think carefully. Would you rather have $15,000 of scrap metal or a fifty-fifty shot at $30,000?"

Everyone looked at me and seemed surprisingly interested in my answer but the stare of my questioner landed on me with ponderous significance.

In every group, no matter how large or small, there is one person who is clearly the center of gravity, the body that keeps it from being a random collection of mismatched egos. In that little group, it was obvious that my interrogator was at that time, in that bar, in that group, the fulcrum which the rest of the smaller egos orbited. The people hovering around him resembled more an audience than participants. I wasn't sure exactly how you could tell, it wasn't in the number of words spoken or the level of voice, it was just there, and as immutable as laws about gravity and physics.

"I guess it would depend on how bad I needed money."

He scoffed.

"That's not the issue, not the issue at all. Everyone needs money, all the time. No one ever thinks they have enough. Forget that. Which would you *rather* have?"

"Well," I said, and interrupted myself to take another pull at my beer, worried I was milking the little drama of the moment too much, "a fifty-fifty shot at thirty grand sounds pretty good to me. You can't win if you don't play, right?"

It was clear I'd said the wrong thing for his little coterie at the bar, but he laughed extravagantly.

"Exactly, that is it exactly. You cannot fucking win if you don't play. See douche bags, there you have it. This is a man after my own heart. I'm going to buy this guy a drink and all of you whiny wussies can go to hell."

That's how I ended up not buying drinks for the house.

There were introductions, the rapid-fire drinking shorthand of young people abroad getting the Cliff Notes on one another, and then I got to hear the story. Aaron had won a car, the scrap metal in the proposition, in a drawing at the Prague Casino. It was important to keep in mind, he said, that he didn't need a car, didn't even want a car, but his number had been drawn. His response had been to bet the sticker value of the car on roulette.

"Red or Black?" I asked.

"Ah, therein lies the rub. What do you think?"

"What color was the car?" I asked.

He eyed me skeptically.

"What does that matter?"

"Everything matters," I said, wondering if it did, indeed.

"Silver, it was silver."

"Red," I said.

He thumped his hand down firmly on the bar.

"That is exactly what I said."

"Only that's not what the roulette ball said, is it?" a girl whose name I hadn't caught retorted with vengeful vindication. I'd seen that often in Vegas. People thrilled at watching strangers win but took perverse pleasure in friends losing. Schadenfreude held a strange appeal.

"That is not the point, that's just detail," Aaron said, brushing her off.

I don't know if it was the beer or the shots of Becherovka he'd bought all of us, but I felt myself agreeing with him. The details were not the point.

The night then began to gather the easy inertia of intoxicating provisional friendships. There was a freedom in carousing with people you'd only just casually met and would never see again, the appealing liberation of no expectations and no demands. The details.

I forgot about the fact that I hadn't eaten or changed clothes and that I was so far from any home. I found myself drifting along with my new comrades-in-drink, most of whom had been living in Prague for some time and were more or less professional expatriates. The quintessential expatriate Hemingway had long ago told us that expats drank too much, talked too much, were obsessed with sex, and spent all their time hanging out in cafes, so in that regard he was the prophet and we the newly-converted acolytes.

Perhaps that lost generation lifestyle was just what we were all seeking or perhaps Papa had been right that all generations were lost by something.

I'd heard it said that Prague was the Paris of the '90s and it seemed little matter that it was no longer the Nineties as the new millennium hadn't defined itself any more than any of us had. We were all behind schedule in that regard.

I particularly appreciated that none of us talked much about home and no one spoke of work or their jobs or the future, the fodder that was the folderol for such conversations in the U.S. It was a pure enjoyment of the moment and I drank it up with the thirst of one who didn't know his place in the future and hadn't yet fully figured out his past.

The only serious moment of the night was when Brian, a drunken and chiseled Marine Lieutenant from South Boston stationed at the U.S. Embassy in Prague, was asked his thoughts on war in the Middle East. Was he likely to be sent, did he worry, what did he think? Like my father, whom I did not let interrupt our revelry, he wore the dark blue dress uniform of America's most vaunted fighting force during the day. No one there, including the token Marine, thought the U.S. would gain anything by flaming the already-raging fires of terrorism, and with the absence of any argument, we went on to the lighter task of having fun. He seemed kind of enthralled by the idea, though, that there would be a war, however brief, and more than a little regretful he would just be moved to some other embassy. He knew it was a prestigious assignment, guarding the embassy, but expressed dismay that the diplomacy he guarded was nothing more than dignitaries and dinner parties. Everyone, it seemed, wanted to put themselves in a role where something happened, even when no one knew what might happen.

Most of the rest of Aaron's crowd, except he and myself, agreed that he was crazy for having lost the car, given up the sure thing. Nevertheless, the argument of what kind of gambles you were prepared to take was good intoxicant for the well-lubricated revelry of being far from home.

∞ ∞ ∞

Two a.m. found us back at the bar where I had watched the sunset earlier, Lavka. Only now it was crowded with the thrum of techno, smoke, and a melange of Czech, German, English, and French voices all sharing the international language of youth: the illusion of infinite choice and unconquerable immortality.

Pam was the arts editor of the Prague Post and the most disgusted with Aaron's loss, seeming to have taken it as a personal insult, and kept posing more ridiculous gambles for him to lose and learn the error of his ways.

"Okay, you two are the big risk takers. I dare you to go up and not saying anything, lean over and make out with one of those girls." She gestured at a table of young, haughty Czech women who defiantly looked at no one but seemed to work hard at being looked at, and they were good at it.

"I dare you to do it, Pam," Aaron said.

"I'm not the risk taker, you are."

It was easy to tell there was some sexual tension between the two of them. She seemed to dislike so much about him that it was clear she liked him altogether more than she wanted to or thought she should.

Just then the Czech girls in their shiny short skirts and skimpy summer dresses got up to leave, perhaps to go away to another bar and be kissed by other more daring men, or perhaps to get away from men altogether.

The question of kissing strangers became moot and I bought all of the makeshift little group shots of tequila, and we all found ourselves drunk and dancing together, all with one another but none of us with anyone in particular.

I was well drunk enough to look out and note the golden lights that shone on the Charles Bridge and the Castle on the hill and tried to remember that this was one of the greatest settings for the sport of getting drunk that I'd been privileged to enjoy. I swayed along with the thumping techno as well as I could trying to fight down the feeling that comes with age, the inevitable generational dismay of how do these kids dance to this kind of music, and did the best I could. Then a conga line developed. I don't know where it started or who led it but we all joined on, and before I knew it we traced an inebriated path around the outdoor patio and down the stairs into the disco, my hands on the bare-midriff of a tall blonde woman and I could feel the sweat of her sides and it felt good to be me then and in that place and following I didn't know who. We circled around downstairs and the line twisted in on itself. It must have been several hundred people long, it was like a wedding party, only without the relatives or the gifts or the social niceties that slowed the festivities down. An unencumbered wedding party.

At some point before the line wound back up the stairs to the patio, the pretty blond with the sweaty waist disappeared and took several people in her wake and I found myself with my hands on Aaron's shoulders as we twisted our way back upstairs.

He looked back at me and smiled.

"We lost the girls," I said.

"Casualties of war," he said.

We kept on and I wondered how many people followed along behind us and was surprised to find that when we reached the previously crowded patio, it was now empty. Everyone in the place must have followed us downstairs and then back, the whole line trailing us. We were leaders of men.

"How far do you think we can take this thing?" he asked.

"Well, how much bigger is the bar?"

We'd already circumnavigated the patio and wound down through the downstairs dance floor and there didn't seem to me any other available spots.

I looked back and there was a very short dark-haired girl behind me, her face alight with laughter.

"With the right music, we could go anywhere," Aaron shouted over the techno.

There was a stone ledge about four feet high that divided the patio from the river below and Aaron jumped on top of it, so I followed him, and the brunette me, and the rest of the people us.

Aaron turned around, raised his fists, and shouted, "*Na hradcany! Na hradcany!*"

A thirsty mob loves a mantra. The chant was picked up and I joined in as best I could and we walked precariously along the wall, me thinking I was altogether too drunk to be walking, dancing, swaying along a ledge over a dark river in Central Europe.

"What's it mean?" I asked.

"To the castle," he said, "it's what they said to Havel."

Of course, the beloved poet president. Or was it playwright president? Anyhow, he'd done something before being President besides sponging off daddy's name and fortune and bankrupting a series of companies.

We circled the patio wall and found ourselves back near the entrance to the disco downstairs, only instead of hopping off the wall, Aaron shouted, "*Na hradcany*," and jumped onto a table some four or five feet from the ledge. He landed triumphantly in the center of the table, perched atop the crowd for a brief moment until suddenly both Aaron and the table collapsed in a crashing cacophony of himself and broken emerald green beer bottles. A small group of suddenly concerned friends quickly surrounded him, festivities, conga line and merriment all screeching to a halt.

As he stared up, his voice rang out above their ministrations.

"I'm all right. Ain't a party till something gets broke," he said, "*Na hradcany!*" He got up and I noted his shirt was ripped and he was bleeding a bit where a new hole in the fabric opened up. He hastily untucked the remains of his shirt.

"Come on, you better take the lead," he commanded.

I turned around and it seemed like everyone was looking at me expectantly, even the brunette, and I wondered where the blonde with the sweaty midriff was when I needed her, the one who seemed like she'd known where to go. You have to do something when everyone is looking at you, so lacking a sweaty blonde guide, I grabbed the brunette's hand and spun her around, dipping her as far as I dared. Then she placed her hands on my shoulders, anointing me, and Aaron grabbed on behind her, more people behind them, and I saw a bouncer or bartender coming over to us but I kept going, down the circular stairway to the dance floor.

Inside the bar was almost deserted, everyone, I guess, was still behind us. I heard someone further behind shout in Czech to one of the bartenders. Whatever was said, he left us alone and I led us on, past the DJ booth and the small bar in front and out the entrance, all along, all with whoever and how many ever were behind us, all shouting "*Na hradcany,*" or as close an approximation as we could, with our various liquor and language limitations.

As we wound out the door, the thump of the music that had sustained us grew dim, and I worried that having lost our melody, I might be leading us to oblivion but it seemed important to keep going. Behind me the group was smaller, maybe twenty people or so, but I was buoyed by the familiar faces from earlier. We all kept chanting as we danced out the bar, our delirious chorus growing louder as the music grew more distant, filling up as much space and silence as we were able. I and the line along with me, all of us together, veered left toward the bridge and the castle atop the honeyed hill beyond and it was beautiful, breathtaking, all of it.

There were very few people that still hour of late night or early morning on the bridge, but it rang with melodious laughter and the softer sounds of the forsaken bar below. Nearly halfway across, I hopped on the wide stone ledge of the bridge and so did everyone else, and on we went, each haphazard step taking us closer to our dubious destination. Perched on the parapet, my focus switched from the faraway castle to each measured step on the ledge until forced to pause at an impasse where a sooted statue stood in our way.

When I looked down, there were floodlights aimed up at us and the bridge, as if our performance had been expected and we were suddenly bright and all aglow and anything was possible.

The river below was dark and a long ways down, but the castle was further beyond. I didn't actually know the way up the hill to the storybook castle and the water looked suddenly so inviting in this luminous light that shined upon us. When the thought struck me it seemed irresistible, even inevitable, and I barely worried whether it was too far and too dark and I was too drunk. It was all perfectly preordained, there waiting to be done.

"To the river," I said loudly. Then more quietly to Aaron, "Can you swim in this river?"

"You can't swim if you don't jump," he said.

"Castle or river?" I asked.

"Red, black, castle, river, it's all the same to me. Don't sweat the details, man."

And we linked hands, our little line standing on that bridge nestled close between the sentinel statues, swinging them together once, allied by joyous abandon, all of our motley, sweaty group, and when I last looked down below, I couldn't see the water but I didn't feel we, any of us, could do anything wrong and together we leapt.

In that weightless fleeting instant, my mind matched our free falling velocity and I thought of everything, momentarily insatiable as we flew feet first into destiny. I even had time to miss the hands I'd held and lost in the air as my arms reached skyward and to remember to hold my breath and brace myself for landing, legs together for protection from the blessing of the hungry baptismal waters.

There was both release and surprise as that long instant ended and my body plunged into the water, then the bracing embrace of the river that had waited for us all this time.

Suddenly thoughts were different, doused in immediacy and singularly focused on descent and how to stop it. The hurried necessity of action, kicking and swimming upwards, craving the liberation of air and the surface. The yearning for emergence was intensified by the invigorating cold that surrounded everything and remained, even intensified, when in closely choreographed synchronicity, one by one, each of our eager heads ruptured the water, buoyant again, mouths eager for breath.

Having made it to the bridge and into the water together, we paddled towards one another, drawn instinctively together as we splashed ourselves into a small circle of shadowy heads, dog paddling to stay afloat and stay together.

Even as the breaths restored us, the cold intensified, and as soon as we were ready and able, we found ourselves stroking after Aaron as he splashed his way to the closest bridge embankment. We swam after him and one by one each scrambled up on the stones and huddled together, shivering and laughing, chilled and soaked and savoring the remains of that brief glorious suspension of rationality. Then reason intervened and Aaron quickly started a head count to make sure that everyone knew who'd jumped in next to them and that we were all accounted for. We were, we all were, and it was goddamned cold and wonderfully ridiculous even, taking roll call in the night on a bridge buttress but we did. I craved a hot shower and dreaded jumping in the frigid river again, but there was nowhere else to go.

Also I knew it would be important to leave there before the laughter stopped. Laughter and joy, even, have limits

Aaron stood up on the buttress or embankment, whatever it was, and said, "This way," and dived in smoothly, making barely a ripple before kicking up a frothy trail with his shoes. The last time I'd swum in my clothes was for a life-saving merit badge in Webelos and yet I had never saved a life nor acquired much confidence in being meritorious. Life happens no matter how prepared you were or what badges you'd sewn on a small-size khaki shirt, so you floated along, doing the best you could.

Somehow, following one another's splashes, we found ourselves at last on the shore, helped by being borne along by a slow but strong current that cut between a small island downriver from the bridge and the fairy tale castle. All of us drenched, shivering, and still laughing, sharing the communal camaraderie forged by drinking deeply of defiance of the everyday. Whimsy and irrationality made for a potent cocktail. We had sipped eau de vie and slurped up some of its magic. And it was good.

No one seemed to know what to do next, how best to relieve the coldness and loss of purpose, until the group was galvanized by the sounds of one of the rare night trams going by and most all of them rushed towards the nearby stop and the yellow lights of the orange street car. The adventure quickly came to an end.

The little brunette who I'd twirled took a few steps away from us, then stopped and came rushing back towards me saying something in what might have been Czech, but I wasn't sure. She put both her cold hands on my cheeks, kissed me quickly and firmly and I could taste the waters of the river and the essence of confident femininity along with the consternation of a new kiss from a new girl whose name I didn't know. The streetcar clanged to a stop in the darkness and someone shouted to her from the stop and she turned and ran off, saying only, "Good morning, sir," with funny, ill-timed English.

Then in a squeal of metal on metal, the orange car carried off most of our sodden group.

It's challenging to figure out what to do when you've just finished a foolhardy adventure and missed a streetcar. Maybe it was yours and you didn't even know it. It was dark and wet and cold and only the three of us; myself, Aaron, and Pam; stood there shivering and dripping on the stones of a dimly lit street. A dampened and diminished triad.

"So," Pam said.

"So."

"Right."

"Uh," I put forth hesitantly, "do you guys know her name?"

"Never saw her before in my life," Pam said.

"There are so many girls whose names I don't know," I said, because it seemed so true and so sad, as if knowing this mysterious girl's name might have helped me somehow in the matter of another girl's name, from another bridge, in another town, with another man, all so very far from me in the here and now. Strange how here and now could be so far from everything.

"Innkeeper, a bottle of your finest cognac, fresh water for the horses! Tonight, we ride!" said Aaron. I was trying to remember what book or movie that was from.

"You say that altogether too much, you know. It's ceased to be funny. Time for a new act," Pam said.

"Guy's got to say something."

Pam took off her sweater and started wringing it out. Her lacy and sodden white bra did little to hide her breasts or her nipples and as she faced us you could see the damp shadowy circles of her areolae showing through. When she looked up and we all became aware of what we were looking at, she quickly regained her inhibitions and turned away. Inhibitions are usually there waiting to be restored. Though why she had them and why we had a natural curiosity to see what we weren't supposed to see was more confounding. I wondered again why the flesh of a breast was so different from the flesh of a shoulder or a knee. And would any of us have been inhibited or overtly curious if we, all of us, overcame our unnecessary inhibitions. We were all dependent victims of prevailing proscriptive behavior. When she turned away and all of us were properly shamed, Aaron pulled me aside and whispered conspiratorially.

"Listen, Mark, my man, do me a solid. Pam and I had just went through kind of a thing. She doesn't really get that it's over. Just do me a favor and go along with me, whatever I say. Don't leave me alone with her tonight, all right? Promise?"

I was a regular guy, I'd whiled away enough nights assisting other regular guys in their efforts to pick up girls but fewer were the times you were asked to thwart the possibility. I was pretty sure I could do that. I might even be good at it.

"Nipple is a funny word," I said, just because it was on my mind and I felt that among strangers in a medieval movie set town after you'd jumped off a bridge, well, you should be able to say any damned dumb thing you thought of. I wondered for a minute if the world would be a better or a worse place if we all said everything we thought, and truly, I didn't know.

"Funny ha-ha or funny strange?" Aaron said.

"Not sure. Just funny."

"Nipple. Nipple. Nipple. Nipple," Aaron said, and like any word you say too much, the magic went away from it with the repetition. Maybe the mystery was the magic.

Pam turned back toward us and strands of her dampened hair were glued messily alongside her face.

"Very mature, fellows," she said.

"Maturity, I find, is highly overrated," Aaron said.

I thought it was a good thing to say.

Pam scoffed. Not everyone scoffs well but this girl had honed her skills. She had scoffed before and probably often.

"Shit. I left my purse, my cell phone and all my money, everything, at Lavka."

Reflexively and simultaneously, both Aaron and I patted our back pockets, and both were pleased to find we still had our wallets. It was mature to have your wallet with you after you jumped off a bridge, damned mature. Maturity. You couldn't avoid it, sometimes.

"Walk me home?" she said, looking at Aaron, and I was suddenly acutely aware of being the interloper.

Aaron took out a colorful 1000 koruna bill and handed it to her. I tried to remember the conversion rate and how much that was in dollars that he would send her away with. What was the going rate?

"Listen Pam, he doesn't know the way back to his hotel. We'll get you in a taxi and I'll show him back and give you a call tomorrow, all right?" he said.

"Forget it. Never mind," she said, snatching the bill from his hand in the way that Jane Jetson from our childhood was going to do in the future.

"Nice meeting you," she said to me, with more scoffing. And then she walked away.

I felt a little awkward.

"So," he said.

"And then there were two."

"Two washed up wastrels, wet and without nipples," he said.

"Technically speaking," I said, "I should guess we have four nipples between us."

"Not quite the same though, is it," he said.

"Maybe not," I said, "Hey, you think there's a language that has a different word for male nipples and female nipples?"

"Probably. There must be."

"The Senegalese, you know, have no word for snow," I said.

"That would be a good list, a list of words of other languages that don't exist in others. They say Eskimos have like a hundred words for snow."

"Someone should write that list," I said.

"You'd have to speak a lot of languages."

"Yeah, I struggle enough with one and a half," I said.

"Litost is one, a Czech word, there's a whole spiel somewhere in one of the Kunderas," he said.

"Yeah. Most don't. Speak a lot of languages. Do you know the Czech word for nipple?" I asked.

"Nope, I am not privy to that information. I've seen some, though."

"Nice?" I asked.

"Yeah. But all nipples are pretty nice in their own way."

"True enough. And very apolitical. Nipples."

"Maybe. I guess Lady Godiva's nipples were kind of political," he said.

"Why did she do that?" I asked, not really remembering the motivation.

"No idea. But the older I get, the less I understand the reasons people do anything. Even myself." he said

"I feel that way, too. Sometimes. Lots of times."

"Ours is not to question why," he said.

We stood there as the muffled clomp of the forsaken female's heels on the stones grew fainter, the only slight sound breaking the stillness of the night. She probably thought we were talking about her, the way anyone thinks you must be talking about them when they leave a group, but maybe in a way we were. I wasn't sure, but it could have been the drinks, the dancing, the jumping off the bridge or the bracing cold of the water, could have been all of those that made me unsure. Or it could have been just that I lacked certitude.

The rhythmic patter came to a stop and I could barely make her out in the murky distance, but we both heard her clearly shout, "I never liked you, Aaron Schonberg."

Then she turned the corner and disappeared. I looked over at Aaron.

"Funny thing is," he said, "I like her a lot. She's great. Pretty, smart, funny, nipples, the whole package. She just doesn't know when to let go."

I felt like I was supposed to say something, but I wasn't sure if I wanted to hear the whole history.

"Never trust a girl," I said, "who says she doesn't like you."

"Or one who does, for that matter."

We laughed.

"That was one hell of a jump," he said.

"One small step for man," I said.

"From a bridge over trouble waters..."

"Never look before you leap."

"A bridge too far," he said.

"A bridge over the river—hey, what's the name of this river?"

"The Vltava."

"Vltava. Good a name as any, I guess."

"In the all-important category of meandering Middle European rivers starting with V, it's tops in its class. Competition is fiercer than you'd think, too."

"Indubitably," I said, because I wanted to use that word and didn't get to often. So many things were dubitable.

We started walking off, laughing and tossing about clichés that seemed to us at the time terribly clever and were mostly just terrible and neither of us, though both of us tried, could remember if it was Billy Joe or Bobby Joe who jumped off the Tallahatchie Bridge. Someone did, though, we knew that for sure. We were dripping and cold and pretty drunk and hoping to find a bar open to dry out in but none were, and as we walked on, my shoes made a funny squishing sound on the stones like I was walking on saturated sponges.

We continued rehashing the night and the jump, refining and reworking the reportage for the future tellings that were part of the weaving together of the colorful tapestry of an interesting life. There would be nostalgia in our future because that's what futures were.

Along the way, we shared some bits and pieces of our own past adventures and the trivial stories and secrets that were the mortar that cemented a drunken bond of new friendship. We finally made it back to the bridge where we'd started and stood staring out at the blackness of the river. The Vltava. Across the way the lights were out at the club, Lavka. Fun was over.

∞ ∞ ∞

"Prague. This is a pretty good place," I said.

"Praha, they say, in Czech," Aaron explained. "Isn't it weird how we rename cities? Praha. It is good, though. I keep meaning to leave but can't quite ever make up my mind to do it."

"Can't let go, huh? Sounds kind of familiar," I said.

"Wiseass. Yeah, it's a damned good place. There's lots of them, though, don't you think? Sometimes I think of how many places I want to see and how boring it would be if you ever did, ever really did, see them all. I mean what if there were no more good places to go and see. Wouldn't that just suck?"

"Venice is a good place, too," I said.

"Shit, Dubuque is probably a good place to someone. The Mayor of Dubuque probably thinks Dubuque is the goddamn greatest place ever."

"You from Dubuque?" I asked.

"No, why, you?" Neither of us were.

"Maybe the mayor of Dubuque hates his job. Maybe he never wanted to even run, got roped into it and all he wanted to do was move to Chicago and be a commodities broker," I said.

"Or a poet," he said, "maybe he would've been a fine poet, too. Damn shame. World could use more poetry."

"But just think, somewhere, sitting in Dubuque right now, is the smartest girl in town, the prettiest, the guy who loves her more than anyone, the best teacher, the toughest sonofabitch in the whole county, the biggest loser, the town drunk, the richest family. It's all there, all in every town," I said, because it was a thought I'd had before, even if I'd never said it, or maybe I'd said it a lot of times, it didn't make a difference. That was the great thing about new friends. I had a whole economic theory of new friends and recycled thoughts and stories. It was very sound. You could only get so much mileage out of a single thought or anecdote with the same old friends. I was about to regale Aaron with my hypothesis when he started speaking.

"Places are big. Cities, towns, places. There's tons of places to see, I've seen some good ones, but what I really like, what I like to collect," he said, "are moments, great moments in great places, things you wouldn't change at all. I've got a little collection. It's the only thing worth collecting at all, I think."

"Gimme one."

"Okay, few months back, I was going through some crap, blah, blah, blah, life is hard, having some problems, et cetera, et cetera."

"Et cetera et cetera ad nauseum," I said, wondering if I'd made a Latin sentence. Did anyone study Latin anymore? Probably at Eton or Oxford. I thought again about sometime, somewhere, there had to be the last person who spoke Latin as their only tongue. I wondered who that was and how they'd lived, when they'd died and what all died with him or her.

"So I packed a bag and took off, just went to the Prague train station and hopped on the first one. It took me to Munich so that's where I went only, well, it just didn't feel right," he said.

"Well you're not the first one to say that about Germany."

"Right. Exactly. The place is filled with Germans. It was more a place to run away from than run away too and you could feel it. So I went back to the train station and got on the next IC train and it took me to Salzburg. And I had a collection of moments there. I stayed in a hostel, befriended a bunch of Aussies and we got liquored up every night and talked about, well, matters of no importance, but great interest and the second night I got in a fight with this South African guy and he didn't even hit me and then this one day they all wanted to ski. Only none of them had and none of them had ever driven on our side of the road before and I was the only one who'd done any of it, I spoke some German and I used to be a ski instructor."

"Where at?" I asked.

"A winter in Killington and part of one in Telluride, long time ago, where I got fired for sleeping with this crazy wealthy widow but that's another story. Anyhow, so I drove us to Kitzsteinhorn, some long-ass German mountain name anyway, and showed them all how to ski and for awhile, they were my best friends, like I was their hero, only they didn't even know I was the one who was grateful because I needed some friends just then."

"Who doesn't," I said.

"Right. So they kept asking me to show off on the slopes and I did and they fucking loved it. They were the most enthusiastic group of guys ever even though they couldn't ski worth a damn and didn't take lessons very well, just sort've kept throwing themselves down the mountain."

"I've always found gravity to be reliable that way," I said, to keep him going.

"Exactly. There are some things you can count on. Not many though, come to think of it. Anyhow, after awhile I grew a little, well bored, I mean it was a great day, but how much fun can you have before you start thinking about it too much?"

"I've no idea. How much?" I felt sure that he would know.

"Not sure, yet. But I keep trying to find out. So I left them on their own for a bit to get in some good runs on the tougher slopes before everything iced up in the sun, and on the way down, I was going straight down, as fast as I could, a little out of control, but in that perfect way where you don't care, and off to my left as I zoomed by, totally out of place, in the middle of the damned slope, I saw a blur of a wooden bar, people gathered around drinking, just a bar in the snow, no building, nothing. But I was going by too fast to stop and I knew right then that it would have been a perfect place to have a beer and I'd missed it, even started to wonder if I'd imagined it. You can't ever get those moments back. By the time I got down, all the Aussies had given up on skiing. They were all struggling to get their skis off, ready to go out and get pissed, and I'd missed out on that one drink I was meant to have."

"It's always the things you don't do you regret the most," I said, because wise people who died were always saying things like that. I hoped to say some good things before I was a wise old dead guy, but you never knew when you would get wise or when you would die or which would come first.

"Well, I don't have a lot of regrets but this was a great bar and I was missing it as I unstrapped my rental skis and I just happened to mention to them that there was a bar up there on the slope, you know, cause it was kind of unusual.

"I never saw a tired group of guys get such a hearty second wind. They were all determined we had to have a drink there. So we got our gear back on, hopped on the lift, all of us, and all of them real thirsty and excited, except one guy, I forget his name, were ready to give it a go, 'God loves a tryer,' they said, only this one guy, though, he looks down at the slope and decides no way he'll make it and asks Der Herr Meister Ski Lift man can he take the lift back down.

"He takes some ribbing, but ski lift meister lets him go down the lift and we head down the hill and by the time me and the rest are finally making it, them falling all over themselves but eager, time we're just skiing up to the bar, there he is above us on the lift, heading down the mountain all alone, and he sees the bar and all us and he just shouts 'Bloody hell,' and jumps off the fucking lift. It must've been fifty feet and this guy couldn't ski for shit.

"He's lucky he didn't break both his legs but he landed in a big messy pile of skis and poles and he's wearing Levis and we're about to go and help him up and he picks himself up and just says, 'I forgot it's my round.'

"We stood there," he went on, "and had one of the best beers in my life and there wasn't one thing in the world I could have thought of that would have made the moment any better. That's one of the best of my collection. In recent history anyway. You have any?"

Well sure, we, all of us, had moments, but which did we collect, which ones left a deeper impression than the others? I wondered what indelible ink inscribed it on one's consciousness. Did just choosing the right moment make it so? How many passed, how many fateful choices and moments fleetingly rushed by, unnoticed on one's journey through life?

"There was this girl, once. I never found out her name. And well, there was this rainy night and this long walk and this perfect kiss on a stone bridge in Venice and she ran off without telling me her name, ever. But it was a helluva kiss. I remember I shouted after her, 'who are you?' and she stopped and looked back and said, 'don't confuse me.' Then she was gone."

"That's a tough question."

"Ain't that the truth."

"But," he said, "like the guy said, better to have loved and lost."

"Right. It seemed like that at the time. Or the moment, anyway."

"Sounds like a moment."

We stood there for minute, both thinking about our own moments.

"Maybe you've got something about bridges," he said.

"Or impenetrable anonymity," I said.

"There's a spot on the Charles Bridge, I should've showed you before we jumped off. Anyway, this spot, this star, is supposed to be some karmic center of the universe or good luck totem or something mysteriously powerful. You're supposed to put your hand on it and touch all the points at once. I do it all the time."

"You superstitious?"

"Damn straight. Who isn't?" he said.

"No one isn't, I guess. Maybe some aren't."

"Religious?" he asked, packing all the mysteries of humanity into one word.

"Not really. Well, Catholic school and some church when I was younger, but lately, well, Catholic is just the church I don't go to. I've been giving God the finger. He rings the church bells at these insane times right outside my apartment. No sense to it at all."

"Flipping off God, guess you could go to hell for that well as any other thing," he said.

"So, that mean you believe in him or you don't?"

"Who knows," I said.

"Superstition, religion, I think it's all the same thing. I'm thinking of becoming a Muslim. Changing my name to Hassan, maybe Kareem. Hell, I might even go the whole way and just become Mohammad. That could be pretty zen."

"So you're gonna be the Zen Mohammad."

"One god's as good the next, I figure," he said.

"Thor seemed like a pretty cool god, as gods go."

"But he wasn't the boss, was he? Wasn't it Odin?"

"Apollo, he was cool and he wasn't the boss, either," I said.

"Maybe when gods are second best, they try harder, like Hertz."

"I think it's Avis who tries harder. Or maybe it's just a big cosmic game of good god, bad god," I said.

"Or maybe there's nothing, and it's all just a game."

"Maybe we should buy berets and hang out in cafés on the Left Bank of Paris talking about existentialist dread. Be gods of nihilism."

"People here used to be fond of saying Prague was the Paris of the '90s," he added wistfully, done with being profane to the sacred but still sacred to the past.

"I've heard that. What happened?"

"The '90s ended. Then I heard it was St. Petersburg. I don't have any idea where the new Paris is."

"Shit, maybe Paris is the new Paris," I said.

"Paris can't be the new Paris. The new Paris is probably in Asia."

"What if Dubuque is the new Paris and nobody knows it?"

"Guess we won't always have Paris."

That was the first night I met Aaron Schonberg. And I too started collecting moments and we shared more than one. But some were later and I little expected what things I'd end up doing at his behest. But he was the type of guy that needed to lead and I was a willing follower at the time, lacking any other path than my own for so long and not feeling I'd done so well with it anyway.

Having dug into lots of things and figured out none, we finally parted at my hotel, drunk, less damp and feeling all together full of ourselves.

"You know," Aaron said, "my sweet, judgmental grandma asked me more than once what I would do if all my friends jumped off a bridge."

"Now we know the answer," I said, relieved we'd figured out one thing at least.

"Or maybe we are the people dear old grandma warned me about."

"It's not a bad gig, huh?"

"Not too shabby, my friend," he said, thumping me on the back and solidifying our new camaraderie.

There are strange and sometimes sad moments abroad when your life's path intersects with another's, when destiny tosses you along with kindred spirits, maybe someone who bet a car and lost and was proud of it and pleased with your approval and then together you led a conga line of people out of a bar and jumped off a bridge for instance. Or just someone who you feel you can and should be friends with, but you know you may never see again, what with there being so many paths and so many people and with all of the paths seeming to so often lead away from the people and things you might have meant to do. Or at least might have done. Every path that led someplace led away from some other.

"So," he said, "how long you in town for?"

"Till Wednesday. Then back to Villetta Vandermar in Venezia."

"Tomorrow," he looked at his watch and shook his wrist, "not a Timex, but still ticking, shit, four in the fucking morning. So today actually, your presence is requested, nay mandated, at the Martini Bar in Obecni Dum. Big beautiful building on Na Prikope street. Everyone knows it, just at the bottom of Vaclavske Namesti. Can't miss it. You won't, I'm sure. Brunch and Bloodies. Be there, why don't you."

He didn't say what time and I didn't ask.

TWELVE

LIKE KINGS OF BOHEMIA

I WENT TO MY ROOM and took a hot shower and felt too excited for sleep but too drunk to stay awake.

When I opened my eyes again, it was to the light of the morning sun and the now unfamiliar noise of the cars and traffic below. The bothersome noise of automobiles was always particularly jarring on one of these trips after you'd acclimated yourself to Venice. Another shower. A red taxi came and grouchily deposited me at the bottom of the sloping, tree-lined Vaclavske Namesti and I found Na Prikope street and walked in the direction that seemed right, which was left.

The street was just a few blocks long, and at its end, where three large streets came together, were several yellow and red streetcars, and one that was painted all over with the red colors and flowing white script of the Coca-Cola logo, and they clanged along in the grooves of the cobblestone street past one another heading different directions and a Coke sounded pretty good to me. I don't know if it was because I was hungover and dehydrated or because I saw the tram and was just impressionable. It crossed my mind that some thousand miles away there was a church in Venice missing an old painting, but also that there was nothing I could do about it from where I was. That made me more thirsty and seemed to accentuate my hangover.

Where the streets came together, on the left hand side, was a large, ornate baroque building, all yellow and flowing intricate architecture that stood out from the rest of the buildings as having been recently redecorated, or at least well tended.

There were large picture windows along the street, and downstairs there were fancy people sipping some of Prague's more expensive coffee in opulent surroundings. There were white tablecloths and suits and dresses and hats and a little band, an orchestra maybe. I wasn't sure when it stopped being a band and became an orchestra, but there was a harp, and that was pretty. I walked in hoping my rendezvous was not at the fancy place. There was a man in a tuxedo standing beside a wooden door with frosted glass windows leading in to the fancy place, I could hear the music but not the harp and the clicking of spoons on fine china. There was a red carpet in the black marble foyer and a small sign at the bottom of a large curving staircase that said simply Martini Bar, with an arrow pointing up.

I trudged up the stairs, glad to be leaving the fancy people and the band behind but daubed with self-pity for the effort required to urge my tired and hungover feet upwards, and I thought of Steinbeck and how he'd written he'd always taken his hangovers as a consequence, never as punishment and this was a reassuring thought.

Inside the Martini Bar, there were empty red leather booths along the outer wall overlooking the square, and Aaron was alone sitting on a large and rather gaudy but plush stool at the bar.

On the bar beside him, there was a disquieting symphony of a pint glass of coffee, an empty shot glass, a half-filled bottle of Jägermeister, and a half-emptied green bottle of Pilsner Urquell conducted by a crushed pack of Spartas, the ubiquitous, cheap Czech cigarettes.

"Breakfast of champions," I said.

He looked at me, eyes bloodshot and bleary and I wondered if I looked as bad as he did, and for a minute I felt flustered thinking he didn't remember me.

Then he smiled. "Some night, huh? Coffee?"

I sat down on the neighboring red felt bar stool on the far side of the Jäger and the Pilsner, wanting to be as far away from both as possible in my current condition, but glad to be someplace, nevertheless.

He got up and went behind the bar to an imposing brass and gold coffee machine.

"You work here?"

"Work might be putting to fine a point on it. I come here on Sundays and do stuff. Something to do. Keeps me out of trouble, helping some friends."

"How's that going?"

"Keeping out of trouble or helping friends? Seems to me trouble and friends, they kind of go together, don't they? You want one, you take the other, simple exchange of values."

He steamed some milk and took great care preparing a double portion of coffee and pouring it into a pint glass and topping it with a cap of frothy whiteness and set it before me. I grabbed it eagerly and took a long, deep taste that burned my tongue but didn't daunt my enthusiasm for the much needed caffeine it contained.

"So what have you done today? Because I have done something quite amazing. I served coffee this morning to a guy who wasn't Joe Strummer."

"Who's Joe Strummer?"

"Well not the guy I served coffee to, that's for sure. Joe Strummer, the Joe Strummer, The Clash."

"Ah," I said, "Rock the Casbah."

"Right. Anyway, so I got here first thing, I was too hungover to sleep, through some fault of yours, I might add, but I'd promised Mirek I'd open and I remembered Joe Strummer was playing tonight at Radost and he's staying next door at the Hotel Parizsky and the place wasn't open yet and I was just sitting here fighting with my hangover then in walks this guy who was very sure of himself and looked, well, exactly like Joe Strummer. 'Good morning,' I say, making sure not to seem like an annoying fan, who wants that too early in the morning am I right? Anyhow, he says, 'Good morning, sir,' in this perfect Joe Strummer voice with the right English accent and asks for coffee, even though I'd already figured he'd want tea, he is fucking English, after all. So off I go, make him a nice coffee and say, as you do, 'Here you go, Mr. Strummer,' all casual as can be, just to let him know I knew. 'Pardon me?' he says, and I figured he just didn't want to be recognized this early in the morning and I mean, who does, right? So off I go and I look over and he takes out a pad and pen and I'm thinking he's working on his set for tonight, this is fucking absolutely great, like a private look inside the artist's mind."

He sat back down and lit a cigarette while I waited to hear about the now not anonymous Joe Strummer. I'd learned someone's name, at least.

"So I just sat here and watched, it was pretty damned cool. He puts his pen and paper away, finishes his coffee, asks me how much. I tell him it's on the house, just to let him know I wasn't fooled. Then he takes out his cell phone and goddamn that motherfucker was not Joe Strummer at all."

"Who was he?" I asked, beginning to get caught up in the tale and its telling, even though I didn't care about The Clash or had never spent this much time thinking about Joe Strummer, incapable since I'd not known his name before that morning.

"He was some fucking real estate fucker and he was talking to a broker, some big development deal with the Germans. It was all very depressing. Very damned depressing, I'll tell you. Anyway, I gave coffee to a guy who was definitely not Joe Strummer. So I got that going for me."

"Which is nice," I said, because if you were thirty-five and had watched Caddyshack a million times like we all had, you knew, no matter where you were, that was what you were supposed to say to an American guy. It was pointless but social.

"And now here you are and you're not Joe Strummer, either."

"Not as far as I know."

"Seems to be some sort of epidemic, this not being Joe Strummer."

"Well," I said, "most of us aren't, huh?"

"Good point. Enough about that. So, you got any special plans today?"

He had a way of making you feel quite important. I'm not sure what it was because I didn't think he really cared so much what you were going to say or if indeed you had big plans. Maybe he was just used to shaping the world to his own tastes and he was good at it and you felt it, somehow.

"Nope, none at all," I said, which was true as anything I'd said and truer this morning than a lot of other things I'd said and done other hungover mornings in other places.

"Let's get started then. In about an hour this place is gonna be filled up and I don't know where the damned waitresses are, bunch of good-for-nothings and I can't take all that pressure, not hungover. So the thing to do is stop being hungover. Let the battle begin."

He filled two glasses with the syrupy Jäger and slid one toward me and we toasted, me rather more reluctantly than him.

"We're hunting and shooting to kill," he said. Then he explained that Jägermeister meant Master of the Hunt and I understood. Our hangover was our prey and the revolting shot was our first assault. It wouldn't do the trick but perhaps it would herald, à la Churchill, the end of the beginning.

He opened up his brown bag, but it wasn't lunch. It was a long, white root, unfamiliar to me.

"Fresh horseradish, picked this up this morning. I make the best Bloody Marys in Prague. Maybe even the best in Eastern Europe, or Central Europe, or Middle Europe or whatever they're calling themselves nowadays, they keep changing their fucking minds."

He rimmed two pint glasses with lime, rolled their edges in what he called his custom spice mix, celery salt and some other Czech spices he didn't know the English names for, liberally doused the bottoms with Worcestershire, Tabasco, fresh ground black pepper, some squirts of fresh lime and then grated out fine strands of the fresh horseradish root into the mix, and then added two healthy streams of clear Russian Stoli, tomato juice and ice.

"A Bloody Mary of my own construction," he said, sliding one towards me. He was well-armed for the fight, you had to admit.

And he was right, it was the best Bloody Mary I'd ever had, even if I wasn't Joe Strummer.

My stomach was sour and still protesting and gurgling from the affront of the Jägermeister but the pounding in my head started to recede and I began slowly to even feel pretty good about the day and its many possibilities there in this dark, empty upstairs bar above the fancy people below on a street whose name I couldn't pronounce. Then two tardy Czech waitresses arrived and made the day look even better. There were introductions and more Bloody Marys and then the people started coming and Aaron tossed me an apron and he was Tom Sawyer and I was compliantly painting his fence in the form of dispensing drinks and we went to work.

I had never tended bar nor wanted to, always preferring the customer side of the wood, but it was a compelling thing to not be a bartender and not be an employee and yet be a bartender, and it was a seductive sort of pretend world that day. At least it seemed like it after a couple more Bloody Marys of my own construction, in the Aaron Schonberg fashion.

And then the day disappeared without any warning about the morrow.

THIRTEEN

SMALL FAVORS FOR REVOLUTIONARIES

MONDAY'S HANGOVER CAME AGAIN and much the worse for wear but enriched by experience, I remembered to heed Steinbeck's sage advice. So there were consequences. I went to an internet café in Stare Mesto, Prague's Old Town, and sent some emails to the office in Venice and copied them to Brussels, to Strasbourg, and San Francisco. There had been a lot of changes in the EU tourism account and I wasn't really sure who I was working for anymore, but it didn't seem to matter to anyone so I didn't let it bother me.

Tuesday was the conference. I donned my suit and tie costume and spoke easily and fluently of the need for travel and overcoming fear and making Americans feel comfortable and safe abroad, all the minutiae of my job, saying what I was expected to say, and it being what they expected to hear, it was right and I was done and there was a plane to Marco Polo the next day. All very simple and even having included some interesting diversions along the way.

Only Aaron talked me into staying another day and some emails and my evident utter dispensability at the office, combined with the fact that I don't think they knew any more than I did who I was working for, along with the easy-going European attitude of holiday time, made it easily achievable. Even easier not to go to work than to go. Though I was pleased to extend my sojourn, it is somewhat less than flattering to face your own insignificance.

That next day, I awoke like any other in Prague, only less hungover, and I had no idea at all as I dressed that I was getting married that week.

Aaron introduced me to Pavel Sokol, his best friend in Prague, a Czech hero, a young man who had made a deep mark in his country by having been one of the three student organizers of Prague's

1989 protests that had inspired some quarter of a million Czechs to gather on the broad avenue of Vaclavske Namesti, clamoring for freedom. Which, unlike local custom dictated, the Czechs got. Still in his early twenties, Pavel was quickly elected to the new democratic Czech parliament, greatly celebrated throughout the land, a friend and confidante to Vaclav Havel, the former Czech dissident and now revered playwright president. That was right. Playwright. Havel, a man who Mandela-like, had been persecuted by the regime for his political views, imprisoned for years, and then quickly gone from having no control over his own destiny to controlling an entire nation. Fortune was fickle as even I was to come to learn.

I was awed by this man, younger than myself, perhaps half a foot taller and who had already cut such a large swath in the world. Who had the ear of the beloved President and had himself spoken for hundreds of thousands of people and had been instrumental in forging their freedom. He knew who he worked for and it was everyone.

The three of us: Aaron, Pavel and myself, lunched outdoors on a rooftop balcony restaurant called Divoka Voda at the bottom of a tree-lined avenue just off of Vaclavske Namesti and beyond the new Kmart, overlooking the brash Little Caesar's that had crossed the Rubicon of Communism. Cheesy capitalist outlets aside, the view was actually quite inspiring. People stopped eating and cheered as he walked out onto the patio. He nodded casually, clearly used to it, if a bit embarrassed about it. How he still found time for humility was another thing.

We ordered three pilsners and sat there in the sun and when the beers came, there was also an iced bucket of champagne someone had sent over. The waiter said something in Czech and aimed the bottle off to the edge of the balcony, popped the cork and everyone applauded again and I couldn't help but hope some of the importance of him might rub off on me.

"Yes," Pavel said, "of course it was interesting, fascinating even, at first, to help organize things, to get the people out, to help the people to say what everyone wanted to say, but what until then all had been afraid to."

He took a sip of his beer while we waited.

"It was a problem of faith, you see. There was no faith left. It had been bred out. Our grandparents had the Nazis and were unable to do anything about them. Our parents had the Russians and some of them even believed in that new ideal but then were betrayed by it. Then in '68 they tried to rebel against that betrayal and were overwhelmed with tanks. But my parents remembered that feeling of Prague Spring, the possibility, the hope. I was born of it. All I had to do was help others find it. When one has faith, he must pass it on if he is able and it turned out that I was able. I was, myself, perhaps as surprised as anyone but it is fine to be taught that people wish for more. So perhaps I can be proud of helping in that small regard."

So that's all it was. Simple, really, when you heard him tell it. But then you never knew, maybe that's how it was with all revolutionaries.

"But then wanting something better becomes the normal. It becomes the business of everyday life," he continued. "Then there are finally the elections, and it was just politics, debates, the making of new laws and still by some of the same people. And it did not seem as enough had changed. In the end, it was again about money. It wasn't at first, you know. Only I didn't care about money so much. I became addicted to the excitement, the adrenaline of new things, change."

"Tell him about Cuba," Aaron said.

"Cuba was something. A marvelous place. I mean it could be a great place, it wants to be a great place and the people with so much to say. We Czechs, you see, can understand the Cubans."

"About the jail," Aaron said.

"That is a complicated affair and in the end the jails everywhere are all the same, it seems," he said, as if everyone had spent their allotted time in some jail for their political ideals. I remembered a friend back home who'd spent two days in jail for a DUI, but I didn't think that counted.

"For another time," Pavel said, brushing off Aaron easily, like a pitcher brushing off the catcher's signs from the plate, asserting who was really in charge, who could really bring it and what he would bring when he wanted to bring it. And not until then.

Aaron, you could tell, knew his tales and still found fascination in them. It was easy to find sometimes.

He looked at me seeking an ally to inspire Pavel to speak more.

"This guy," he said, gesturing with his champagne glass at Pavel, "besides being friends with Havel, has met Clinton, Gorbachev, Putin, Mandela, Castro."

"Some just a few times," Pavel said, "and not to forget Jaromir Jagr. What a hockey player. That man is a god on the ice."

We sat there sipping gifted champagne in the sun with a hero who had broken bread with some of the greatest minds and bigger villains in the world, speaking of hockey gods, whom I hadn't even known existed. Perhaps god was everywhere and maybe he even drove the zamboni, who could say? My hockey theology lesson was put to rest when Pavel aimed his next words at me.

"More to the point, Aaron tells me you may be in a position to help me out."

I was a bit taken aback to think there was anything such a person might want or need that I could help with. And more than a little bit flattered.

"Denissa."

"His sister, she's beautiful, a beautiful human being," Aaron said, and I believed him because right then it seemed like everyone in the world was a beautiful human being and all of them should be sitting in the sun on a rooftop in Prague sipping bubbling Bohemia Sekt in a world filled with heroes. Looking down over the edge of the roof, I could see a Lancôme ad adorned with the graceful smile of Isabella Rossellini.

"See, we have some trouble with her here and I'm afraid it's my fault, mostly, and I should like to fix things."

"I would do it myself, but I'm already married," Aaron said.

"Dude, you're married?" This was rather surprising.

"Sure. Long story. She's in New York at college. She couldn't get a student visa and it seemed like the least I could do, sign some papers. I mean, why not, right?"

It began to dawn on me what type of favor might be asked of me and there was more than a little awkwardness creeping over me, rising quickly like the bubbles in my flute. Isabella kept enigmatically smiling and staring at me from down below.

"If it had not been for the Cuba thing," Pavel said, "she would have no problems, I could get her a student visa or an H-1, and she could go to America, like she wants to do, like I want her to do. But with September 11th and the Republicans, the visas are now almost impossible to get and everyone I know is no longer in a position or with the inclination to help after the minor international incident I caused."

The little favor loomed before me and seemed vaguely altruistic and more than a little interesting, I admit. Maybe she even looked like Isabella Rossellini.

∞ ∞ ∞

I made some calls to work and arranged to stay for long enough to fill out the mountain of paperwork that marriage abroad called for. I met Denissa, and she was young and beautiful and blonde and had wide, rouged Slavic cheekbones and we had absolutely nothing to say to one another, though her English was good. I got the feeling she wanted me to do this thing for her but resented me for doing it. I guess you didn't thank someone for something like this, or maybe you did, but who did you ask? I don't think Miss Manners ever even once touched on the etiquette of this particular situation, or if she had, I had missed it and evidently so had Denissa.

Anyway, I liked Aaron and admired her brother Pavel. After all, if he'd given himself for a whole nation, I could give something to one person. I'd been seeking to be more irresponsible and this was that, and they were so caught up in gratitude and so busy arranging things and putting more paperwork in Czech and English before us both to sign that our presence and getting along were of little importance. I was pleased, at least, that I was helping someone out who had helped so many other people. I wondered briefly if this false marriage might tarnish my otherwise unblemished bachelorhood, but I'd done other things to tarnish myself and didn't fret too much about it. It seemed a hell of an out of the ordinary thing to do, and to have done. Ordinary had become pretty tiring, just by the sheer prevalence of it.

Denissa and I had a civil ceremony in the magistrates' building near Castle hill in Mala Strana and then fourteen of us went out to dinner. I remember counting and trying to remember everyone's name and being pleased with whoever it was that kept us from being a group of thirteen. I wondered for a bit, twelve apostles, plus Jesus, and if that was why thirteen was unlucky or if just being Jesus was unlucky enough. Anyway, I didn't wonder long because everyone kept putting new drinks and shots in front of me and it was a wedding night of sorts and we got gloriously drunk and I didn't know if I was doing the right thing, but it seemed right. Though I spent most of my wedding night at the bar with Aaron and Pavel drinking cinnamon tinged shots of Becherovka. There was no bride and groom first dance or father of the bride or chicken dance, but I didn't miss any of them. Really it was just another piece of paperwork and I thought it strange that signing your name to a piece of paper could be so important to the living of life, but it was, in that time, at that place.

Denissa came up to me alone later that night and I wasn't exactly sure of the protocol, but she thanked me and hugged me and kissed me lightly on both cheeks. For want of anything better to say, I told her we should go out for dinner some time and she agreed, perhaps for the same reason. Hell, maybe we'd fall passionately in love and stay in Prague forever and get a mortgage and raise a whole brood of Czech kids. Anything was possible.

Before she left, I said,
"So Denissa, do you want kids?"
She looked at me with pursed, pouty pink lips and I guess it wasn't funny, but I thought it was. Maybe my new wife didn't have a good sense of humor. That's important in a wife, I think. I hadn't even been married for 12 hours and I was already learning a lot and having dashed expectations. No doubt about it, I was a natural.

"Someday," she said, and walked away.

Newly married, I flew alone back to Venice, oddly aware of being a solo newlywed in the world's most romantic city. I had to make up for lost time at work and had agreed before leaving Prague to go back in three or four weeks to sign more papers and go with Denissa to the U.S. Embassy to obtain her visa so she could go off to the States. And maybe to take my new wife out to dinner, at least for symbolism's sake and to get an idea of what all had to be said at the Embassy. Though I didn't see any reason why it should be any foreign service officer's business where or why I signed my name, but I guess it was. What a job.

If the questions got too personal, I could always take the Fifth. I'd always wanted to take the Fifth, just never had had the chance, but I didn't know if you could in Prague, but I guess an embassy is like a little piece of its home country wherever it was, so if you could take the Fifth at home, you could've there too, it seemed. I wish I'd known exactly what the Fifth was but I couldn't remember the last time I'd read the Constitution.

Once, long ago, in another time and another country, I had whiled away hours before a delayed flight in an airport bar. I remember, at the time, I was drinking Whiskey Sours, because I thought they were pretty cool and that I was over beer. I think it was in the St. Louis Airport, but I'm not sure, and it doesn't matter, all airports and most people in them being pretty much the same. I found myself sitting next to a middle-aged bald man with a large, bushy beard, all white and gray, and he kept stroking it, that full, overly bushy beard, clearly proud some part of his body could still sprout, he clung on to the whiskers as if they were some sort of life-preserver. I don't remember his name, but like the airport, it doesn't matter, in these things, these anonymous bars and people modern life briefly tosses our lot in with.

What I do remember is that he was an actuarial scientist. At first I thought it was just insurance, his were the Good Hands or the guys with the Peanuts characters, or whoever they were. But he, I recall, was greatly offended by that. He was a scientist and as proud of this as he was of the whiskers on his cheeks and chin and neck. All in all he was a thoroughly boring guy but like so many such, he seemed blissfully unaware of this as he pontificated on his science, which I've found myself, eager as I was to get away from him at the time, thinking of more than once.

"Take a group of 100 people, any 100 people, it doesn't matter," he'd said, and I guess, being a scientist and all, it didn't. "I can tell you how many of them are going to get married, and if they got married since 1990, I can tell you 50% of them are going to get divorced, that most of them will be fired from more than one job, how much their average savings account balance is, hell, I can tell you how many of them are going to die in 10 years, in 20 years. It's all science, pure science and this is what I know, I know the science of people."

"Well, far as I know, the mortality rate is still fixed at 100%," I'd said.

"Oh, sure, in the end, everyone dies, but I can tell you where and when and of what and how much their heirs will get or owe. The only real question is which ones it will be."

"Seems a hell of a big question," I'd said.

"To them, maybe. Not to me, the specifics, see, they don't matter at all, just the generalities. It's all just numbers. Pure science is what it is. That's what insurance is. People are willing to bet a small amount to accept a guaranteed loss, to cover them for the possibility of a bigger loss. And that, that's where the science comes in. Everybody wants to cover their asses. But they can't, cause I know everything that's going to happen to them in advance. That's how the big fortunes are made. Trust me."

It was clear this man had marked out his little realm of understanding, like my father had, and maybe for him it was all he needed, this assurance in numbers and percentages and death rates. It was also evident with his pager and large outdated laptop and rumpled cheap suit that the big fortunes he spoke of had not floated down his way. That he was but a little puppet in the big scientific game of life and death and disaster, waiting to be ordered about by those higher up in the echelons of the big fortunes. But he was secure in his understanding of the world. Science. The science of life and death. This guy wanted to buy me a drink and for some reason I knew it would be bad fortune to let this parasitic son of a bitch buy me anything, so I pretended it was time for my plane when it wasn't and got the hell out of there. I bet the percentage of guys who didn't want to talk to him was much higher than he thought it was, but it didn't deter him in the least. Besides, you couldn't get a policy to protect you from insufferable boors.

He was telling me something about the numbers of plane crashes and the percentage likelihood of them being greater at certain times or certain flights, some such shit, and as I walked away, he was still talking. I just remember that I was disgusted as hell with him and damned glad to get out of there.

For some reason, I think of him, a lot, though. Strange I thought of him on my wedding day, which, being many years after 1990, left it an even fifty-fifty chance of success or failure. Unless the odds had changed in the twenty-first century or were different when you married someone you didn't know at all just as a favor for someone you'd just met. Fifty-fifty seemed to me about as good of odds as you were likely to get in anything in life. Damon Runyon had said all life was six-to-five against, so maybe some of us were beating the odds. No matter the odds or how rigged the game of life, it was the only game there was. So you played it even when you did not know the rules.

I didn't mind them, those odds, but I wish like hell I'd never met that guy all the same.

FOURTEEN

PEOPLE PASSING IN GONDOLAS

BETROTHED BUT STILL ALONE, I fled Prague and my forged matrimony and returned to Venice under a moon that was not honeyed. This time with a new determination to apply myself to the life I was leading or at least better understand its convoluted course. My exile, instigated by a messy affair, had itself become a messy affair. Ostracized back home then banished to Venice, I'd succeeded at ingratiating myself with the various Venetian tourist boards then been repeatedly relegated elsewhere. With each move I made, I kept finding a way to unwittingly complicate my life.

Everything I gave, it seemed, was unrequited.

Missing a girl whose name I did not know had incited a series of unsatisfying incidents; I had dived into too many more random encounters that did nothing more than dilute my own sense of self. A longing for connection and seeking friends in Prague had led me, unsuspecting, into a marriage of convenience. Even as my own inconvenient yearnings remained unfulfilled. Weary of repeatedly being reminded that desire led only to disappointment, I figured maybe it was time to try and learn to want what I had, lest life continue its recurrent theme of unattainability. The tangled mosaic that made up my life, like myself, lacked clarity. It seemed the more I moved, the more muddled things became. It had become difficult to differentiate between returning and retreating.

I had been buffeted by my first Venetian winter then spent much of the spring singing the simple songs of Venetian tourism under other skies. I had set out purposefully to enjoy some meaningless encounters and failed at making them enjoyable and keeping them meaningless. My life, like Venice itself, had grown too fluid and I was unsure of its proper shape. Making so many mistakes was at least teaching me how very much I had to learn.

I was not grounded and I decided to dedicate myself to seeking some semblance of stability. If Venice would be where I worked and lived, I would dig deeper into Venetian life. Seeking roots in a watery city that supported itself on nothing more than submerged wooden piles seemed no more impractical than anything else I'd been doing. But if Venice, precariously perched where it did not belong, had somehow managed to contrive a way to fashion such a strong sense of self, maybe some of it could rub off on me. Maybe by learning to love Venice, I could learn to love.

Even as I attempted to forge a sense of permanence, Venice became more besieged by transients. Summer was brighter and busier but not Venice's finest facade. The chilling winds and low-flung fogs of winter and spring had departed. This season's sun shone brighter and longer but also illuminated things better left unseen. The winds grew hotter and heavier as the bracing Bora withdrew and the Sahara's Sirocco advanced up the Adriatic synchronously with the onslaught of teeming tourism that was the unloved lifeblood of Venice. The tourism that I was both a product and producer of.

Summer and busy season had settled strongly on Venice and the walkways and cafés were always filled with a cacophony of foreign languages. Despite the talk of war abroad by those who sat in well-appointed offices and made such decisions or huddled in caves or desert palaces raptly watching CNN and hated other people and their ways, tourists—regular, lucky everyday people—as they always had, came to Venice. Venice took their money and served up some beauty and memories. These treasured trophies were expensive, prices having risen with the tides of the high season, but Venice will sell whatever people will pay at whatever rate the market will bear. In this tumultuous world, the business of beautiful memories was a seller's market. The city and its café tables and coin purses seemed to be as filled as they were capable of being, though the reactions were conflicting.

Signor Contarini took me out one afternoon to designate my summer duties. As we left the office, I followed behind him, hurrying to keep up. Real Venetians strode nimbly through the crowded maze of summer tourists, with no need to gawk at what they saw every day and no time to dally. He wound us through numerous twists and turns until we found ourselves finally freed of the masses and sat at a table in a quiet cafe off the beaten track.

He ordered us two spritzes, a bottle of sparkling water, and a plate of assorted tramezzini and sat there complaining of the crowds that prevented us from choosing a cafe closer to the office and then went on to tell me what a fine job I was doing on the tourism account.

"Still early to tell, but so far summer tourism arrivals are way up," he said.

Then he explained that I would have some additional responsibility in August because he couldn't stand the oppressive heat and the crowds, so he would be spending most of the month at his villa in the cooler and quieter mountain climes of the Dolomites.

"So beautiful. Fresh air, so much peace and quiet. Hardly any tourists," he said, wistfully.

We finished up the sandwiches and as we got up to leave, Contarini fielded some complaints from the proprietor about how the tourism board didn't do enough to promote Venice's quieter sestieri. There was truth in that, too. Venice was one of the most touristed and under-explored places in the world. As we made our way back to the office, Contarini added his own voice to the chorus of the crowds, all declaiming the very crowd of which they were themselves a constituent part. Venice was both too busy and not busy enough, depending on who you spoke to, and it seemed that there was no one truth, just different versions of the same truth. And the voices of discontent led the chorus.

The place I knew as Venice, overwhelmed by holidaymakers, had its very beauty blemished by the admiring hordes. It seemed a bit like losing the forest, or not even seeing the forest, for the infestation of the trees. Only the trees were tourists in shorts, all comfortably shod in Tevas or Nikes, coming casually dressed to wander along the world's most hallowed canals. They came bearing guidebooks and video cameras and busied themselves with the writing of postcards, boasting about how lucky they were to be there while complaining about the cost of coffee and food. And the forest, unseen through the throngs, was the beauty that had been the slow and quiet grandeur of Venice when it was not besieged and maybe when I had not been married to someone I didn't know and had been desperate to get to better know someone I could not have.

With the warmer weather and the water came the humidity, the fetid smells, the dampness and the crowds. You had to look harder to see the beauty, but still you knew it was there. You would be reminded when the right breezes refreshed the waters of the canals and then when they were freshly cleansed by the Adriatic tides, the canal waters were all manner of bright greens and bold blues and beneath the sea of tourists you could see the rippling reflections of palazzos and people passing in gondolas. The reflections were the best part, even if they made me think about Plato's Allegory of the Cave and how reality, perhaps mine and everyone's, was elusive. Then thinking about caves made me think about Bin Laden and how the world was rapidly going to hell. Every silver lining has its cloud.

Even as the city grew more crowded, the office grew quieter. I started taking particular pleasure in having a place to be alone and unsupervised. Surrounded by loafers, I took to strolling into the office at my leisure, taking along books to work rather than reading reports that didn't beg to be read anyway and which no one was awaiting my wise response to, Europe having for this time left its environs to tourists and gone away to enjoy the month. Funny that during the heights of tourist season, real Europe was effectively closed and the world was rushing to war yet still more people came.

So I stayed and enjoyed myself best I could by staking out my little claim. I left my sweltering suits and ties unmolested in my closet, started wearing jeans to work and studiously avoided the crowds in the Piazza San Marco and the lines at the Guggenheim and wandered instead in the outlying areas of Venice never reached by most tourists even when the city was filled beyond capacity. The public gardens designed by Napoleon at the upper reaches of Venice's landfall were lush and green and filled with the Italians who stayed to cater to the tourists, and the Via Garibaldi, the long wide street out there, was a pleasant place to stroll during the day and be among the Venetians.

Even if I was indeed less Venetian than tourist, it was fun to feel otherwise. I didn't fool them of course, even with my now practiced Italian. But I did a pretty good job of fooling myself, which I managed to feel smug about. Smug, unsupervised and irresponsible, that was me. I began to feel, while malingering in some café busied with sundry afternoon libations, that my doing nothing was something of an accomplishment. Things like reading and having a drink, or even better, reading while having a drink, worked their way to the top of my to do lists and I was diligent about them.

During the hottest days of August, Venice buzzed like a molested bee hive, and contriving more ways to get more people to come seemed pointless, so I loafed more. The gondolas kept passing me by, their coveted seats continually replenished by new versions of the same people. The gondoliers never sang anymore, the tourists took the same pictures on every different day and they all started to seem like one another and I started to feel I lost a bit of my tenuous grip on reality. I didn't much miss it, having decided the reality of the world was highly overrated. Venice was in fact as fine a place as there could have been to utterly ignore reality. It was designed for the sport.

Disdaining work, I studied up more on Venice but this time toward my own ends. Needing to admire something, I dedicated myself to learning to admire the place I lived, which in Venice was an easy thing to do. It has eternally been locked in its own embrace. It is easily the most narcissistic place on Earth. Most every Venetian edifice, public and private, boasts at least one print or picture of the city on its walls. All the bookstores are filled with throbbing tomes heralding the long history of the city, available nowadays in any language any tourist might speak. I decided it had something to do with three things, this narcissism: that it was like nowhere else, that it had once been great and powerful but was no more, and that the city constantly faced its own reflection in the quiet waters of the canals. It was a good theory, even if a bit unrefined, but some things didn't need refining and I was glad to have explained it to myself.

Mired in my own solitude, I sought any such simple distraction.

I found respite from my thoughts on the far side of the city, where the bar I called Sancho's—where the dog I missed never was— remained a good place even through the heights of busy season. It wasn't on any guidebook-driven tourist thoroughfare nor near any important church or must-see museum. It was frequented by the denizens of the insular little Sestiere Dorsoduro and blue and white striped-shirted gondoliers off work for the day, done overcharging tourists and having accumulated good thirsts and full pocketbooks from stroking their sleek craft through the canals. Some afternoons, I would go there for a simple Italian lunch of a glass or two of wine and a porchetta panino or two, due panini, and eat them there sitting at the tables where you had to pay extra, so hardly any one else sat. Most Venetians, staunch and thrifty, stood.

Outside in the late afternoons, there would often be three or four little motoscafo launches of the fine, polished mahogany wood turned out by Venice's shipyards on the Giudecca and used to take the wealthy visitors to wherever they wished, along with as many as eight, or one day, even ten gondolas. Which might not sound like much, but the gondolas, as black and sleek as they looked floating through the wide Grand Canal, were a good twenty feet long and the little canal in front of the bar that was not Sancho's and had no dog, not nearly wide enough even for them to turn around in. So they came from both directions and tied up to one another, blocking off the canal until someone outside in a boat sounded their horn.

When the horn sounded, you would look around to see who would drain their glass and go out to make a small shipping lane so the untimely intruder could pass and it was a thoroughly engaging spectacle. Much better than sitting in an empty office. So I sat, ate and drank and counted gondolas along one of Venice's many small clogged arteries.

∞ ∞ ∞

One sweltering sunny afternoon, I decided to celebrate the arrival of each gondola with a shot of Averna, a little to the dismay of the light drinking Italians. After having had my typical repast of a fresh sandwich served on a cutting board and fêted the arrival of each gondola with another shot, I found myself wishing for no more. But not willing to give up the game. Every time one gondola left and another came to take its place, another Averna came to me. It was a pretty good drinking game even though I had no one to play it with but myself. It would have been nice to have the right woman to play it with, but it would have been better to have the right woman so I could busy myself with better things. But I had neither the right woman nor better things to do.

I was glad when the gondolas began to depart, some off to evening cruises in the Basin of St. Mark and underneath the Bridge of Sighs, others done for the day and going home on their dark, asymmetrical crafts. The gondolas look so sleek and majestic when slipping past palazzos in the Grand Canal that you don't notice their peculiar design. When they sit silent and unmanned in a little canal, they're uneven and unbalanced, with the back left side wider and larger to support the standing weight of the gondolier. Unmanned, they float clumsily off kilter, as if uneasy with idleness. Without a gondolier, they looked something like an ungainly ostrich, sporting all the right equipment to soar but unable to take flight. There was something sad and wrong about it, as if evolution had robbed them of their true purpose.

Finally the gondolas took flight and I paid my bill and left. They never gave me a receipt there. This was a place for the locals and the Italians went to great lengths to fight the muscular arm of the bureaucracy of Rome which tied and taxed each and every cash register into a central bank. Not getting a receipt meant that you had somehow become an accepted part of the charade. It meant they wouldn't report the sale, would not pay tax on it, you wouldn't be charged the full amount and everyone would part a bit happier having pulled one over on a meddlesome taxman in a far away office staring at a computer screen. It was a popular pastime in Venice and being included in the game made you feel somehow an insider. Like everything they did, the Italians approached this dodge with a sense of style. It was all a game, played with a careless nonchalance, the famous sprezzatura that made it seem effortless and natural.

Not born with this sense of style, this easy abandon was not a natural part of my demeanor. I sulked and agonized over all my steps and missteps, especially when I kept seeming to find myself walking back to the church at San Pantalon and the scene of my crime. Even in the sober light of day when the church was open and I didn't have to furtively sneak in, my guilt still made me furtive.

It was strange that when I went in, I could not see where the painting that still sat in my bedroom was supposed to have been. The walls were filled with large old religious art, not so colorful nor so beautiful as the one I had sitting at home in the Dorsoduro. The ceiling was the colorful bright blues and luminescent whites of heaven that had been painted on by some artist in the 18th century whose name I did not know, but that was a long list, artists whose names I did not know. A long list marked predominantly by one particular artist I would never know.

I thought about going in and just telling them I'd found the painting. Perhaps I'd be a hero, having discovered a missing work of art. Only no one told me it was missing and for the life of me there were no blank spots on the wall and no one looking any more aggrieved than old Italian men and women generally look when they go into a church.

In my bad Italian, I asked a janitor, after waiting for him to finish dusting off the altar, if this was not indeed the very church where the recent art theft had taken place. He told me that nothing had been taken from his church. I knew the painting had been, having been the one who took it. But perhaps no one cared about it but me. No one missing it made it harder to do the right thing somehow, even confused me as to what was the right thing if I could not find an easy way to do it.

I had grown rather fond of the horse painting and started to feel as if perhaps I was indeed the only one who cared at all about this accidentally orphaned artwork. Well, not so accidentally. But in my mind it had been an accident. I'd meant to put it back and would have, but I had no wish to risk getting caught returning a purloined painting to a church. I learned the Italian for thief was ladro but I didn't feel like a ladro, and anyway it had a nice ring to it, that word. I had taken a painting of a horse. A cavallo ladro. A horse thief. I tried to throw the term into a conversation down at Franco's Bar to see if horse thief was even a workable term here in this city of water-filled streets. But it didn't work, didn't go, and it had been, I guess, too many centuries since horses had set hooves on the stones for it to be a term they understood or used. Good thing I wasn't out west. Cavallo pazzo, crazy horse, was a common and kind of endearing curse term in Italian rather than an Indian chief. Who was Crazy Horse and had he perhaps been a horse thief, too? Anyway, it was certain that he'd been stolen from. If you look hard enough, you can find rationalizations for almost anything.

Unable to easily disentangle myself from my accidental art theft, I became obsessed with finding out more about the painting. I looked everywhere, to no avail. The study of history is the study of sin and this is more clear in Venice than in most places. Feeling guilty enough, one finds guilt everywhere. Venice was built on dreams but it was decorated with crime. Her most revered icons came with a tarnished provenance of greed, larceny and looting. Doge Dandolo, after conniving the Crusaders and plundering Constantinople, was instrumental in destroying the Byzantine Empire.

The great bronzed horses that were supposed to have sat before the Basilica San Marco were likely looted from the Hippodrome, though neither the Hippodrome nor Constantinople bore those designations any more. In any event, the bronze horses were not believed to have been indigenous to Constantinople, having likely been forged on the island of Chios. Their travels had been long, and like myself, their homes temporary. Only somehow we'd all wound up in Venice. After Constantinople was thoroughly looted, the horses were loaded on Venetian ships and sailed to another new home.

There the horses stood, silent and displaced, atop the Basilica San Marco, hooves poised motionless over the Piazza, for seven centuries. Then Napoleon, the little emperor with the purportedly small penis but large acquisitive instinct, had conquered Venice, liberated the horses and taken them further from home, where they sat in Paris for thirteen unlucky horse statue years. Fated to be bounty, after Waterloo, the Austrians took them, and finally the machinations of European horse-trading and infighting brought the horses back to Venice where they supposedly belonged. They bestrode the Basilica for years until they were tucked away for both World Wars. Then cautious as ever or perhaps growing to believe in the regularity of wars and danger, the Venetians hid the horses away in a conservation or safety measure. They placed them inside the Basilica and had replicas made, which were the ones now poised outside the Basilica and probably the most photographed horses anywhere, though mere replicas of the proud steeds that had, in perfect still life, lived and traveled further in Europe than any real horses. The replicas had come to represent the reality.

The more I looked, the more subterfuge I found. The winged lion that was St. Mark's symbol was the very emblem of Venice. Everywhere I went I saw the lion: in the Piazzetta, chiseled into churches and government buildings, pictured in paintings, stamped onto tiles, stitched onto flags, even imprinted in our everyday office stationery. It was good marketing, plain and simple. Which is probably what the Venetian merchants thought on their ninth century trading trip to Alexandria when they connived the priests there into letting them steal away the revered relic that was the corpse of St. Mark, ensuring that only they could protect it from Muslim hands. Worried about being caught in their smuggling by Muslim officials, they hid the corpse under layers of pork that no Muslim would investigate. And off they went with a new religious reliquary and the beginnings of a marketing campaign that would stand the test of time and still did today.

Pilfering had a proud pedigree in Venice and I began to rationalize that perhaps my liberation of the painting was merely the adhering to the dictates of local custom. When in Venice.

Turns out you didn't have to believe in much of anything to be a religious looter. Sometimes it could even be considered an accident. If you do something you know is wrong and you live in an evil world, you can even convince yourself that if you didn't do it, someone, somewhere would. I knew much better men than me had done much worse things. And that much worse men had done better things. Frail, fragile, flawed and imperfect, I began to embrace my missteps. Sometimes that's all there was.

No matter how hard I tried, I couldn't find any information about my painting. The painting. It was not the makings of an auspicious career in the art theft business, and anyway it was, like most businesses, one I had no wishes to be in. Morality and a guilty conscience make for poor business bedfellows.

The painting was unsigned, seemed unmissed and began to look proper leaning against the wall of my bedroom overlooking the Church of San Trovaso. Whether you intended to adopt a stray painting or not, once you had taken responsibility for letting one in your home, you felt obligated to name it. America has already been through the desert on a horse with no name. Sancho Panza was already taken by the liege of Don Quixote and by the wandering shepherd who had left me to catch a ferry out to the Lido. I roved my mind searching for famous horse names. Secretariat, Man o' War, Seabiscuit were all too racy. There was Robert E. Lee's gray companion, Traveller, who had famously survived the Civil War but it was impossible to get away from the fact that he'd done it on the wrong side beneath a military mastermind who'd fought for the wrong reasons. You didn't want to saddle a horse with a burden like that. Not if you liked him. I was pleased at remembering about Alexander the Great's Bucephalus, but I was afraid I might have learned it from my father and didn't like all that implied. This was my horse, this was the horse of a valiant knight, a grand cavallo, not a conqueror of worlds, more a thing of chivalry and grace. I could not remember the color of Don Quixote's horse but after a couple of Camparis and some further obsessing, I finally recalled his name, Rocinante.

Mine in the painting was white but somehow glowing and there could have been no grander name then Rocinante, an innocent beast that wanted to be better than it was. And so he was. My own Rocinante. Gray, I recalled, the real Rocinante had been, an old and bony gray mare. But of course, not real at all and mine may well have been. Real, that is, not gray. It was an appropriate name for my morally inappropriate acquisition. Amid all the wrongness, at least I'd found the right name, one that lent the misdeed an unjustified sense of propriety. If you modified your outlook enough, you could justify most anything, and I knew my outlook needed a lot of modification.

I thought a lot about my mistakes in behavior and my own complicity in conniving to make such a mess of my life while I waited for the tourists to go home, back to work or school, and to simple streets filled with asphalt and pavement instead of water. They began to stink well before the aphorism of three days told you they would. Thinking of fish reminded me that it had been many weeks since I had seen the bright colors of the fish market in my own Campo Santa Margherita. That meant, if you didn't know the schedule of the fishmongers in my campo, that I had taken to never rising and walking to work before lunch time. I missed the fish and the calls of the mongers and the smell and the colors, but lunchtime for everyone else was a damned comfortable time to start the day when you didn't have much better to do. And I didn't then have much better to do but at least it was good to know that, unlike so many things I missed, those fish and those mornings would always be there when I was ready for them again.

Maybe the secret was only to miss things that were accessible.

FIFTEEN

CAMPARI COUNTS

BEING A MINOR INTERNATIONAL ART THIEF of no renown, along with possessing a purloined painting of a noble steed now officially christened Rocinante, gave me a strangely excessive sense of self-confidence. It was as if the liberated painting was some sort of totem that had just been waiting to find the right confederate. Together we were conspirators, I just didn't know what against.

As Venice heaved with masses of tourists that far outnumbered the local population, I became the sole summer inhabitant of an otherwise empty tourism council office and my impudent sense of self-confidence grew to fill up the space allotted.

Keeping a bottle of Campari and carting a fresh bottle of soda to work with me in the afternoons helped in that regard as well. I wasn't sure when I became that guy who kept a bottle at work, but I liked it and it was certainly a fine accoutrement to my desk. The bitter crimson-colored liqueur, invented in nearby and staid Milano, sat nobly there to the right of my laptop and released a fine glow when the late afternoon summer sun caught it. The soda, boring and translucent, sat there beside my desk atop a bookshelf. Together we waited.

Like myself, the Campari seemed to enjoy being unsupervised. Sitting impertinently out in the open on my desk, it called for attention when the afternoon sun slanted through my office window and it began to cast a beckoning red-hued shadow that generally stretched out to touch the back edge of my computer at about three o'clock. And that's when cocktail hour began there in my little office. Sartre had said that three in the afternoon was always too late or too early for anything you wanted to do, but he probably drank translucent Pernod.

The little tripping of the red light fantastic lent an air of ceremony to my otherwise unceremonious days. There was not much to be done in the office then and I expended a lot of effort finding ways to fill the hours. Since there was no one in the office to miss me, I could have gone out for cocktails but everyone else was out everywhere else in Venice. Except those that knew better who had left Venice. Venice in August was like Yogi Berra said, no one goes there anymore because it's always too crowded. Anyway, I didn't have anyone to see.

One day, particularly hungover and hot, I cheated and moved the Campari closer so it caught the very first rays of early afternoon sun. But that lacked grandeur. There was no nervous anticipation of awaiting an uncertain outcome, the very sweetness that made the game worth playing. So I didn't make that mistake again and positioned the bottle back in its proper spot and sometimes had to sit and wait as long as a full hour until that fine moment when the red shadow slowly seeped to the edge of my black laptop. Even if you make up the rules yourself, they demand some reverence.

Only when the Campari shadow completed its course would I retrieve the Murano crystal tumbler I kept in my upper-right desk drawer, toss in three ice cubes, and adorn them with a liberal douse of Campari and a small splash of soda and raise the glass and say, "Salute," to the sun and the shadows of myself and my empty office. Once I got the schedule down, if there weren't any clouds, I could have the soda and ice all prepared and waiting for the right moment, but there was no nobility in it if you got the ice too soon and it started to melt while you waited. It was a very precision operation requiring careful attention to detail. Rather like heart surgery or defusing a bomb.

While I sat there reading and waiting, I kept anticipating being disturbed by the phones, expecting Signor Contarini or one of his minions to check in from their holidays in country houses in the Dolomites, villettas by the shore, and other parts of terra firma, but they were so spectacularly dedicated to the month off that they never did, not once. Sometimes in the afternoon, I would even raise a glass to them and their healthy respect for leaving work behind where it belonged. I began to like my office colleagues much more during their absence than I had during their presence.

The summer tourism figures, I knew, were to be released in late September, as they always were, by Signor Contarini, to all the necessary publications and councils and everyone who cared about such things, which, travel being what it is even when the world is on the brink of war, is many more people than you would think.

The only real thing I was expected to accomplish during the month of August was to gather hotel occupancy figures from the major ones, which were, despite the hoteliers' lamentations, always completely full. So eventually I stopped bothering and just studied the previous years and rather ingeniously, Campari in hand, accentuated them to suit my needs. It was a simple maneuver that seemed easier for everyone.

One afternoon in the last week of my August autonomy, when the Campari shadow had just about reached the F6 button on my laptop, which meant I probably had about an hour to go, the phone rang and disturbed me. The problem with being in the office at F6 o'clock in the late afternoon was that it meant it was early morning in New York where all the important travel industry magazines were.

Venice as a hot tourist destination had been copy as long as there had been printing. The same people kept going to the same places and reporters kept writing the same stories about them. I was expecting to trot out some of the usual platitudes, thinking it would be the typical Condé Nast or Travel Industry Holiday Trends scribe, but was surprised to find that this was a very earnest and serious sounding man from a business journal of note on Wall Street.

This guy was actually seeking news and I had very little of import to share.

He apologized for not speaking Italian, and I quite gracefully, I thought, told him to think nothing of it, that he should find my English quite adequate, which I believe he did. It was a good thing it was already F6 o'clock because I could do much better Italian-accented English at that time, after a couple of Camparis. I was fortunate to be so well equipped for the task.

He did go on and on, this guy, despite my speaking very fluent English to him, all about accounting scandals, the effects of a war in Iraq on European travel, bankrupt airlines, and budding new destinations. It was all very official and very boring and it took me a couple of Camparis just to wait him out. But I was patient.

I had to interrupt him at one point to get some more ice and he was very good about that, especially after I explained to him that it was the long tradition of my family, who had once been Doges and were of course well listed in the Libro d'Oro, to take a small cocktail in the afternoons at precisely this time.

This guy, despite being such an educated, informed, and earnest man, didn't know anything about the Doges and he had never even had Campari. It was pitiful. I tried to explain to him about the red shadow and where to place the bottle on his desk if he would like to develop some good ceremonial office habits but I think the precision of the whole operation was just too much for his bureaucratic mind-set. Not everyone's cut out for heart surgery-like precision endeavors, it's just a simple fact.

"That's very fascinating, that about the Doges, and I wish I was doing a piece," he blathered on, "about the history of Venice so I could get that in. But that's not really, you see, *the focus* of this piece," he said. I don't know exactly how he managed to speak in italics across the ocean, but he did.

So there you had it. He wasn't entirely lacking in ability to focus, he was just focused on more narrow things and gathering facts to confirm the story he wanted to write. Which was, according to all his fine research on European travel spots, that this had been the slowest travel season in many years. He was very clear on that part and here it was almost F3 o'clock and he just needed some good quotes from a spokesperson, so wasn't it lucky, he said, that I spoke such good English.

"Ah, yes, well, thank you," I said, "it has long been the tradition in my family to study the important languages of the world."

"Afraid all I have is a little high school French," he said.

"Bravo, trés bien," I said, "la belle France. I had a great uncle killed there on the Maginot Line in World War II and, of course, lost many noble ancestors in the Great War, but we hardly ever speak of that anymore," I told him, for no reason at all except that by now it was almost Escape key time and I was out of ice and ready to go home and see Rocinante and get ready for the evening. I was thinking perhaps of some mussels as a starter and then a simple pasta, perhaps laced with coniglio, which I had discovered went perfectly with a bottle of Valpolicella and made you almost forget you were stuck dining alone, the combination being such good company.

"We will not, under any circumstances, at this time, speak of the Fascisti, that is understood, is it not, my good man?" I said, because it was actually quite a pleasure to be a fake and eccentric aristocratic old Venetian gentleman even if you weren't. I do respect, obviously, that the Campari was no small assistant in the endeavor. Living in a world that survived on credit, I always tried to give credit where credit was due.

"Yes, of course," he agreed, quite amicably, I thought, my fake aristocratic family having probably been well riddled with fascists, but damned if I was going to tell him any of that, not about my fine and phony ancestors who had most certainly not fought with the French anytime, anywhere, anywhen, even in my mind.

"I shall tell you what, we here at the illustrious tourism office in Venice," I said, as you do at Escape key time when you're out of ice and stuck talking to an earnest journal reporter calling from Wall Street who is drinking coffee in the morning in New York, "are not only so pleased with this year's tourism numbers, which, of course, we make a habit of not releasing officially, you understand, until September."

"Right," he said, "well, I don't necessarily need precision numbers."

"Allora. So then, unofficially, I can tell you we are not only so pleased by the not yet released numbers, we are in fact absolutely astounded by them, and well, toward that end, we are working on a rather, I think, bold and interesting agenda for the next year which I only wish I could release to you at this moment in time, but alas, I cannot."

I was pretty sure that was precisely ambiguous enough to be too tough to parse down into a quote for an esteemed business journal and would get rid of him so that when I was fully sober I could perhaps zap him an official email. But there was just no getting rid of this guy, none at all. Dio mio, he was nothing, this young man, if not persistent, I'll say that for him. And even though I was out of ice, the sun-warmed Campari was not too bad after all and this guy was very eager to file his story. He was working on something for the middle column of the journal, that one that was always kind of interesting that I myself had glanced at on occasion. Even if I and my fictional family were not titans of industry.

"If we could perhaps get some indication, for the article's sake, of this year…"

I took another sip of the warm Campari, and well, it wasn't all that good either.

"I'll tell you what, I'm in a gracious mood today, my good man," I said, very magnanimously, "and since, although I do not have the pleasure of reading your publication, I do believe that your journal is indeed one of some repute, is it not?"

"Well, of course, influencers and opinion-shapers turn to us for…" I don't know fully what he went on and on about, just how important he and his job were and a bunch of unnecessary detail I didn't much bother with. I got it and who in the hell didn't know it, anyway?

Did he think a family with the blood of the Doges coursing Campari-like through their veins didn't know about high finance? Hell, Venetians had practically invented high finance. Even a pretend aristocrat knew enough to know that and as much should be expected from an informed business reporter.

While he droned on, dripping in self-import, I stared at the Campari, which was nearly empty by now and threw but a bland and hesitant shadow across my laptop. It was well after Escape key time and I was getting bored with my little game. Amusing yourself only worked for so long.

I thought of dinner and eating alone again and it came to me in a rush.

"I should be willing to give you some details, in rather strict confidence, of course, if you were able, in keeping with the esteemed ethics," I was careful not to fall out of my accent here, it having almost slipped by me with my excitement, "of your profession, to keep things, as it were, under your capello, that is to say, hat. I could, however, in exchange for a small favor of a more personal nature, offer you a very special, how do you say, 'scoop?' for your fine publication, fully attributable," I wasn't sure if that was a word, but it was great being a pretend aristocrat because it didn't matter.

"My journal, sir, has a very strict policy about payment for stories."

"Oh, not that my dear boy," I said, "money is so, how should one put it? Pedestrian? Philistine? So, well, American. One never likes to speak of money. I am referring only to a simple favor that perhaps you might bring your charming skills to bear and do for me this small thing. All very discreet, I should think. For which, in exchange, I should be willing to offer you the most delightful, what is that charming American word you use again? Scoop, isn't it?"

By then I was committed and I was giving real thought to actually becoming an eccentric foreign aristocrat. Maybe I could sell Rocinante and buy a title.

"It's not actually, um, customary, sir"

"Count, actually," I said, "but not to worry, dear boy, I hardly ever use the title any longer. Not since the Austrians left."

I should have planned my family history a little better in advance, but who knew an important business reporter from Wall Street was going to call in late August during cocktail hour and need to know all your fake bona fides?

"What I need, all that I am speaking of, I should think would be but a trifling matter for a young man of your position and obvious influence. I should like to obtain a list of all the female graphic artists in Los Angeles, or failing that, at the very least, a list of all the graphic design firms there and their phone numbers and addresses.

I should think, being so close to Los Angeles, that it should be likely something one such as yourself might even have right there in one's own desk somewhere, were one to look."

"Actually, sir, uh, Count,"

"Posh. Do call me Nicolo, my dear boy," I said.

"Thing is, you see, we're in New York, which is about three thousand miles from Los Angeles."

"Miles," I said, trying to make it sound quaint and provincial, "I had almost forgotten you Americans still use those charming little measurements. Surely in real distance, in kilometers, that is not so very far, is it, my good man?"

It was starting to seem as if the hiring standards might have been as loose on Wall Street as they were in the Ufficio Turismo but at least we had gotten on a first name basis. Names had taken on a ponderous importance to me by then.

"In any event, if you could obtain for me such a list and have it sent here to my personal home address, well then, I should be willing to release this bold new information which, I guarantee on the blood of my ancestors, is not going to any other publication for several months to come."

"I think that might be possible, Mr. Nicolo" he said, warming up to the game at last.

"Nick, if you find it easier," I said, for no reason at all.

"So, I believe that the Federal Express takes some three or four days to arrive from the United States. It's rather a long ways in kilometers and the moment I receive it I shall be happy to either take your call or to send you the full details by way of facsimile, which, if you don't mind me saying, is an Italian word, from the Latin, I'm sure you knew that, though."

"I could definitely look into that, but I would have to get some idea of what type of information it should be, you understand, of course, Nicolo," he said, "to make sure it was indeed fit for publication."

Shit. I had hoped to get the list, find the girl's name and have some time to think up something harmless and interesting that wouldn't have too many repercussions now that I was so well ensconced in my little job here in Venice and I probably could have gotten that damned list myself online if I'd tried. Or could have caught the next goddamned direct flight from Marco Polo to Los Angeles, if I'd had the guts. Something I'd thought a lot about but not done. But this seemed somehow a serendipitous sign to help fill the void that lie in the space between my longing and my listlessness.

I had to give him something to get what I wanted.

"As for the season, I can facsimile you all the numbers if you should like, or have my very capable assistant do that, but the big news, the real story is…"

What indeed would be a real scoop for the Wall Street reporter? What would he find worthy fodder to dish up to all their highly-touted shapers of opinion? At least they boasted no famous strictures about "All the News That's Fit to Print." The news of Wall Street was rife with fiction and innuendo, so I was limited only by the constraints of my Campari-lubricated imagination.

"I should perhaps let the Prime Minister's office speak on this, and indeed I would do so if I hadn't dined with him at Florian's just last week and discussed this very matter in some detail."

That did it. I could palpably feel him perk up from across the ocean. Practically speaking, it turned out that the dropping of prime ministers into conversation generated far more interest in business reporters than titled nobility and Doges. I imagined that this would be a source of great disappointment to my illustrious and much admired phony ancestors, but there it was, all the same. The modern corridors of power are much less concerned about pedigree. The world was filthy for its love of lucre.

This was getting to be a pretty expensive phone call and I was glad the Wall Street paper was paying for it and not me, because for some reason the phone bills to America were the one single thing that the vacationing Signor Contarini complained about when in my presence. Something I found doubly strange because he didn't have to pay for them for one, and for two, I had stopped phoning friends and family back home in the States many months ago. Indeed, stopped missing them almost entirely.

There were emails, of course, but they were always the same. Somebody had bought or built a new house or birthed another dribbling infant with a very creatively spelled name or here were some pictures of their kitchen remodel and they'd chosen Chesapeake Sunset for the walls or maybe their oldest had earned another participation trophy for showing up to something. Nobody cared if you'd gained a new part-time profession by becoming a semi-successful art thief abroad or lost a bit of your heart and didn't know how to make sense of it. These were not the things that constituted the news that was fit to print. Not in emails.

I realized that both I and the earnest young reporter were losing our patience.

"The hint I can give, of course taking you at your word on the other minor matter of the more personal nature, has to do with Venice's plans as regards to an ill-advised war in the Middle East. We can not," I said, "be expected to sit by idly during such times."

Sitting by idly seemed to be exactly what we were all doing but I'd had enough.

"What we've decided," I said, "is to take the step of closing Venice, at least perhaps to Americans, for a period of time, should the United States choose to proceed with initiating a war."

My pronouncement was met with transatlantic silence, so I went on.

"We here in Venice, you see, have learned from our history and all we are saying," I continued, trying not to burst into song, "is to give peace a chance."

Instantly I began to feel better about my charade. Why the hell not close down Venice to anyone who was starting a war and killing abroad, Christian, Muslim, or Atheist? Why not let regime change, like charity, begin at home? Why not wish to be better, for everyone to be better. Why not take some step, however futile or fictive, at attempting to forge peace? I'd grown so disgusted by the jingoistic platitudes passed around in the American press and my own country's notions about vengeance and revenge masked under a cloak of patriotism. It was an ill-fitting costume.

Maybe acting as someone else I could say what I wanted somehow, whether anyone wanted to hear it or not. Venice was the quintessence of beauty and surely each and every war diminished beauty. It all sounded right enough to me, just then, in the simple confines of my little office.

"You can't mean not allowing any visitors at all there? Surely tourism is the number one economic factor in the region," he said, with some authority.

"My dear boy, that is, I'm afraid, all I am at liberty to say right now until which time I speak with the Honorable Mayor of Venice. Who happens to be my nephew, by the way. And of course, again to the Prime Minister. I should, alas, like to go into further detail. But you understand how these things go, a savvy young man such as yourself." I said.

Surely there were fact checkers who would know better and check out such outlandish things. All of this, I knew, would never be news fit to print and I would never hear from the earnest young man again and never receive the list of graphic artists in Los Angeles. I would never know who she was and never see her again and nothing would happen about it at all and everything would go back to normal.

Although of late, normal had been rather atypical for everyone, not least of all myself. The status quo was in a tumultuous state of flux.

I reminded myself that I had determined to make my normal everyday life less normal and less everyday. It was a Quixotic quest but a quest, nevertheless. That reminded me that I'd been meaning to reread that book, and I don't know what it was about Venice that set me to thinking about Cervantes so much, being that he was one of the few Europeans of any note who had not left much of a lasting imprint on Venice.

Of course, he'd visited Venice when he was soldiering in Italy and said all the right requisite things about how beautiful it was. But then he'd sailed away with the Venetians and the Spanish in their Papacy-sanctioned Holy League to fight the Muslims in another earlier era of Islamophobia, before finally returning back to Spain to settle down and write.

I'd been to Spain in simpler times of my own, and despite having enjoyed Cervantes and sangria and late nights and dark-haired women and tapas, had not learned to love it like everyone said you should. It wasn't just the witnessing one afternoon of the killing of several bulls, though that did little to endear the place to me. I wasn't some Greenpeace activist or anything. Hell, I ate cows, I wore their skin. I knew what a hypocrite I was. I just didn't like to watch them be senselessly killed right in front of me. It seemed so sad and pointless and nobody around rooted for the bull and how could everyone not secretly want the bull to win the fight he'd been unknowingly forced into? Not in Spain. The rabid crowds wanted the bull to be fierce and strong, filled with fight, but to lose. Then there was blood on the bull and on the sand and frenzied applause at death. And you were a part of it, a race of ravenous bloodthirsty beings. And you knew you were in the wrong place.

It seemed so Roman at the Coliseum, but being distanced from America had lent me the perspective to see how much there was: Ultimate Fighting, Toughman, Survivor, MMA, Cage-fighting, the WWF, leaders of the Army serving as Secretary of State, idiots of privilege at the helm of presidential power because of their bloodlines, well, just how much utter depravity there was in modern America that was in fact so strongly reminiscent of the decadent and foul fading days of the fall of the Roman Empire.

Sitting there spilling my own propaganda in my sun-splashed office in Venice, where Doges had ruled the republic for a thousand years before falling into decadence and becoming a Disneyesque parody of themselves and their former glory, made you think more about what could, what might, and what would befall every empire, of every sort. And yet we people kept relinquishing our rights, handing over the keys that hastened our own annihilation.

Empires, like people, fell from grace. You just didn't want to dictate your own demise, nor to fiddle while your empire burned. I decided that I should think more about this, there was one of my theories in there struggling to sort itself out but it and my brains were a bit addled by the afternoon Campari and the self-imposed ordeal of being a pompous fake aristocrat and the too long talk with the earnest journalist from Wall Street.

∞ ∞ ∞

So I left the office and my own little lies and stepped out into the steaming heat of late-August Venice thinking about crumbling empires and religious wars and how not to be the architect of my own demise. There was much to mull over but I had a lot of time on my hands and figured I could fill it with thinking about things I did not understand. First I had to find some things I did, like the simple need for some food. Maybe a plate of steamed mussels and some Valpolicella. First a Coke, though, definitely a caffeinated cola to invigorate me. Coke and Campari, the idea occurred to me, might not be so bad. In Spain once, in San Sebastian which some past reading of some pedestrian guidebook had told me had been Bridget Bardot's favorite beach town, I had drank calimochos, red wine and coke. So the colors were right. It was something else to note. It's good to keep an open mind, as long as you could find the right things to fill it with.

I wished I'd carried around a little notebook. I'd always meant to, but never did. There were so many things you never had the time to do in life. Like take a purloined painting back to a church. So much there was not time for. You couldn't even have hoped to get a notebook big enough, even though Venice boasted an excellent selection of lovely little leather bound notebooks that would have sufficed. Another note to self: get good notebook, I thought, as I was locking up the little office and walking out into the early evening of Venice.

I went a bit out of my way to the traghetto stand where I could catch one that would whisk me away from work and across the Grand Canal.

Unless your timing was just right, you often had to wait ten minutes or so, but the traghetto helped avoid all the crowds going to and from the Guggenheim and the tangled summer lines outside the always packed Accademia. Besides, at only one euro, it was a much more satisfying commute across the canal than jostling across the bridge. Taking the traghetto made you feel like an insider.

I stared out at the traffic of the canal, captivated by the stately spectacle of the world's most majestic thoroughfare until the traghetto returned. That meant it wasn't yet eight o'clock, which was when they usually stopped for the day. It had been much earlier in winter but I had never taken them then because the wooden bridge of the Accademia hadn't been crowded and had itself been a pleasant commute. The way home in Venice was seasonal. Another reason for the traghetto was my compulsion to check on the graffiti on the British Embassy, which was right near the landing. You could see it while you were crossing if you were up front, but unless you were pushy, you usually weren't.

After the traghetto emptied out, I got a spot standing in the back. Only tourists sat down and we all looked askance at them when they did. Standing required more effort and balance than one liked on a Campari-sodden summer evening, but sometimes you had to concentrate on doing things the right way and just go with the prevailing current.

There I was just standing around minding my own business, kind of wanting a cigarette though not having the room to reach into my pocket and knowing I should wait, despite the fact, much to a few tourists' disdain, there were several people on the traghetto already smoking. I could wait and would, and I was standing there waiting and wanting when I saw her, that very day, the artist of all my many dreams, just across the Canal, walking along with her chestnut hair and a sketch pad in hand, moving ever further away from me even as we slowly advanced.

I was watching where she went, silently willing the gods and the traghetto guys to hurry up, trying to think of what to yell before she disappeared from view. What words could be shouted across a canal to someone whose name you did not know that strolled uneasily across all your thoughts and looked again as if they were vanishing and might be lost to you again, forever? What words would carry across the water and cover all the distance between water and shore, between longing and anonymity?

I could not conjure the right incantation, though I guess anything might have worked and been better than nothing, but at last the boat swooped in gracefully and I made my way, utterly without grace, pushing past some older tourists who were too slow to wait for and someone shouted at me in French and I pushed by, stepping over the seat of the traghetto, rushing to follow her, and he pushed back and I didn't hear what he said, I think it was French anyway, and I could smell the garlic he'd had that lingered on his breath but couldn't tell for sure what words and what language he threw at me because the next thing I knew I was falling off to the side into the Grand Canal and the garlic smell and foreign words were lost in an inauspicious burst of gravity.

As I splashed into the canal, thoughts came flooding to me in a rush. Get up, get out, get ashore. *Get to her.* While thrashing in the water, I remembered hearing that the canal water was less than ten feet deep and I had always wondered, always meant to check, and wished I had but I didn't have time to wonder or to check anything, I had to get to her. Only so many things could be known for sure, no matter what you'd heard.

I scrambled up and out of the filthy water, and as I reached both my arms up onto the edge of the floating dock of the traghetto stand, the pilot was laughing at me or maybe with me as he reached his hand down. I didn't have time to care, just clasped his strong arm and he pulled me out of the water onto the dock, and I scrambled off in my wet, clinging jeans, uttering mi dispiace, grazie mille, grazie. Outside, it was suddenly colder now that I was all wet and he was saying something about the euro I'd forgotten to pay him as I ran off after her, down the Rio San Trovaso, pushing and shoving to make my way through all the people between us, assaulted by all manner of angry comments and exclamations in various languages, and not caring and damn these tourists, get the hell out of the way, no time for excuse mes in any language, just shoving through and then, at last, right in little Campo San Barnaba, I caught up to her.

I was afraid, panicked for a moment, that I'd been wrong and it wasn't her at all, she had her hair all tied back and was in shorts and looked so different from the teary-eyed, dramatic, red-haired artist of winter Venice and my many dreams and the swift traveling of time might have changed her in my mind, maybe everything I thought I'd believed was false.

But there was the note she had left me and the other man I'd given her the courage to go back to, but there was also the truth that there were so many artists in Venice in summer and the possibility that it wasn't her at all, that maybe she lived only in my mind and elsewhere and that it wasn't her, and I was crazed and had had a weird day and drunk too much. My wet jeans were stifling me and my shirt, it was an orange one, was all gooey and dripping, and I was cold and remembered how ridiculous I looked and maybe even how foolish I really was. Still I ran up to her, just like the crazy person I felt like and utterly unlike the pompous aristocrat I'd purported myself to be to the Wall Street reporter, just a canal-crossing few moments long ago.

And I came to a hesitant halt before her, hoping, and she stopped drawing and looked up at me.

I stood there swept away with relief that it was really her, noticing that she had some freckles I had not noted before sprinkled across the bridge of her nose and maybe in winter that had not been there, and I thought about the fresh freckles and their appearance on her nose, and her appearance here, and the reality of my wet and disheveled demeanor, feeling cold and self-conscious at my inauspicious arrival, not knowing what to say, I finally said exactly what I'd been thinking to myself but hadn't known for sure if I could, or would get to, ever say.

"I love you. Whatever your name is. I love you."

The saying of those words right there and right then made me wonder when exactly, at what moment in time, had I decided they were true. Had it been only right there and right then, or if not, at what precise moment had it become my truth? Could anyone who'd been swept away, overcome with this feeling, have looked at a precise moment or placement of hands on a clock and call out the minute that love had commenced? Or should one even be able to? Love, after all, was far older than timekeeping.

She looked up at me, poised, sensible, self-assured, everything I was not, and said simply, "Sophie. It's Sophie."

"I love you, Sophie," I said, emboldened by knowledge of her name and the fact that she was here again and I was here for the first time and I'd taken the right traghetto at the right moment and skipped so many other necessities and didn't know what else to do, so I repeated it.

"I think I love you," I said.

"You think?" she said.

"I believe so. Yes. It's true, it's my truth."

"When did this happen?" she asked.

"I'm not exactly sure. Maybe just now. Maybe when you fell asleep next to me on the couch and I woke up and you were gone. Maybe some time in between. Maybe always."

I kept standing there, not exactly waiting for her to say the same words I'd said, but it crossed my mind, and having said that, not knowing what else to say after, feeling I had skipped ahead to the end of things and missed out on a few parts of the middle.

She looked up at me and smiled and it was the right smile, the best and purest smile I'd ever seen, and I decided her hair was chestnut and it matched those little freckles that sprinkled the curve of her nose. There are quintessential moments in a man's life. Maybe for some it's getting married or having a baby or discovering something or winning something, but that smile, that pure and radiant smile and the wondrous white teeth and the little lone dimple on the side of her cheek and her sad, green eyes that lit up when she saw me, that smile of hers was mine. An award, however unexpected or undeserved, to cherish and keep forever in mine own arsenal of things to make my world better than it was.

She leaned toward me, crinkling up her nose, animating and rearranging the freckles that danced across her nose.

"You, uh, kind of stink," she said.

"Oh, the canal, I saw you, I was swimming, I mean, on the traghetto, I was at work, talking to a reporter from Wall Street, about you, actually, I mean sort of, well, I was…"

"Slow down, slow down, take a breath," she said.

I stood there and slowed all the way down to an awkward moment of silence, pondering the proper gestation period for a pregnant pause.

"I think I could use a hot shower."

"I wanted to return your shirt," she said

"Oh, thanks. Right. My shirt."

If you've ever stood and declared your love to a woman you didn't know so well while you're dripping wet from having been pushed in the Grand Canal by a Frenchman reeking of garlic, and she's told you in response that you smell and she's returning your clothes, then you know exactly how I felt at that moment.

Somehow sort of extraordinary.

"My apartment is just down this way," I said, stupidly, waiting, hoping, she would stand up. Maybe she would stand up and start loving me. Why shouldn't she?

"I know. I actually tried to visit a couple of hours ago but the gate outside was locked. I left you a picture in your box, actually. I think it was your box, anyway."

"Did you really? You did?"

"You're not calling me a liar, are you?"

"No, not that. But you said I smell."

"Well you do, pretty badly. I wouldn't lie about a thing like that, I promise. Why exactly were you swimming in the canal? Is it some hip aquatic aerobics routine?"

"Come with me, come home, let me clean up so I don't catch the Bubonic Plague or anything, and I'll tell you all about it, everything. There's lots to tell."

"I believe you would, wouldn't you?"

"Anything. Everything," I said, marking more truths that I did not yet understand.

At last, she stood and together we made our way through the sea of people, slowly and purposefully. It was too crowded to walk side by side, to talk or try to hold hands, even though there was so much that needed to be said. It gave me time to try and acclimate to her being there again, to being near her again and reflect on what all I'd been doing without her and why I had let myself be without her and how I could avoid ever being without her again. And what I'd just said.

The walk to my house was not far and there was not much time but there is never enough time. The tourists were all heading the opposite way from us, away from my apartment and towards more vaunted sights than little San Trovaso and we were, it occurred to me, like salmon swimming upstream, driven by instinct beyond our understanding. Maybe driven to spawn, though I wouldn't have put it that way to her. There were limits, no matter how stupid and drunk you were, to what you would say to a woman you'd just brazenly declared your love to early on a late summer evening. Even in Venice. There were limits to everything. Maybe knowing the limits was enough, maybe you didn't have to abide by them.

As we turned down past the bookstore and neared my house, I remembered suddenly that I was newly married and it seemed so sublimely funny, so spectacularly ridiculous that I couldn't help laughing out loud, and she stared at me while I unlocked the gate, and I laughed then laughed some more and my sides even hurt a little bit, not just from the laughing but from where I'd perched my chest on the traghetto dockside planks. I felt how my chest hurt while I laughed and it was a good hurt.

She looked over at me and I remembered about the drawing that was supposed to be in my postbox but I didn't have the key to it with me since I so rarely expected, wanted, or checked for mail anymore.

"I, uh, have been drinking a bit," I said.

"I suspected that might be the case."

Seeing her had sobered me up but I was drunk on many things and I reached out and wrapped my arms around her and she embraced me back and I squished against her, all wet, and she crinkled up her freckled nose and said:

"Yeech. You really do smell, you know. I mean, you really reek."

"Sorry," I said, kissing her cheek, and she smiled.

"Now I need a shower too," she said.

And we went inside my building and I forgot about the drawing she might have left and unlocked the downstairs door and wished that I had drank less that afternoon but maybe somehow it had helped get me, get us, here. I retrieved my key from my wet pocket and unlocked the door and let her walk in front of me, following behind her.

Then we were back in my apartment again, only this time it was bright and sunny and all the windows were opened and before it had been dark and cold and raining and she had been sad and now everything was different, and we showered together and kissed under the water and laughed and sprayed each other and then went straight to the bedroom, naked and damp, and made love with an ardor and intensity that left me breathless, and then we lay there together in the dark, spent, and speaking in soft whispers of newly discovered wonder until we drifted into sleep. It occurred to me that there were many things, so many more things to say, so many things both of us should have known but that maybe there would be time for all of it.

And in the morning when the church bells rang, she was still there.

She stirred but slept through the bells, and whatever combination of contentment, exhaustion or jet lag made this soundness possible, her soft, sleeping murmurs gave them benediction.

I crept out of bed quietly and grabbed a pair of khakis and a shirt and went to the kitchen and wrote a note and then left it on the pillow next to her head, where her hair, all reddish gold in the morning sun that slanted through the windows, was splayed across her cheek and the white casings of my pillows.

"Do not leave! I shall return," the note said, silently, as I tiptoed out of the room, and there were no bells ringing anymore and I didn't give God the finger, not that day.

I walked across the Rio San Trovaso to the small shop I frequented and bought a bottle of prosecco and some blood orange juice from Sardinia and some brioche and two oranges and then ran down the fondamenta to the little flower shop and bought a bouquet of something, all yellows and reds, to complete the color scheme and ran back through the eager early morning tourists as fast as I could carry my purchases to make sure when I got home that she would still be there.

I peeked in and she was still sound asleep, so I set up everything on the little white wrought iron table on the balcony, found a bowl to serve as an ice bucket for the champagne and a vase for the flowers and then I undressed again and crawled back into bed beside her. She stirred drowsily and reached out for me, and I remembered again that I had gotten married and hoped that besides being beautiful and having the right smile, and having come back to Venice, that she had a terrific sense of humor.

"What's so funny, mister?"

"Nothing, well, everything. You're even beautiful in the morning," I said.

"Don't joke so early. It's evil, I'm jet-lagged and I must have coffee. Kiss me," she said.

I did. She got up and kept the sheet around her until she dropped it and put on a pair of red panties I had not even noticed from the night before that had a little lace front that pushed back the hairs but was quickly covered from view by the shirttails of a blue oxford she grabbed from my open closet. I liked the confidence she displayed by just grabbing a shirt and not asking, just taking, and liked even better the fact that she only buttoned the bottom three buttons, which was perfect and afforded me still a good view.

We went, together, both smiling and quiet and probably with much to say but without saying much, to sit on my balcony and we sipped prosecco and orange juices, mimosa's of our own construction, and the world seemed just about perfect and I didn't even consider going to work and tried to remember for a second if it was indeed Friday or Saturday, but let the thought slip away when we clinked glasses and just savored the moment with all my senses.

While we sipped champagne, she sat with her legs tucked underneath her on the iron chair and the tails of my shirt almost covered them and it was just hot enough that little beads of perspiration formed on the glasses and above the high, light-haired arch of her eyebrows. I noticed that her toes, all ten of them, were polished a bright red.

She broke the small silence of the day after the infernal bells finished clanging again.

"The bells, the bells," she said, with a smile, covering her ears with her hands like Quasimodo, which lifted the shirttails a bit and made the view more exciting for a brief moment.

"So, here you are. How? Why? What happened?" I asked.

"Aren't we Mr. Inquisitive?"

"Now that we're on a first name basis, my curiosity is limitless."

"Let me see. Where to start? So I left Venice," she said.

"I noticed."

"Hey, do you want to hear this story or not?"

"All of it," I said.

"So like a real grown-up I went home to put the pieces together. I dedicated myself to sorting everything out: job, boyfriend, life in general. And, well, I guess I was just not so good at sorting and being dedicated actually kind of sucked. Everybody wanted stuff from me I didn't want to give. The straw that broke my back was, there was this pension plan thing I was supposed to enroll in. My boss, my boyfriend, everyone was all, 'you have to think about your future, Sophie.' Everybody said it was a very smart move, y'know, planning for your future and all. But I couldn't help thinking I was missing my present. Then there was going to be this big round of layoffs because all the mucky-mucks are cutting their ad budgets and everything was just, just dismal. So I decided instead of staying there and hanging my life up on a hook in the hallway, I would take my retirement in little bites. Live my life now and worry about later when later happens. That's my new credo. So I sold my car, untangled myself from my love life, quit my job, bought a ticket, and voilà…"

"Career, car, boyfriend, in exchange for a ticket to Venice. Let me just tell you that I think you made a very good trade," I said.

"So far you're the only one to tell me that."

"Besides," I said, "who wants to spend all their best years working at something they don't like so they can retire with a little pension and play golf?"

"Do you play golf?"

I smiled.

"I am proud to say I am not at all a golfer. My friends, though, they're all golfers. All very good and very serious about hitting that little white ball up and down the green."

"I never got the allure," she said.

"Me neither."

We finished the champagne and nibbled at the brioche and when the orange juice was gone we went inside.

We spent the rest of that day in bed, somnolent after champagne, being awakened at random times by the bells, and I forgot to flip God off again because we made love instead, again, which seemed better, and we caught on to each others' rhythm and wants and discovered ways to make them our own. We explored one another inside and out, talking as much as we touched, and I couldn't help noticing the talking made me feel even closer to her than the touching and wondering if that was indeed what love was, the touch of talking and the love of touching, all together.

Later in the day, we ate and drank and slept more, and I was relieved that of the many things I had let go in my house and in my self-care, that I was well provisioned with groceries and that I still had her note sitting on my dining table beneath the red Murano glass bowl centerpiece that sat there in the middle of the round wooden table. I noticed her raise her eyebrows when she saw it as she brought the bouquet I'd bought her inside and set it on the table and it made me pleased, and, I think, her too. We smiled at one another and it was another of those moments.

It occurred to me the next afternoon that I might should have gone out and gotten a Wall Street business journal, that some strange and stupid things had been said by me. But I didn't seem to care at all and so I didn't, though I told her a bit about the silly fiasco and my attempts to trade propaganda for knowledge of her whereabouts and she laughed and told me the name of her former firm. And I wondered if I would even have gotten a list and if so, how I would have handled it, and what it would have driven me to do and also, if perhaps, I would soon have a former firm of my own. I was relieved that they were all things I did not have to worry about now. And no matter what I had said or what might be written or what lies might be told so that war might be started, Venice would not close, and beauty would still be diminished. But maybe, just maybe there was enough of it, if you believed and you were very lucky.

SIXTEEN

BRIDGE OF THE HONEST WOMAN

THE FIRST DOSES OF REALITY reared their heads into our cocoon by Sophie's necessity for her clothes.

Not having made hotel reservations in Venice, she had left them in her bags at the train station. I felt more than slight swellings of pride that she had taken for granted the fact that she wouldn't need a hotel. I knew that could have meant many things, but I liked to think it meant she took me for granted and I rather enjoyed the feelings of being taken and being granted.

We left my apartment, her wearing a pair of my khakis that she had to gather up baggy and belted at her waist and rolled up at the bottoms so they transformed into fashionable Capri pants rather than the boring khakis they were at heart. I marveled again at how adroitly she made things better than they were without trying.

We walked together northward through the crowded calle to the left luggage at Venice's least attractive edifice, the stazione centrale, where we retrieved her two bags, both soft canvas with wheels, and rolled them along through the crowds and stopped and had lunch in the sun in the Campo dei Frari. It was far too crowded for my taste and altogether too touristed, but it was two in the afternoon and soon most everyplace would be closed and it happened that there were two empty tables sitting in the sun, which seemed fortuitous.

We sat down and had prosecco and a green bottle of still Pellegrino and shared a cold insalata di frutta di mare and both had simple pasta primavera, foregoing secondi in favor of caffè macchiati.

We were idly finishing up our little coffees just as the sun was beginning to be shrouded by the looming stones of the Frari. I thought about my earlier trips to the Archives of State that adjoined the Frari and the Titians as well as his tomb and those of several

Doges that sat there inside the large church, but I wanted to embrace life rather than focus on small talk of work or death or history. I was preoccupied with the possibilities of my future, of perhaps, our future.

I had ordered for us both in Italian, not being able to help showing off that these intervening months had not left me utterly unimproved, and she told me I needed a haircut, which I did. And which pleased me, not so much the need as the needing to be told. I forgot all about dead doges and famed artisans which, even sitting there in the shadow of the Frari, is not hard to do when you are next to a captivating woman.

"I've been thinking of a dose of retirement myself," I said, "if I might be so bold as to ask if you'd like some company in your self-imposed retirement scheme."

"I might," she said.

It occurred to me that anyone "might" do anything at all. But usually didn't.

"Do you have any plans?" I asked, feeling things out, not wishing to be too intrusive but wanting to be clear about my availability. Invitations can be elusive. I remembered the scene in Chaplin when he was told that his exile had been lifted and he could return to America, when he declined, saying he was accustomed to invitations. I had meant to read his autobiography after seeing the movie, but hadn't. So much to read.

"Nope. I have clothes, some paints, some vague notions. But no real plans, per se. I'm thinking maybe of Greece but I don't know. It's kind of nice not knowing."

"I wonder," I said, striving to evoke a nonchalance I did not possess, "have you ever been to Prague?"

"No, why?"

"Have you ever seen Chaplin, the movie?" I said.

"Also, no."

"Great film. I didn't know how truly amazing he was. The things he did, the impact. He was the whole package."

"Was it filmed in Prague?"

"No, why?" I asked.

"I thought there might be some connection. Some point," she said.

"Right, of course. Prague, indeed," I said, stretching out the last word, seeking time for truth. "A lot of my stories are in search of a point."

There were always connections but they didn't always make sense.

Or at least, I could not make sense of some of the wrong connections I had made.

"Indeed," she said, simply, not stretched out and perhaps not leaving me enough space for the truth I had to tell.

"So, I was there on a little business trip a couple weeks ago. Actually, some things that I might have to go back and finish up in a week or so," I said.

"Oh?"

"Yeah, just a couple of things, a little favor I did for some friends. Some very nice people I met. An actual revolutionary."

"A revolutionary?"

I told her about Pavel Sokol and gave her my condensed version of his compelling role in the Velvet Revolution, though somehow neglected to get up the courage to mention his sister or the small civil wedding ceremony that now seemed a particularly poor piece of planning on my part and almost tragic in its comedic aspects. If you are not well compensated for it, no one wants to live out their life as if it were a bad sitcom. I hoped that my future wouldn't be dictated by agreeing to a favor in a faraway land that now seemed like a preposterous farce. Many futures had fed on worse sustenance. Destiny had an indiscriminate appetite.

"That's something. I never knew any actual revolutionaries. There were a couple of Fauvists at art school."

"Well you don't meet them every day, I guess." I said, because you didn't, at least not in my circles. It occurred to me then and there that I was completely unaware any longer, after almost a year abroad, of what my circles were or if actually I still had a circle. Geometry had always befuddled me.

"You know, Prague might be a good place to paint. There's these soaring spires, a meandering river, heavy old stone bridges, green copper domes, red tiled roofs, very picturesque stuff. I mean the place looks like a painting. And it's terrifically inexpensive."

"Sounds paintable enough to me. Especially after all the dismal commercial stuff I've been doing. Dreary graphic art during the day and drab, dark paintings on my own time was not a very satisfying diet. I like big banquets of colors and light. Like the Venetians. The reason I came," she said.

So that was the reason.

"My self-imposed black period was getting pretty stale," she said.

Maybe that was another reason. Maybe I was a part of it. I tried to remember if black was the absence of all color or the presence of all colors and couldn't and didn't want to reveal my ignorance by asking.

"Do you like Picasso?" she asked.

I hadn't seen many Picassos and didn't feel on comfortable enough ground to discuss him with a painter and was conscious of not wanting to answer wrong and how utterly silly that was, but knew so much depended on the expression of these early opinions and which ones you shared or which disagreements charmed.

"I don't know him very well. I mean the generic blue period stuff, cocktail party talk, some drawings, kids with too many eyes and such," I said.

"Well, you have to study Picasso, whether you like it or not. There's this story I like. Picasso, that brilliant misogynist—"

"I thought Picasso loved women," I said.

"You don't think you can love women and be a misogynist?"

"Well, yes, like most things, I guess. Not that women are things, I mean."

Silence.

"What I meant was," I tried to add.

"Don't fret. It's all right," she said, "I know what you mean. Take Picasso, who happened to be a huge momma's boy. He used to like to tell the story about how his mother told him if he became a soldier he'd be a general, if he became a priest he'd end up as pope but instead how he became a painter and wound up as Picasso. I would like to wind up as something. Not necessarily as Picasso. Or a revolutionary. Shoot, maybe not even an artist. Just someone else. Someone other than who I've been lately. I got tired of not liking me."

"I've given thought to becoming someone else, too. Only I'm not sure what or where. Or actually, how," I said.

"That's the million-dollar question, isn't it?"

"Not so much 'to be or not to be,' but rather 'what to be?'" I said.

"What, indeed," she said, and stretched the word out as I had and we were closer somehow over something trivial that might have allowed for more truths.

"Work, lately, is well..." I began, until she saved me with understanding.

"I know the feeling. The woman I worked for back at the design studio, where they had me doing these dreadful logos and renderings of artless things like cleaning solutions or cosmetics. Terrible stuff. She'd take the most trifling account, something like contact lenses or stain remover and say, 'This time, Sophie, I want something sensational, something larger than life,' she'd say with a totally straight face. It was all I could do not to get sick all over her. I just couldn't face it anymore, I loathed it. And it was murder on the artistic part of me. It was practically art prostitution," Sophie said, shaking her head.

"Larger than life," I repeated.

"I don't mean to sound scornful. Maybe there are things or people that are larger than life," she said.

"Michelangelo, DaVinci, Napoleon, Alexander the Great, Jefferson, Lincoln," I said, to show that I was paying attention and I was, though couldn't help feeling a bit uneasy, as if nervous that I was performing unrehearsed and wanted ever so much to do well but wasn't sure when the reviews would come in. Or exactly how they would read.

"Hmm. All men on your list," she said.

"Joan of Arc, Cleopatra, uh, Madam Curie...."

"It's okay, it's not a test. So long as you agree that new and improved stain removers and disposable contact lenses are, well, life-size."

"I do, most definitely," I said.

"So it was kind of demeaning, you know? I don't think Renaissance masters or dead patriots would be very pleased being dug up to push detergents or mascara to the masses," she said.

"Man's got to know his limitations," I said, in my best Eastwood, which was not very good. Somehow she managed to suppress her admiration.

"Enough about me and my past. How's everything with you? Your job? Still enjoying being terribly overpaid, making people want to go elsewhere and reaping what you sow, hopping all over, all that jazz?" she asked.

"Funny you should ask. Because things are sort of winding down, the boss here, the evil Signor Contarini—"

"Is he evil, your boss?"

"Not really, but I like to think of him that way. Anyway, everyone here, is, well, not here, really..."

She looked around at the crowded campo, humming with late afternoon activity.

"That's strange, because seems to me like everyone is really here."

"Exactly. But everyone else, at the office, I mean, well, they're all away on vacation. Most of them due back in the next week and I've been the only one here. And truthfully there hasn't been much to do. So I haven't really been doing much. Not much at all, just sort of mucking about. Perhaps mucking things up a bit."

"And that means?"

"Well, possibly, I'm not sure with all the European bureaucracy, it's not exactly entirely clear who I'm working for anymore, but I think, perhaps that there's a little chance my, um, services, shall we say, might not be so required in the future. Hard to tell what's going on."

"Are you trying to say you're going to get fired?"

"It's possible. But, frankly, my dear—"

"Please, no more impressions. Things that are possible have a way of becoming probable," she said.

I thought that a fine note to orchestrate an ending on.

I looked up and caught the eye of the waitress and nodded and she started tallying up our bill.

I paid the check and tipped more than the Italians, even though there was a service charge included. It was important to showcase generosity.

Around us, unnoticed during our repast, most of the diners had finished and departed. Just a few tables nearby lingered on, a large family of Italians whose purer Tuscan Italian sounded more melodious than the shrill tones of the Venetians, as well as two handsome American men enjoying the intimacy of a romantic holiday. And us.

The chef came out and sat down at the empty table by the door with a sweating bottle of water. He was large with a heavy paunch draped in a straining, well-stained white apron. He lit a cigarette and let out a deep sigh before taking a large draft of water and he bore the contentment of a good day's work that I had not known for some time.

The waitress brought my change over. Tipping was confusing to the good Italians.

"Thanks for lunch. I'll pay you back when I change money."

"Please don't," I said.

"Do you insist?"

"I do."

"Okay, I'll let you get away with insisting. This time."

I left the change sitting there next to the empty Pellegrino bottle. As we crossed the campo, a small group of young Venetians kicked around a weathered soccer ball while being chased by a pig-tailed little girl riding a blue bicycle with training wheels, who was herself pursued by a barking brown terrier as she pedaled on gleefully, laughing at the dog or the boys or just for herself, and we were for a moment a small part of their glorious mayhem.

I wondered if I should quit my job or if I would get fired and what might happen and how wise or how foolish I was and how and why and when the simple pursuit of pleasure had grown so difficult. Life had come to a crossroads and no one knew what might lay ahead on the road not taken.

∞ ∞ ∞

I couldn't help but ponder if perhaps, in my still well-schooled seasonal mentality, summer and holidays were over, were and were supposed to be grinding down to a halt. If I wasn't trying to make them last one day too long. When younger, which had been all days before this one, I had always believed that at some point adulthood would mean forgetting about summer holidays and back to work or school in September. But somehow the feeling had never left me and I wondered if you could mess up your whole Circadian rhythm by trying to stretch time and what if it wasn't elastic at all. If time and summer and this feeling weren't relative?

Sophie stopped and reached down into the side zippered compartment of one of her bags and took out a little black scrunchy and pulled her hair back and tucked the strands into the elastic. Ah, elasticity, I thought, a sign. I saw the sign.

We each grabbed one of her bags and wheeled them along behind us, carefully avoiding the impromptu soccer match, and strolled off towards my apartment. Sophie, I guess, en route also to fitting the pieces of herself together and me wondering if perhaps there was a place in the puzzle into which I and my future might fit. I noticed that the little blue bicycle sat there, unridden, leaning against one of the green wooden benches of the campo and wondered where the little girl was and what had happened to the terrier. I sort of missed them but hoped maybe they'd gone off to pursue other playtimes.

It occurred to me that I had no ties anywhere, that my apartment lease was in the Tourism Council's name. That there was no paperwork to sign, no car to take care of, no valuable possessions to crate up. That another winter in Venice in that office wasn't altogether an idyllic choice, and I wasn't sure why exactly, if it was because of her being here next to me rolling her suitcase alongside me, heading to my apartment.

I thought that perhaps my time in Venice had simply wound itself down, that I'd done what I came to do, along with many things I hadn't.

There would be some remorse about leaving just as the tourists did, without seeing Venice in the early autumn, which I had started to look forward to as a reward for making it through the stifling crowds of summer, a victory of sorts. But each choice carried within it another one forsaken, and I was pretty sure the race was more important than the victory party, the journey of more interest than the destination.

As we walked on in comfortable and companionable silence, I bristled with resentment toward the messy and interfering outside world. The petty demands of work, circumstance or convention that could conspire to interfere with us being together.

We left the Frari and its heavy gothic stones behind and walked along the fondamenta until we reached the Ponte della Donna Onesta, the Bridge of the Honest Woman, that would take us out of San Polo and back into my Dorsoduro neighborhood. It was a very small bridge, just a few steps to cross, but by the time we had made our passage, me trailing along behind her, I had decided not to let the squawking and squabble of the outside world distract me from this new little world that might be mine. This world that could include her and for that was far superior to the others I had known. If I could inhabit her world, that was where I wanted live.

As we stepped off the bridge, I thought more about what it means to disavow the outside world. In a certain light, it could have been cowardice, a recognition of the possibility that this new thing, new feeling, might not have been able to stand up against the world.

But I disdained that possibility and decided to view it more from the rosy colored lens of heroism. Not that falling in love or feeling this way was necessarily heroic, but rather the conscious choice to thwart the interference of the outside world from this inner one of my own, our own. Perhaps it was the very lowest rung of the ladder of heroism, or maybe even a higher rung of the ladder towards understanding the heights or dimensions of your own little place in the world, made better by sharing it with the right someone. Maybe that was as well as I could have explained it to myself and I didn't even try, not then, to explain it to her as we walked on, wheeling bags behind us across the stones of Venice and through her quieter streets and then her unavoidable crowds when we could not avoid them.

I led us through the smaller calle where there were less people and more room for us to pass unmolested. Some were so close that we had to go single file, and I chivalrously let her go first and watched her backside which, despite being draped by the folds of my khakis, undulated with a grace never before known by my pedestrian pants.

By the time we reached the Zattere, I had decided to quit my job and set out for adventure, if both adventure and Sophie would have me. And to find out about my wife and what obligations there were to be fulfilled so that Denissa could get her visa during these troubled times when it was so hard to reach the land of opportunity. I couldn't help noticing that the world, the outside world, made her presence known no matter how hard you tried to disdain her. But maybe if you gave the world what she wanted, made some small gesture to help another, the world might help you back. Maybe that's how it worked.

On the Zattere, we wheeled her bags alongside each other, and though it was slightly awkward, I kept turning to look at her as we walked. It was as if I couldn't stop checking to make sure she was still there and I drew strength and confidence and assurance of her presence beside me. Around us, before us, and in our wake, the world went about her business and we made our way through it best we could, sometimes steering past a troop of tourists or a child licking a strawberry gelato or slowing to let an older person cut in front of us.

Sometimes when I stared over at her, she met my eye, looked deep within me, I thought, or felt. But then the moment would pass and the magic of Venice would overtake it as she stared out across the basin toward the Giudecca and the Church of the Redentore. Venice overwhelmed.

It occurred to me that an artist and a beautiful woman embodied a certain dichotomy. Two opposing characteristics in the play of life, with stunning women being habituated by circumstance at attracting admiration, whether willed or not, while Sophie turned her eyes outward, seeking always the beauty that lie elsewhere. It was clear that she was not quite comfortable at being looked at so closely, so much admired. But I kept looking, and she seemed more radiant for perhaps not recognizing her own beauty or maybe, was it possible, not seeing, not having ever seen, what I saw? Perhaps she lacked the perspicacity to appreciate the masterpiece that was herself.

I looked out onto the canal and saw a large, white cruise ship cleave the quiet waters of the basin heading off toward the Adriatic and it came to me, to go somewhere else, as I always had, knowing that in a new place the world left less indelible stamps. That new identities could be forged.

"I've never been to Greece," I said.

"Me neither."

"Seems a good thing."

"Not having been or going?"

"Going. The urge to be somewhere else. That's been my job all these years. Convincing people they should be somewhere else. I don't know how much difference it made to the other people but I've grown to believe in it, being somewhere else. Actually, we missed it yesterday, I don't know how, but every Saturday the ferry to Greece floats right past my balcony. It's a beautiful flag, those white and blue stripes with the cross in the corner, and you can look right into the eyes of the passengers, straight over the treetops and roofs across the way, and you just wait for the flag to float by in slow motion even though it's not, strictly speaking, in slow motion, it seems like it. It's one of the top three flags," I said.

"It is a catchy design. Good colors, too. Of course, I am half Greek," she said, with a little note of unease or even regret. I couldn't tell the difference and I didn't know just how to pursue it or what to say and if I was treading on dangerous grounds and stepping on territory where my feet or thoughts should not be planted.

"Everyone is half something."

"I guess. Only I'm still trying to deal with the fact that there's this whole half of me I never knew about before."

"That's why we explore, right? To get to the other side," I said.

"Maybe to see how the other half lives," she said, and a small smile tugged at the corners of her lips, and I noticed again that they were so very pink and she didn't wear lipstick, nor need it.

Looking over at her, I was pleased again that she was still there, still slightly surprised and proud every time I reassured myself of this, which I had done countless times already in these few days, yet still hadn't grown used to the idea that there she was, right there, walking next to me. Each time it was a remarkable discovery. The times, far greater in number but lesser in magnitude, when she had not been there, seemed already faraway and forgotten.

"My place or yours?" I said.

"Since I don't have a place…"

"Why don't we see what can be done about that," I said, and we went back into my apartment and went straight to bed, skipping dinner altogether and I didn't even miss it, feeling fortified by the late lunch and the beckoning dreams of a new future.

I woke early, the outside still darkened by the absence or late arrival of the sun, and reached my arm around her naked waist and rested it there, her muscles twitched and then relaxed and she let out a sleepy sigh. Beneath my arm in the darkness she was just a pale shape, a shadow form, but I could see her eyes were closed, her mouth, her lips slightly opened. I could feel the steady and slow rising and falling of her breasts with each breath.

I didn't move, just lay there and savored the moment in the darkness, the waiting for the light of day, and the rhythm of her breast slowly grazing my hand, each breath a gentle measure of contentment. In that soft-hearted darkness, it occurred to me that it might be possible there could never be an end to desire, to wanting to be with someone, and it seemed infinitely wondrous.

I moved closer and she nestled up against me and we lay there with our eyes closed and the next time I opened mine the church bells were sounding their solemn alarm and the sun was shining outside in Venice and it was another day and being new, was better than the other days. I knew I had many things to do this day in order that I might have other such days.

The morning light and the peal of the bells reminded me of the tasks that had to be done to make this work. I wished I had email at home so I wouldn't have actually had to go in and let a Monday interfere with life. But I didn't, so I did. Have to go in. I couldn't help feeling like it was dangerous to leave her alone. What might happen when we were apart? The little times we'd been together had been so ideal, seemed and felt so right, but a relationship, new or old, had to also earn merit by how it handled times apart.

We got up, she showered while I made coffee and we drank it together on the balcony and we made no other plans except that I had to go to the office and she was going to unpack and stay with me for a time and go out and draw in the afternoon. We arranged to meet at Sancho's in the afternoon and I drew her a little map and told her about the dog and she had never read Don Quixote and I thought about us reading it together and I didn't know why, because it was a buddy book more than a love story and I wanted a love story.

SEVENTEEN

LATE SUMMER DAYS OF LABOR

WALKING TO THE OFFICE WAS DIFFERENT with the knowledge that Sophie was back at my house and the expectation that she would be there again when I returned. It inspired me to work fervently, dedicated to finish up my business so that I could get back to her. And that day my business was personal.

I called the number I had for Aaron repeatedly and kept getting no answer, but kept trying, thinking he would pick up, he had to pick up, it was important. My future depended on it. He had a machine but these were not things to leave on a recording. My unanswered urgency and the frustrating realization that I didn't have my new wife's phone number or address rather perfectly suited the absurdity of my situation.

I wondered how many husbands didn't have their wife's contact information. Then I remembered the insurance guy, the actuarial scientist of the fifty-fifty divorce rate, and figured it was a lot. There were probably unlisted wives all over the place.

The desk calendar reminded me that Labor Day was the coming weekend. Not that it signified anything there in Italy, but the seventh of September was the day we had agreed I would fly back to Prague to sign more papers and make declarations to whatever foreign service office presided over such things and needed to hear them told.

A trip to Prague with Sophie to work out Denissa's immigration details seemed less than ideal for everyone. I was not eager to risk our fragile new duality by subjecting it to being a part of a trio that would require too much risky triage. It occurred to me that I was the one doing the favor, and it was a rather large courtesy, and perhaps things might be done at the American Embassy in nearby Milan, just three hours away by rental car or train. Or maybe even in Greece.

American diplomacy, however challenged, might be accessed anywhere. After being buffeted around Venice and much of Europe on other people's errands, the idea of actually grasping destiny by the hand and taking over the tiller and being master of my ship seemed a marvelous mutiny.

I gave up on the phone and looked at some websites on Greece. September there seemed idyllic and a good time and a good setting for falling in love. I hoped it was not a mistake to chuck everything and fly off in the direction of all the unknown, of us, her father, all that might be, but there was only one way to find out. Deciding to steer forward instilled a liberating sense of relief, the suspension of indecision was intoxicating. If mistakes would be made, at least they would be my fault.

I searched for Greek villas and found a company in America called European Escapes and sent them an email, enjoying the irony of being just across the Adriatic from the shores of Greece and emailing some company in the U.S. for a rental house there. They had some very good deals for September and I had stashed away a decent portion of my money that sought something special to be spent on. Taking my chances with some books to read and a captivating woman on faraway shores seemed a worthwhile investment. After the bustle of busy Venice high season, the possibility of a quiet Greek island where she could paint and I could maybe fill up some notebooks with thoughts begging to be figured out seemed as good a return as one could desire.

I emailed the company that I wanted a little island house for two people. Something where you could see the sea, where there might be the possibility of staying on for awhile. Not knowing the islands, I asked if there was something not too popular, not too crowded and not too far away from the American Embassy in Athens. Having told them many of the things I did not want, I sent off the email hoping that someone might be able to help figure out what I did want. The world wide web was supposed to have all the answers.

Then I went to work.

I emailed Aaron, my bridge buddy and ersatz marriage broker.

TO: ASinTransit@GoldenCity.cz

FR: MVandermar@VeneziaTourism.it

RE: Honeymoon HELP!

Greetings my pivo-swilling pal, here I am, your friend from Venice writing you from the heavy heat of high season (damn the day-

*trippers and tourists!) and thinking about coming back to Prague to
tie things up and looking at the calendar and I find myself in rather a
delicate position. Did I say delicate? Perhaps serious and complicated
are better words. Or all of the above.*

*Do you remember we spoke of moments (still collecting?) and I told
you about a certain girl whose name I didn't know (which by the
way, is Sophie)?*

*Well she's here now and I'm not so sure your beautiful city and its
bridges and beer, not to mention a marriage there, all bode so well
for this new adventure I'm throwing myself into (I remember you
told me about the Australian guy jumping off of the ski lift—that's
perhaps rather how I feel now—it's my round, I think).*

*Here's the deal. We're thinking of taking one another someplace else
to see other shores and perhaps the sooner the better. No time like
the present, as they say. Who are 'they' anyway?*

*What I'm wondering is, if in your inimitable style, you might conjure
up a plan (the way you conjured up fine Bloody Marys and forced
them on me one hungover morning when I was not Joe Strummer) to
make things easier for me. That is perhaps to arrange a rendezvous
in the Athens Embassy at your convenience with yourself, Pavel,
my newly betrothed Denissa and whomever else you might wish to
invite, perhaps a honeymoon of sorts. Though I shall be bringing a
date, which I guess might be a little less than normal. Normal, I have
decided while cast away here in Venice, is highly overrated.*

*For the moment it seems like a decision I need to make quickly and an
opportunity, like jumping off of a bridge or ski lift, that I should not
like to miss. I hope you understand, and more to the point hope you
might be able to get back to me ASAP with any news and help. I'm
happy to do the favor and say what needs to be said and sign what
needs to be signed but should rather do it in Greece than in Prague.
As you said, Prague seems a good place and a hard one to leave, so
not one for me, for this girl and I, to go to now. I guess I probably
sound kind of whipped and love-struck but the truth is, that's exactly
how I feel. And you know what? It's a pretty damned good feeling
after not feeling too much of anything for far too long.*

*It seems some of my future might be in your hands, so I'm trusting
that they're capable.*

*Let me know if you can conspire to help make this work, my friend.
Seeking solution as soon as possible.*

Feel free to send suggestions and resolutions but don't perhaps mention the situation (I haven't because I'm a stupid coward) should a certain girl whose name is Sophie answer my phone at home.

Anytime, day or night, sooner the better. H-E-L-P!

Your impatient pal,

Mark Vandermar

While I waited for word from the web, I carefully crafted a resignation letter for Signor Contarini in the event that everything might work out the way I wanted and filed it away.

I was so busy that day digging into new destiny that I even forgot about the Campari which, in my haste, I had moved from its regular preeminent place of glory to a spot out of the way of my computer and desk calendar. Damned European desk calendars that were hard to read because they started on Monday instead of on Sunday and still confused my American chronology. The good thing was that they actually showed the weekend at week's end, Saturday and Sunday there together instead of separated by five days of work.

I also neglected to answer the phone and hoped that it wasn't, when it did ring, either the illustrious Signor Contarini or an earnest, misguided reporter from Wall Street seeking out a certain imaginary aristocrat I had hastily invented in a time that suddenly seemed long ago, but which, surprising even myself, had only been several days, several long days, so far in my past.

What I needed was a chronology focused on the present.

I tried calling Aaron again and still no answer and was getting ready to give up and go and meet Sophie at the bar when I received an email from the villa rental company. I was thankful that back in America it was still early morning and somebody was starting their workday while I was finishing mine.

In answer to all the things I did not want, they sent two choices they thought I might want along with pretty pictures and alluring descriptions. Both seemed fully fitting. One was an ocher-colored cottage surrounded by lemon and orange trees on Corfu. It was pricier but did happen to be on an island that still carried the flavor of its Venetian colonial past and boasted a certain symmetrical appeal as Corfu was where the ferries from beneath my balcony floated off to.

The second choice was smaller and cheaper: a little, white stucco, two story maisonette with blue shutters that overlooked a picturesque port in captivating colorful miniature on Hydra. The lady who sent the email mentioned that though Hydra was smaller, quieter, and more compact, it had no cars, which suited my Venice tempered sensibilities, and was serviced daily by fast hydrofoil ferries to nearby Athens. The issue with the Hydra choice was that it had a month minimum and had to be booked right away as she said there were other clients interested. She was very cordial, and though it seemed she was politely trying to steer me toward the more expensive Corfu choice, Hydra seemed more alluring for its unfamiliarity and the house being competitively coveted. The cocktail of unfamiliarity and possible unattainability was a potent aphrodisiac.

I knew which I wanted but couldn't be sure which Sophie would prefer. I thought about going and explaining everything but then remembered the joyful look that had glimmered in her eyes when she'd seen that I'd kept her note, that I'd tried to track her down, and her repeated intimations that she wasn't sure herself what she really wanted. I decided that I could want enough for the both of us, if that's what it took. If you couldn't fall in love with a wonderful woman in a little Greek island house overlooking the sea, then where could you.

I sent them an email of decision, declaiming a decisiveness I wasn't sure I felt, that we would take the little maisonette for the month. They sent a form and a wire transfer request. Having paid most all of my bills from Italy online, I was used to virtual spending and quickly made it a reality. While I waited for the wheels of the web to confirm my plans, I transposed my resignation letter into an email and set it up to be delivered on the date of Signor Contarini's return, hoping that I would not be here then and would instead be safely and happily ensconced elsewhere when he received it. I wondered if he would care or if either of us would by then, but marveled at the wonders of the internet and what a perfectly peculiar connective tissue it was that would let you quit your job in absentia.

I sent everything and by four p.m., it was all done and a good day of work it seemed, though conspicuous, perhaps, by the fact that I didn't do any real work. Though still no word from Aaron, I had an appointment to keep and miles to go before I would sleep. I wondered if she liked Frost. I wondered if I liked Frost, not for the first time. I'd even wondered if Frost liked Frost. It was hard to tell.

I printed out a color picture of the house and wished I had some ribbon to wrap around it, but didn't, so I poured out the rest of the Campari, rinsed out the bottle and rolled up the picture and put it inside and rushed off across the wooden planks of the Accademia Bridge, no time to wait for a traghetto and a more beautiful commute.

It took me about fifteen minutes to get to Sancho's, which I had finally found out was called the Codroma, which did not sound nearly as good and I tried to forget its real name. She was sitting there beside a glass of white wine, doodling on a sketch pad, and attracting entirely too much attention from the gondoliers. I noticed she was the only woman in the place, both literally and figuratively, and hoped it would also be so for me.

I went in, ordered two more glasses of wine and sat down across from her.

"I come bearing gifts," I said, pushing the Campari bottle toward her.

She unrolled the picture and raised her eyebrows and said nothing.

No excited exclamation, no joyful exuberance. Just arched eyebrows, two little curves of light rust colored hairs above her sparkling green eyes. Eyes of such iridescent green that begged to be poetically compared to the waters of the canal at some poignant moment when we stood before them and the sun and the water and the moment were right. I knew it was hackneyed but thought maybe that's what infatuation was, knowing and not caring about how corny you sounded.

"It's a little artist hideaway. On an island called Hydra. Just finished renting it for a month. Starting this weekend," I said. "I thought maybe you could paint there. And we could spend some slow time getting to know each other better. Maybe we could…figure out who we're going to become?"

She took a sip of wine.

"Hydra, where exactly is that?"

"That's the great part, this little island, with no cars, just like Venice, these everyday artistic sunsets, this balcony view, all those little colorful fishing ships, and it's in the Saronic Gulf, so still just a couple of hours to Athens. It's sort of both near and far."

"Certainly looks appealing."

"I should like to see Athens and its Acropolis, shorn though it is of Lord Elgin's marbles, the thieving bastard. Maybe eat some lamb, drink some ouzo. It seems a good way to spend a little slice of retirement, I think. So what do you say?"

"I don't eat lamb, poor baby sheep, but other than that," she said, taking another sip and giving me time to realize I would eagerly forsake lamb in favor of a future. With her.

"I think it sounds pretty damn good, Mark."

Just then the door opened up and a couple of loud gondoliers burst in, and it seemed all the doors were opening up, everywhere.

"It does to me, too. I was thinking maybe get settled on the island and then a trip to Athens around the middle of the month. A vacation from a vacation, the best kind. Maybe some friends of mine from Prague might even arrange to meet up with us there."

"Funny. Back home everything's always all planned out. Work, pension plans, dinner reservations, the whole enchilada. Then all of a sudden I just hop on a plane, wake up here in Venice, and now you want to cart me off."

"Us off," I clarified, "think of it as bouillabaisse, mixing everything up."

She smiled.

"Well, who wants enchiladas when they can have bouillabaisse?"

"Exactly," I said, and took a drink of the white wine, which was cool and refreshing though not as outstanding as the local reds from my wine shop.

"Well then. You have a swimsuit in your bags?"

"Afraid not."

"Me neither. What say we go procure some?"

"You don't have to twist my arm. Just promise not to stereotype me as some female shopaholic. I hate shopping, I really do. And shopping for swimsuits, well, bathing suit shopping is the absolute worst of all the many dreaded shopping hells. You might be getting into more than you bargained for."

"I hope so," I said.

And off we went, hand in hand, and everything was starting to come together nicely, I couldn't help noticing. I tried not to notice but it was tough to be nonchalant and utterly enthralled at the same time.

We ended up peeking in a lot of windows. Venice was not a great place for clothes shopping unless you went to the Merceria, and I was too snobby now about the place to go there while the city was so crowded and share it and her with all the other annoying strangers, so we ended up still swimsuit-less and back in the Café San Trovaso where we'd had our first meal, without having bought anything at all.

The host greeted us with enthusiasm, warmly welcoming us with that gracious Venetian respect they reserved for people who had proved they were more than just transient tourists. There were several groups of hungry travelers gathered in the little foyer and he ushered us along ahead of them. I was pleased and proud of the preferential treatment. I had been a regular, if generally solitary, customer for most of the year. I had paid my dues to be welcomed into the inner sanctum and it was good to collect.

He led us to a small table for two against the exposed brick wall of the side room and I urged her to face the front so she could see the view outside the window and so I could occupy myself with a view of her. I was going to pull out her chair but he did it before I could and she sat down and I did too. We were special and elect. And I liked it. Dinner was wine, antipasti, small smiles, shared secrets of our pasts without speaking of our futures, grilled sea bass, caffè macchiati. And perfect.

She wanted to pay and I let her, noting the host's disapproval as she handed him her credit card. You couldn't get away from the fact that it was a chauvinistic world and Italy was a pedigreed patriarch in this and we all knew she wasn't supposed to pay. It had occurred to me that we had much to learn about one another and seemed something I was ravenous to do, but wanted to do slowly and enjoy it.

We went back to my apartment and opened a plastic water bottle filled with the Nero Rosso from my wine shop and took it and two sturdy water glasses out onto the balcony.

"Make yourself totally at home. I mean if you need to use the phone to call home or anything."

"No one to call."

"I feel the same way," I said, without mentioning the call from Prague I both hoped for and dreaded.

We sat and sipped the dark wine that looked almost black in the dim lights of my balcony but which I knew to be more a deep purple in the right light. Some lights weren't right.

I reached over and filled both our glasses and she tugged her chair a bit closer to me and kicked off her sandals and put her feet in my lap, and the church bells rang and I played with her toes, wiggling each one in time with the bells until they stopped. I ran my fingers lightly across the soles of her bare feet and noted that she was not at all ticklish and was surprised and I don't know why, but pleasantly so. I could feel the edges of the little calloused sides of her heels where the skin was harder from her shoes, and I liked that too, and I felt altogether there in that moment and wished it could have lasted longer, but we were both sleepy and it was late and a lot of things had still to be arranged, I hoped tomorrow, sooner better than later, always.

We went to bed and didn't undress and didn't brush our teeth and didn't make love, just curled up on top of the covers with the windows open, and you could hear far away voices reflected off the waters of the canal and then some fog horns in the distance, even though you couldn't tell if it was foggy from the bedroom windows that looked out onto the church.

I wrapped my arms around her and she nestled back towards me and we fell asleep and woke up both facing away from the window but with our legs all intertwined, and sometime during the night, I hadn't noticed, she must have gotten cold and had wrapped up the covers around her, and the early morning rays lit up the church and it was the first time in a long while I had awakened before the bells, and I just lay there and thought a little about the future and enjoyed not knowing exactly what that entailed, but having some pretty good plans for it.

I had had enough experience with traveling to know that you didn't take a trip so much as it took you and each one defined itself in its own way and there wasn't always too much you could do about it otherwise; it was going to develop its own dimension and character and you either grew into it or you didn't. I looked forward to a lot of growing and to us growing together.

I got up thinking about Prague and emails and Greece and coffee and went to take a shower, and she rolled over drowsily and grabbed my pillow and went back to sleep, mumbling, "Morning, sweetie."

I tried to remember of all the women I'd been with if I had ever been sweetie before, and I didn't think I had but I wasn't sure, and even if I had, it seemed new and special, and I showered quickly with the door open in case she might come in. But she didn't and when I dried off she was still asleep and I leaned over and brushed her hair away from her cheek and kissed it and some drops of water from my hair dripped down on her.

"Time is it?" she said, stretching out her legs and arching her back.

"No idea."

"Good. That's nice."

"Coffee?"

"Strong coffee."

"Un momento, cara mia," I said, and grabbed a pair of jeans and a shirt and took them into the living room to get dressed and give us both some privacy for our newness, thinking still how strange it was that you could sleep with someone, make love with someone, yet still not shed all semblance of modesty.

We took coffee on the balcony, another day started slowly, and we were both quiet and I lit a cigarette and I hadn't thought she'd smoked but she took one too, and there we sat under the sun while Venice around us applied herself to tackling another day.

Usually I'd always felt a need to strive for witty or clever commentary, to entertain or be entertained, but sitting there I was acutely and unusually aware of how easy the silence lay between us, how much more there would be to say and, hopefully, how much time and opportunity to say those things. But for now, for that time, the silence was comfortable, and we drank the coffee and smoked slowly and watched the birds prance around busily among the treetops: several boring black crows flitted about, the busy drones of the bird world; one flighty little bluebird I'd seen before, alone; and as always, the pigeons cooing noisily along the eaves of the church. Above this private pageant, we could see the slow-moving, sailing along of several white and gray seagulls that drifted overhead. The seagulls were the aristocrats but the bluebird the more beautiful, even though it looked lonely among the large group of other busy birds.

I went to work and gave her my keys and she said she was going to bathe—I liked that, bathe not shower, she said, it seemed fetching—and then go shopping and make lunch, if I was coming home for it. I agreed, and would have to anything, right then that morning, but all she asked about was lunch.

I went to the office and several emails awaited me. I scrolled through some boring work stuff and forwarded it to Alexandra to handle later, everything could wait or go on without me and would no matter what I did, I knew. I was abundantly pleased with my utter dispensability. There was a more interesting one from the American villa rental agency. It confirmed the receipt of my funds and included simple instructions about arrival times, ferry schedules from Athens, and less simple ones about a bar called Delfini, where the donkeys met the ferries to carry your luggage if you wanted, and where we were to meet and pick up the keys from a waiter called Panos who spoke English and was said to be generally accommodating.

I printed that out and most importantly read Aaron's, which I looked forward to with some trepidation and excitement as we had come to feel quite close and traded many amusing notes since our meeting and made some plans which I was now abandoning in haste. He wrote in a quick, sort of telegramese shorthand, simple and direct, that I liked.

Message received, my friend. Have spoken with all parties. Embassy in Athens, September 7, perfect. I shall be delighted to attend, and look forward to meeting the girl of the bridge. Knew you had something about bridges, kid. Will be especially pleased to be there while you introduce her to your wife. You are either very foolish or very foolhardy.

Pavel, as always, knows some people and is arranging all appointments.

Expect 'husbandly duties' to take all the day. Nights free. I may try and rustle up a girl for Greece myself, but have to see what's hatching and who's rustleable. As you do.

Let me know where and when to confirm with you.

Looking forward to it. Till then, drinks and laughs,

Aaron.

∞ ∞ ∞

So this thing, that I wasn't quite sure what it was, was done. I was leaving. Again. I packed up a few mementos from the office, a little gondola paperweight I'd picked up and a wooden Venetian lion resting his paw on a pile of books and roaring to the world, a lion that would like to see Greece. It occurred to me that I needn't take everything, even though I hadn't much to take. I agonized over the self-imposed choice of a boat or a lion and decided that a gondola had no business anywhere but Venice and put it back on my desk where the Campari should have sat and squirreled away the lion with my things. After this momentous decision, I thought only briefly about all the paperwork and references and emails and stuff I might should have done but didn't feel like it, and it was lunch time and I had a date at home waiting for me, with a girl and a future that might not wait.

She had shopped well: picked up produce, not from my guy in the campo, rather from the surly seller on the boat on the Rio San Barnaba, some light green melons, some sliced prosciutto and spicy capicolla, two green apples, several cheeses and baguettes, and had tied it all together in one of my blue and white checkered tablecloths.

"What sounds yummy is a quiet picnic, don't you think?"

Venice. Summer. Quiet. All pretty challenging. I thought briefly of gondolas, then all the tourists and the rush and the crowds. The stuffy, overfilled summer vaporetti, too busy and pedestrian. There was the quick ferry to the Lido, but that, on a sunny late summer day, would be too crowded, by far, and the ferry to Murano took too long with all the tourists going to buy the requisite crystal.

Then I remembered the sleek mahogany boats. The private motoscafi that I'd only had reason to take on my mundane airport transits, alone, but never for their finer intended purpose of exploring the lagoon. They were perfect, if a bit pricey, and would take you quickly and elegantly, together, anywhere you wished to go. And I had meant to see Torcello, meant to do a lot of things in Venice I hadn't done when I had not known I was leaving.

But now it seemed I was.

"I know just the place."

Near the Rio Foscari, we found a private launch with a small, faded red, white and green Italian flag and white leather banquette seats in the back and a paunchy, avuncular looking pilot of about sixty well-lived years sitting on the bow.

Torcello, sure. The whole day, return? We hopped on the boat and asked him to stop somewhere where we could pick up some wine along the way, he nodded agreeably and maneuvered us out through the twists of the smaller canals and onto and up the Grand Canal, the world's single most prestigious sweep of water.

We stood behind him and our sunglasses and watched the activity of the canal unfold before us and drift off into our wake. We crossed the Canal and just past the Rialto Bridge, he cut north through a smaller canal, pausing briefly to glance up into a round mirror to look for oncoming boats, and I leaned over and kissed her lightly on the lips and she opened her mouth to me and placed her hands on both sides of my face, and when we stopped kissing, we were moving forward again and the old man looked at us and said, "Brava, brava, che belli ragazzi." Beautiful kids. And I felt very lucky and that he was right and perhaps we were. Then, leaving the upper reaches of Venice's landfall, he stopped at a little shop I hadn't been to and told me to go in and buy wine, and very Venetian-like, told me what kind to get and how much it should be, just to be sure. I did as instructed and returned. He and Sophie were there waiting right where I left them and he said, "Avanti. Now we go," knowing we spoke English and proud to show off that he had some, and well done, I thought, and we were off.

He steered the boat between the wooden pylons that marked the channels and gassed it and she sped up and caught the plane of the water and it splashed a bit around us and he looked back to check if we were okay with the speed.

It was too loud to talk over the engine and she smiled and nodded slightly and I saw his lips but couldn't hear him, but could tell he said either brava or bella, and either suited me fine, and it seemed natural that he and I should both so want to please this girl. We pushed forward, and in seemingly no time, less than an hour of light spray of salty water and wind blown hair, he guided the boat gracefully up to the small wooden dock of Torcello where several others sat, and I had forgotten to look back at Venice and now it had disappeared behind our horizon.

Our pilot called out to a younger man sitting on the dock, something in dialect, I guess, I didn't catch it, but it galvanized the young man into action and the line was thrown to him where he caught it easily overhand, a practiced and easy maneuver made graceful by being so natural to him. He tied us up to the piling beside another boat, finer and newer and much less beautiful than ours, and the old man, much spryer and more agile than I would have thought, cut the engine and hopped up onto the dock and reached his hand down to Sophie while I picked up the makeshift picnic basket and wine.

By the time I got out, she was standing up on her tiptoes and kissing the old man on the cheek and he lit up and looked over at the younger man and made a joke, something about an old rooster being beautiful because it was loud or strong, I didn't quite catch it, but they both smiled and I could tell our pilot, Giuseppe, his name was, had been pleased.

He said he would meet us there at four but not later than five, with the perfect elegance and disregard of the Italians for numbers on a clock, and I realized that I had forgotten my watch but didn't care and we walked off.

Unlike the other islands of the lagoon I'd visited, there was no little canal entry for the boats nor any buildings there where we landed. Just a dusty tree lined path which we followed along, Giuseppe having told us, in the way that Venetians always give directions, with a simple gesture of his hand, just to go "sempre diretto, tutto sempre diretto," and we did, simply straight on.

Farther up the path, there were a couple of older villas with a certain sad and worn elegance that looked uninhabited. But you couldn't tell for sure. There was so much quietude, and the land and large horizons that spread out before us reminded me of how long it had been since I had stared out at wide open spaces. I found it surprising to find them here, having read that Torcello was the first island settled by the future Venetians back in earlier times, whenever exactly it was, which I knew was still a matter of some mystery, as much as where those people had come from and whom they were fleeing.

Some said the islands had been settled by Romans fleeing the Goths and the Visigoths and the Vandals; others, the Huns fleeing the Romans; some even put forth that the islands of the lagoon had been settled by Slavs fleeing the Huns; or even by Britons fleeing whomever they fled; or perhaps just simply by Etruscans fleeing terra firma and seeking new horizons. No one knew, but guidebooks had to give a date and it had been decided that 421 AD was that date for the founding of Torcello and the beginnings of civilization in the lagoon. Probably about two fifteen, I guessed, because it had to be before three o'clock, Sartre's empty hour.

A little less than 1600 years after that inauspicious beginning, Giuseppe moored his craft to the dock and told us to go straight on, so we did.

About half a mile down the pathway, there was a small canal stream or the stream of a former canal but with no boats in it. It was crossed by an arched stone bridge on the right and to the left of the bridge on the other side of the stream was on outdoor patio restaurant, Il Diavolo, right next to a sign with an arrow pointing ahead, sempre diretto, that said Chiesa, Kirche, Church, Cathedral in the languages modern man had deemed necessary to declare such things. I enjoyed the close proximity of a house of God and the Devil's restaurant and thought it would have made a good picture but didn't have my camera and didn't want to stop there anyway, so on we went, passing by the Devil's place and heading for God, though it didn't seem exactly like that at the time. Just for fun, I turned back circumspectly and flipped off the Devil's restaurant and didn't think Sophie saw me and didn't know about God or the Devil but it was sort of a gesture of equal air time. I was not one to discriminate against God or fallen angels or places that nourished the body or the soul. I was utterly impartial. At least I felt that way then.

We wandered in front of the sunken, circular stone ruins in front of the old church just beyond Cipriani's Restaurant, which I had forgotten was out here and which was filled with well dressed people sitting outside underneath a panoply of purple bougainvillea. You could hear the light clanging of cutlery and coffee cups and conversation. Beautiful people busily lunching in another time, and I had meant to go there and do so too, but had lacked someone to go there with. Now I had someone and was even happier to be passing it by, forsaking all the melodious sounds of eating al fresco under the flowers to look for a tranquil spot to spread out our picnic.

Just past both of these sights, I began to feel the weight of the picnic makings in my left hand, my right hand comfortably interlaced with hers and she carrying two bottles of the wine Guiseppe had instructed me to buy in her other hand, which somehow balanced us. We reached a large river with several boats drifting along its center and several more modern ones tethered to its shores, and there were wide open fields beyond the church and across the river, but no bridge to cross that you could see either way up or down the river. Venetian life acclimates you to automatically hunt for bridges and it was unusual not to see them where they should have been and undoubtedly had been some time before. I unlaced my fingers from hers, pleased that our hands fit so nicely together. There are some girls you can not hold hands with, not comfortably, and some you can. Perhaps girls find it the same or maybe they don't think about it at all, I didn't know, but I knew I was happy that ours fit, and they did even after I let go.

We walked through the field where there were already a lot of people sitting, sunning, picnicking and even a group of old men playing bocce ball like you saw everywhere else in Italy, except never in Venice, there being so few places of bare earth where you could well roll the old balls. We continued on and found a quiet place by the river and spread out the tablecloth on the grass, which was mostly all dry and thirsty, much as I was, and I opened the wine while she unpacked the food.

We ate hungrily and enjoyed the simple foodstuffs and the out of doors and talked about a post-prandial visit to the church but neither of us got up and it seemed fine, the church having stood there 1000 years took away any urgency or obligation to go and visit it. Instead, I opened the second bottle of wine while she cut a melon in half and got two spoons for us. I wished we had some salt for the melon because I liked the salty taste against sweet melon but everyone always thought I was strange for doing so, and there was no salt, anyway.

She put on some sunscreen, her skin was very fair, and I'd found she hated the little freckles that the sun brought out and I couldn't convince her otherwise, but sunscreen was good, like the song that wasn't a Kurt Vonnegut commencement speech said. She took off her top and had on a sports bra beneath it, an orange one, that looked pretty much like a bikini except that it mushed her breasts down and made them look smaller than they were, but I had seen them otherwise and knew better and was pleased at that too. I helped rub the lotion onto her shoulders and she lay down on the blanket on her back and her breasts, with gravity and the sports bra, almost disappeared and I missed them but put my head down on her stomach.

The sun had traced down to about the middle of its afternoon arc, and from my vantage point, bounced lazily up and down as my head rose and sank with her breath, which was slow and content, and I tried to make sure my head was light and not too heavy and wondered if it was too heavy and how much did a head weigh? Mine, then, was too heavy with thoughts of my Prague secret. It seemed an inauspicious beginning to a relationship, matrimonial secrets.

"Have you ever been married?" I said, ruining the silence.

"No."

"Have you ever been asked?"

"Why?"

"Idle curiosity."

"Killed the cat," she said.

"Ah, but eight more lives."

The engine of a motorboat cut through the stillness also, and I glanced toward the river but couldn't see where it came from.

"Yes, twice."

I turned my head up toward her and could see the line under her chin and a little curve of scar tissue I'd have to find out about and the fine tendons of her neck pointing in the direction of the river as she stared up toward the sky and I wondered if her eyes were opened or closed but didn't ask and couldn't tell.

"And you said no?"

"Obviously."

A boat passed by. I saw it was powered by an American made Johnson Outboard motor and heard the loud sounds of Italian over the noise of the engine, and then it was gone and fading away, heading towards Murano or Burano but probably not Venice, not from that way, I thought, but wasn't absolutely sure.

"Obviously." I said, though it wasn't, not fully.

"Was one of them, the proposals, recently?" I asked.

"Might have been. That'll be another life for the poor little kitty."

"I can handle seven."

"Okay," she said, "it was. You're dead, you serial kitty killer."

"And you left, exit stage left, pursued by a bear," I said, quoting Shakespearian stage directions from one of his plays, only I never remembered which. Maybe it didn't matter since a lot of people weren't even convinced that Shakespeare even wrote Shakespeare's plays. If he hadn't, he'd sure missed a hell of an opportunity.

"And," she said, "I left and I came here to Venice."

"Which, as I've said, was an excellent choice."

"Says you."

"Reason I ask, is..." I hoped to be able to do this thing without springing it on her like it was too big a deal, without taking it for granted that she should indeed even care about it unduly, but also without wanting to keep it hidden and striving to tread carefully, so that she would know I wasn't about to be proposal number three, not right there and not right then. I knew how many swings you got, after all.

"...is because, a funny thing happened to me in Prague."

"Is that a question?" she said.

"No, just an observation."

I sat up and poured some more wine for each of us. She drew herself up and leaned back on her hands and I noticed that one of her arms bent back further behind than the other and wondered if it was a double joint and if it was her painting hand. I thought a bit about how the word sinister came from the Latin for left, sinistra.

She slid her sunglasses up over her hair and squinted at me, facing the sun behind me. There was a little spot of white suntan lotion just below her ear that hadn't been rubbed in and I wanted to reach over and take care of it, but didn't.

"Well?"

"It's quite funny, really," I said, without laughing.

"Do I want to hear it? I'm not a wanton kitty killer like yourself."

Good point, well taken. Did she?

"I don't know. Do you?"

"I guess," she said, without much enthusiasm, I couldn't help noticing.

"Thing is, it's really very funny."

"You mentioned that."

"Yes, well, it was, see there was this guy, and then this other guy," I said.

"The revolutionary?"

"Exactly. And well, he had this sister and she needed to get a student visa for school back in the States and since September 11th, well, there's been all these problems and all these restrictions and he was in jail in Cuba and with the Czech Republic not yet in the EU, she can't just go and study anywhere, and…"

"And…"

I thought perhaps I detected a note of jealousy, but I wasn't sure. Not yet, nor if there should be.

"And anyway, long story short, we sort of, well, got married. Ha."

There were no boats or other sounds to break the silence while I waited for her to say something.

"Congratulations. I would have sent a toaster or a Crock-pot or something if only I'd known where you were registered."

She sat forward and took a long pull from her wine glass. I took a small drink, then another. She was still squinting off into the sun and I couldn't read her face because of it. Damned sun: silly, freckle-inducing, squint-causing sun.

"Simple ceremony, little celebration, just a favor, really, for some friends."

"How generous of you."

"Generous to a fault."

"And pure of heart."

"Pardon?"

"Pure of heart, that's what you told me that first time we met. That day in the rain. I liked it, pure of heart," she said.

"And here I am and it's still true."

She took another drink.

"Since idle curiosity and diminishing cat lives are today's theme, did you consummate this marriage?"

So there was some jealousy but jealousy necessitated interest.

"No, not at all, not even a little, I mean I just barely even met the girl."

"Oh, really?"

"Really. I don't have anything to hide, not at all. I mean, like I said, there's nothing I wouldn't tell you," I said.

"So you say, Mr. Pure of heart."

"Kind of funny, isn't it?" I said, not knowing what else to say.

"That you're married or pure of heart?"

"Well, the whole thing, I mean."

"Oh, sure. Hilarious," she said, without laughing.

I smiled and reached out and poked her nose and she scrunched up her face at me and put her sunglasses back on and leaned forward.

"So, I'm like the other woman, a mistress."

"If you like."

"That could be interesting, being the other woman. So long as I don't have to participate in too much more senseless kitty slaughter."

"I promise."

She leaned forward further and gave me a kiss, first slowly and lightly, then she bit my lip pretty hard, and it hurt a little, but then she was kissing me and I her and it seemed everything might be okay or at least be interesting, and interesting and confusing and kind of funny were all far better than boring.

"Stolen kisses from a married man on a little island in the sea," she said.

"And sweeter far," I said, quoting someone, but unsure who.

"We'll see."

"Shall we get Giuseppe?" I said.

"I don't know if I can handle the scandal. Suppose he sees right through the veneer and figures out how you corrupted me."

"I have a feeling Giuseppe won't mind."

"If he doesn't and you don't," she said.

"I most definitely do not."

"Then I guess I can handle it."

We packed up our stuff, threw out the garbage: melon rinds, white paper packaging from the prosciutto and capicolla, and the two bottles of wine—one emptied, one halfway there but warmed from the sun—and deposited it all in the trash can in front of a little souvenir stand beside the hollow of the original stones of the old church. The doors of the "new" church, which was only a thousand years old, were already closed and the patio of Cirpriani's almost emptied, the laughing people gone, joining the procession towards the dock.

We followed along with them through the little path along the stream, everyone leaving a few steps between one another as if in some tacit agreement to respect the revered silence. We all had our bits of privacy and things kept to ourselves, and some mystery and intrigue and satisfaction settled down between us.

As we walked back to the dock, off to our left, I saw a group of people sitting outside an old, classical Italian country estate, the villa all pinkish or dusty rose colored, and there was music faraway, but I couldn't tell where it was coming from, it was like a distant silent movie, and we kept walking toward the dock and I wondered what people who lived on this quiet island with no town nor stores did for fun or for work. Wondered, what they did besides sit outside their lovely old villa on Sundays on a sunny afternoon. Wondered, when you lived in a place like this, what did you look for when you wanted to see other places, what did you romanticize, or did you even dream of other places at all. Wondered, if maybe there were people out their who were living their dreams. If it was that simple.

Knowing the way, the walk back was shorter than the walk out had been, even though they were the same distance.

At the dock, Giuseppe was asleep in the back of his boat, his face aimed toward the low, late afternoon sun. I noticed that there was no name painted on the back of the boat and wondered if all boats in Italy were shes like they were in America, and why were boats shes, anyway?

I coughed quietly and he didn't wake up.

"Ciao, Giuseppe," Sophie said.

He hopped up quickly, at your service, positively reeking with goodwill, dispatching smiles and questions all over us: had lunch been good, what had we thought about the mosaics in the church, molto bello, no? Ah, we had not seen them, oh, it was sad, they were some of the best, the mosaics there, he said, tutto bello, truly fine, then he smiled and elbowed me and said something about amore and laughed and I agreed and we hopped on the boat and he held out his cheek to Sophie and said, "Ancora baci, Signora?"

She kissed him quickly on the cheek, and he smiled all aglow and proud again and winked at me, and she corrected him quietly and, I thought, with a note of amusement, "Signorina."

"Avanti, Signorina?"

"Si, si, avanti," she said, the Siren steering our little ship.

I would have climbed the yardarm or hoisted the mainsails or even walked the plank, if she had said. But it was a small boat without any of these things, and maybe the generosity of her spirit and the grace of Guiseppe's goodwill, as we embarked on a journey together, would help absolve me of my penance.

And with that we were off, skimming along the watery trail marked by the sun on the lagoon, heading swiftly back toward Venice, and the spray of the water felt good but a little cool along with the wind, but on we went until we could see more and more of Venice fill our horizon, and from the right angle, we could even see beyond Venice and glimpse other horizons.

I told him my address in the Sestiere Dorsoduro, and yes, he could take us right to the door, of course, niente. A very reasonable amount of money changed hands and we departed—all smiles and ciaos and grazies and buonaseras and a final belli ragazzi, as we walked away.

In the campo, we stopped and contemplated gelato, which seemed like a fine idea but too many others had already had it and the line deterred us. Not that we were in any particular hurry, but who wants to wait for pleasure if you don't have to?

We went inside the patio gate and up to my apartment together, as natural and comfortable as if we'd been doing just this for some time.

On the way to my apartment, I didn't stop at the kiosk and didn't buy the Wall Street reporter's paper, so I didn't even read the little article that said: Venice Voices in on War in the Middle East. If I had, I think I would have enjoyed it then, and by the time we went to sleep, it was old news, even though it hadn't really ever been news at all before I had made it up.

EIGHTEEN

TASTES OF TERRA FIRMA

THE NEXT DAY WE WENT to Mestre and both bought swimsuits, though I didn't see her in hers, not then, nor she in mine, but it was as good a reason as any to take the train across the causeway and then a taxi to get to the square of Mestre and away from the ugly factories and refineries that lined the shores.

Mestre, far bigger than Venice, was the neglected sibling of her famous sister in the sea and no one knew about her except businessmen or errant tourists trapped there during high season when Venice's hotels were full. Lovers were all heading toward Venice and harried businessman to Mestre, so we traveled against the natural flow.

Most people who did know Mestre didn't like it anyway. But if you went beyond the shore and ventured to the inside of town and made your way to the square, it was like any big European workaday city and had everything, fountains and cars and Benetton shops and McDonald's and Chinese restaurants and cafés, and you got your business done, bought your swimsuits, then had a coffee in the square because that was what you did in squares in Europe, whether they were called piazzas or campos or places or plazas or platzes. The squares could be any shape and go by any name but the formula for figuring out their area was usually the same.

Back in Venice, we stopped at a travel agency. I wanted to take the ship I had watched so often from my dining room window. There was a sense of harmony to it, but the days weren't right. Timing is crucial in matters of escape. Sophie had decided that she would let me pay for the house for a month, saying it was only right if she was going to be a kept woman, only that she was going to pay for our transport there, which was all right too, especially if I got to keep her.

I told her about my obligation and meeting and the Embassy stuff and we decided, in the way you did these things if you had to meet your new wife with your lover at an American Embassy in Athens, that the only way to make it work was to fly. That meant we had to take a train west to Milan, to catch an airplane east to Athens. I hated going the wrong way to get the right way, but I didn't even know which the right way was, not exactly, so I guessed it didn't matter and wasn't technically backtracking.

Airline tickets in hand, having studied one another's passports and sneered at each other's photos, I realized I had to say my goodbyes to Venice. There is a time in life, in all lives, when you realize that what you have been doing has perhaps just been prelude to something else and rather than an ending can be a beginning, and it seemed one of those. It occurred to me that anyone in today's world who does not have a passport is literally a prisoner, someone who can't leave. It was good to have the blue American passport I carried, though hers, from another bureaucratic vagary, was green, which was not nearly so right for the Red, White and Blue, but worked, nonetheless.

We walked back through the Campo Santa Margherita and stopped at the bridge where we had first kissed and kissed there again, this time knowing how one another kissed and which way to turn our heads, and with the absence of mystery there was still the excitement of having everything understood. There are people you can kiss and people you can hold hands with and people you can love, and I felt lucky to have found one of them there in this city and hoped that love, if that's what it was, would weather travel and newness turning to familiarity well, but you never know for sure about these things and perhaps it is the not knowing for sure, the recognition of it, that makes it all the more valuable. I tried to put it into words but didn't succeed, though she told me she understood exactly what I meant, which seemed like an important proof to me at the time. Of something, anyway.

Back at my apartment, we agonized over where we should spend our last day in Venice and she asked about the painting on my bedroom floor, and I realized I had almost forgotten, during all the new activity of leaving an old place and loving a new face, that I was an art thief.

Having told so much, we were at the promontory where I had to tell the truth, though I didn't want to, not about this and what I had done because I couldn't actually explain the reason I had done it, though it had indeed seemed the only thing to do at the time.

I related the sordid saga.

"I wish it was signed, I'd like to know who painted this. You can tell, see," she pointed to the background of the painting, "that it's at least as early as the 15th century, the perspective here isn't quite right. They didn't start getting perspective right until the early Renaissance. But it's beautiful, a really lovely piece."

"You mean it's actually five or six hundred years old?"

"No doubt. At least. A lot of times, old works of art have been cut and trimmed down. The artists were nobodies, just craftsmen, while they were alive. People thought nothing of just lopping off a few inches here or there to make a painting fit the right frame or the right wall space, the signature wasn't important. Not back then. Then the picture was the thing. It's funny. Today, the signature is so much more important than the picture."

"You didn't sign your picture, the one you drew of me," I said.

"My signature isn't important."

"Not yet maybe," I said, "but it would have been to me."

"Anyway, you can tell from the colors, god, what wonderful colors, that it's Venetian." she said, gesturing at the canvas.

"See how you notice the colors more than the shapes, how they take over the painting with their power. Marvelous. They were the big innovators of color then. No one had ever utilized them, mastered them in that way up until the Venetians. The play of light and shadow, the way you see the tones and the shades before you even notice the shapes. Layers and layers of different hues that create something you almost can't believe you're seeing. Really something. But it's an odd painting for a church. I mean no religious pandering or anything."

"Maybe I did the church a favor," I said, without conviction.

"You've got to return it."

"Well, when I took it, see, it was a quiet night, no tourists around, nobody anywhere around. Taking it back, during this time of the year, well that would be much more challenging, I think," I said.

"Still."

Of course she was right. Something would have to be done about the purloined painting. I wasn't too worried actually about the theft from the church or even really the morality of the thing, just what she would think. Maybe that was morality. I had to make it right by her. Because I cared about what she thought, I cared about what was right. It was a step.

"Her name is Rocinante, the horse," I said, "like Don Quixote."

"Hmm."

I knew Don Quixote was the first modern novel and couldn't remember what century it was from and wondered if it was written before or after the artist painted the horse I had so christened.

"I guess a painting so old must be worth quite a bit. What good, after all, does a painting do a church? Wouldn't it be better if it sat in some rich guy's study or some museum and for the poor to have all the money that someone might pay for something like this?" I asked.

"Don't be unscrupulous. It's not flattering. Anyway, how would you sell it? You'd have to get it out of the country, have to know the right people."

"Do you?"

"Me, know the right people? No, not at all. In fact, I know mostly the wrong people," she said.

"Myself excepted, of course."

"Of course. Maybe. Though on reflection," she said, "newly married, a thief, about to be unemployed..."

"But pure of heart," I said.

"So you keep saying."

I realized if I kept telling her I was pure of heart, I was perhaps going to have to prove it at some point.

∞ ∞ ∞

So there it was, the painting was in the way of my future and something had to be done to make it go away.

I was not going to get tangled up in returning it and all the possibilities there—so many of which meant trouble for me and my newfound future. Together, with her love of art and me wanting so badly to impress her, we could not just let it go, nor would I have wanted to, but it would have made the problem go away. We could not leave it in the apartment to be found by either the right or the wrong people. Something had to be done. A wrong had to be made right, without interfering with my version of what was right for myself.

"I know a guy," I said.

There were things to be wrapped up. I took out a blanket from the closet that I hadn't used since the subsiding of Venice's fierce winter and covered up Rocinante. We put her in Sophie's art satchel, which she just barely fit in, and I led us out through the neighborhood towards the little Bar Postale up toward the train station. I didn't know exactly why the bar owner there was the right one, but he was Venetian, he understood much about life, and we had commiserated and bonded, and he was the guy I knew, sort of, and I saw possibility and solution there.

On the way, just in case, I had Sophie wait in the campo with the painting and stopped at the painting's home, the Chiesa San Pantalon, to see if a simple solution might present itself. Hope springs. But the church was locked and there were several people milling about. No good, but worth checking. Damn millers about, I thought, surely they had better things to be doing so why weren't they doing them?

I crossed the little bridge again to return to Sophie and Rocinante, we walked back through the Campo Santa Margherita and turned right just past the toy store and headed up the Rio Terra something or other towards Sestiere Santa Croce, where sat the Bar Postale. When we walked in, it was near midnight and the place was barely open.

There was a young couple sitting at the table in front overlooking the little canal and Bruno sitting down behind the bar, smoking and nursing a drink and probably crafting credible stories to tell his wife even though he knew she shouldn't believe them. We all had someone we wanted to impress and went about it in our own ways.

He smiled when I walked in and we set down the satchel and ordered three Avernas, and he understood and poured one for each of us and for himself.

I introduced them.

He kissed her hand. Quiet and unassuming as she was, she evoked a robust interest from men, and I was glad, knowing what I knew about him and American girls, that she was with me and not alone there. But I liked him for liking her, nevertheless.

"Ciao. Va bene? How's things, Bruno?" I asked.

"Ah, things. The same, always the same. Wife, business, children, government collapsing, the world going to war, taxes, everything is always the same."

"Good, huh?"

"Yeah, brilliant," he said, in his lilting accented second language.

The couple at the window seat gestured to him for two more drinks.

He spoke in Italian, but I caught it, "No spritzes after eleven o'clock. Too late for spritzes. Have something simple."

Obviously not regulars, they told him to forget it, set some money on the table, got up and left, either headed home or somewhere else where they could drink whatever they wanted.

Bruno scoffed at them after their hasty exit.

"Spritzes so late, too much trouble. Doesn't make sense."

"Pazzi Italiani," I said, with a smile.

"Yes, it is true, there are crazy Italians everywhere. And all crazy people, I think, everywhere. Only here we do not hide them so much as everywhere else. I think in America you hide them very well, the crazy people, don't you?"

"No," I said, "I don't think they're so well hidden, I think they're just not interesting enough to be very crazy. Anyway, I'm glad they left. I, uh, wanted to speak with you alone."

He nodded at me and then cast a glance toward her.

Even then it was unusual for a woman in Italy to be included in important talk among men in a bar. But I hadn't acquired the convention.

"So," I said, "I have something I want to ask, sort of, well, something to give you, maybe, if you should like it or know what to do," I said.

I couldn't decide in my mind if gift or present or trouble or problem were the right words.

"You bring me a present?" he said, "It is not so often that people come to my bar to give me something. Ah, a terrific surprise in an otherwise very boring night. Shall I close up?"

"And perhaps pour something your uncle made?"

He locked the door and came back to stand before us behind the bar.

"There is bad news about my uncle. He passed away some weeks ago. I went home to Schio for the funeral."

"I'm sorry to hear that," I said. I felt bad now for bringing him up.

"Sorry? What is there to be sorry about? He had a very good life, he was married for almost fifty years, he buried his wife and more than one of my cousins, he saw his grandchildren be christened, he worked, he loved, he died, he was ready. He kept telling us he was ready to die. Why just the last time I saw him on his Saint's Day, you know what he told me? He said, 'you know what is the worst thing about dying? If only all the pretty young women would die at the same time as myself. But they'll all go on living and being young and beautiful and won't even know enough to miss me, those bitches.' He was old and he was ready. He didn't leave any grieving widow around to mourn. Now the rest of his children can fight over his little, how do you say, estate? Life, death, the whole beautiful mess. And the funeral, it was some funeral. We ate like porci and drank like pesci."

The Italians knew a thing or two about life and death and if you got to know them and sat in a bar with them, with the right ones, you could learn a little about celebrating the life of a man you never knew and hoped that perhaps when you passed people might eat like pigs and drink like fish instead of moan and wail, or, even worse, not notice at all.

"Ah, he was a wonderful man, my uncle, but in many ways he was a filthy old son of bitch. My father never liked him. And since you can not ever like your own father too much, for too long, he and I were natural allies. I shall miss him, that rascal. Is it right? Rascal?"

"Sounds right," I said, hoping to someday be so remembered, aspiring to be a rascal.

"His being a rascal, and that was wonderful, too?" Sophie inquired.

"Si, si, si, that was maybe the most wonderful thing of all. And you," he said, pointing at Sophie, "you are just the type of pretty young girl my uncle was so mad about having to leave behind on this earth. And it happens, that while my cousins will fight over his estate, I have all of his brandy. So we will toast him, you will toast him with me, yes?"

"Of course," Sophie said.

Bruno pulled out a green bottle with no label from underneath the bar.

"Just like the pretty young women, he left so many bottles behind that he didn't have time to drink. I will be toasting him for some time, that man."

He poured three hearty servings of the dark and syrupy brew of his departed uncle and we raised our glasses, and there was nothing at all even remotely sad about it and I liked that too.

"Have you ever been to Chiesa San Pantalon?" I asked.

"Pantalon? Might have been, but it is not my church, so far away."

It was all of a mile, but in Venice—where there was a church about every two blocks sometimes even two right next to one another—the church parishes were small and loyal, no matter how religious they were or were not. The relation with God was complicated and largely driven by custom and geography.

"The reason I ask is that I made a little mistake there some time ago."

"A mistake in the church?"

"You could say that."

"You are not the first, then."

"Well, this is kind of a big mistake. See, it was after that first night I met you."

"I remember that night. You gave the Americans the wrong directions, it was funny. I was pleased. My wife she waited up for me."

"And she was not so pleased, I gather."

"Ah, she is not one to be pleased too often. That's how she is. But still, she's a good wife and a good mother. She deserves far better than me, but all the same, we are stuck with one another."

He refilled our glasses and the three of us drank again, this time to women deserving better men, which I couldn't help thinking might have been true, but might have been getting me on even more dangerous ground than I already felt I walked with Sophie.

In any event, she drank with enthusiasm, perhaps more than was necessary.

"So there I was, late at night, I slipped through the doors into the church, and as you know, since you and your uncle caused it, so to speak, I was very drunk."

"Yes, that much is true."

He looked over at Sophie.

"This one, you know, he tells the truth," he said, "unless you ask for directions."

He laughed heartily and he was good at it and his laugh was as strong as his uncle's homebrew and I wished I had known the uncle or had an uncle like that, but didn't, but laughed along with him anyway, because it was that kind of laugh.

I couldn't help thinking it was rather amusing, given what I was trying to tell him about truths.

"And it was dark, it was late, I was all alone, and, well, I sort of, well, accidentally, you see, stole a painting from the church."

He laughed more and I knew he was the right guy for this and would have been for many other things and thought that perhaps his wife didn't need or deserve better, that perhaps his wife thought herself lucky. Perhaps. But you would never know.

I told him about waking up on the bridge, there with the painting, about not knowing what to do and taking it home and then naming it. He too had read Don Quixote and thought Rocinante was a good name for the horse, which I appreciated.

I opened Sophie's satchel and pulled out the painting and we leaned it up on the bar, the horse and the knight rearing up facing the bottle-lined shelves behind the bar as if to fight them.

He stared at it for a long time, maybe one or two minutes, maybe more, and inside the bar there was only the presence of our silence. That is, the absence of sound, a noticeable absence. He walked around to the front of the bar and stared at the painting, then turned the lights higher and moved closer to it and looked at it from less than a foot away, as if he knew what he was looking at. I wondered if he was the wrong guy, maybe he had a son or a brother who was the chief of detectives and floated along Venice's canal in a polizia boat chasing bad guys and maybe I was a bad guy.

"Bello cavallo," he said, "molto bello."

"Thank you," I said, not really knowing why, since I had nothing to do with making the painting so beautiful, but pleased at something all the same, and outside the night was quiet and inside too, after I spoke.

"I thought you might, maybe, know what to do with this," I said.

"Perhaps it could be so that a horse such as this, a horse like this one might not even be happy in a church, maybe he was meant to escape. Maybe he wanted a drink," he said.

The Thirsty Knight. That too would have been a good name for a painting or a bar, I couldn't help thinking. I filed it away where I filed such things.

"I think he misses the church," Sophie said, and somehow the painting, sitting there at the end of the bar—600 years old if Sophie and her art knowledge of perspective was right—seemed to come to life under the glow of all the admiration. Illuminated by the bright lights of the little bar that was not clean, but well-lighted, the painting was happier with all the attention than it might have been for many dark centuries.

"Of course something must be done about this," he said.

It occurred to me he could have picked up the phone and I could have spent a long time getting Italian lessons in a little jail, although I knew that Venice's prison was no longer the dungeon beneath the Doges Palace and the Ponte dei Sospiri, the Bridge of Sighs, did not lead to where she kept her criminals, not anymore. There was a newer one. There always was.

He poured more drinks and looked at Sophie seriously.

"What do you think of him?"

"The knight or this pazzo ragazzo here?"

"Both. Either."

"Him," she pointed at me, "I kind of like. But I'm not sure why."

"You probably deserve much better," he said.

"Probably does," I agreed.

"We all get what we deserve," she said.

Bruno burst out laughing, a loud and heart-felt laugh, a contagious laugh, and the three of us, unheeded by Rocinante, The Thirsty Knight, sat there laughing for some brief, unexplained joyful moments. A new girl. A philosophical bar owner. A stolen painting by a long dead artist. A recently dead uncle. His remaining liquor in his favorite nephew's bar. All the beautiful creatures that he had left behind. And us. A quiet bar in Venice, a previously silenced bar, filled itself with our laughter and I was conscious of the fact that I didn't know what I was laughing at, but that it didn't matter.

"Yes, we all get what we deserve," Bruno said.

Somehow the statement and the laughter didn't quite agree with one another, but that again is common in life, whether true or not.

"So, you wish to give me this?" he said, looking at me.

"If you will have it."

"What if, perhaps, I sell it and it is worth billions of lire, oh, I mean, a million euros. Or what if I keep it and never return it? Or what if I return it and they ask a lot of questions and I have to tell them everything? And what if, someday, someone is to come looking for you?"

"Do you think that will happen?" I asked, thinking of being a fugitive from justice and whether it seemed exciting and intriguing or preposterous.

"No, not if you do not wish it. I can solve this. I think perhaps I can solve this very easily. I know some people, Venice is, you know, still a small town. One always knows some people and such things can be taken care of. It might even be," he said, tipping more of the potent uncle's brew into our glasses, "that there might turn out to be a nice reward for someone who knows the right people to return things to their proper place. I think it will be a fascinating little adventure. Even my wife may enjoy this. She loves the church. It might even spare me from mass. And it will give us something to talk about, which is always good. Why don't you come by and visit me in a week or two and I will let you know how things are going to turn out?" he finished.

There was a catharsis in giving away a problem, an appreciation for being able to hand it off to someone who would let you know how things turn out.

"That's the reason we're here tonight. We're leaving tomorrow. We have a plane from Milano Malpensa to Greece," I said, knowing that fugitives shouldn't give up their hideaway, even if justice is blind.

"Here is my card. You must send me a postal carte. I will try and sort it out in English, but it has been a long time since I had to write in English, so you may not make jokes at my expense."

"Oh, I promise."

"Do you think," Sophie asked, "that it'll have a happy ending?"

"What the painting? Or you?"

"Both," I said.

"Why not?" he said. "We shall drink on it with the spirit of my uncle."

We did and I was done with all I had to do in Venice and very happy to have given the wrong directions to some snotty tourists some time ago in an out of the way bar.

It had helped me find the way to what might be conclusion, though as for that it had also been the fount from which all this had sprung, so perhaps the scales of justice remained exquisitely balanced.

NINETEEN

Toward Distant Shores

THERE WAS A WINSOME FLAVOR OF DOMESTICITY in the air as we finished packing the next morning and closed up the apartment.

The excitement of bags in hand and anticipation of a new adventure animated our way to the train station. Along the way, I stopped at the Rio San Trovaso and pitched in a Campari bottle which carried a rolled up note saying, "Ciao, Venezia." and watched it drift down the canal and would have liked to know where and when it might end up, perhaps it would drift onto a little island in the Atlantic years hence, but knew that probably it would just be aimlessly buffeted back and forth with the tidal flows of the basin and the lagoon, as everything had since people had populated the islands. My mark on Venice would be as fleeting and illusory as the reflections that dispersed into nothingness. All you could take with you were the memories and not even all those were portable.

And we lit out for the territory ahead.

The train station was packed. Disordered clusters of confused foreigners gathered around all the service windows, asking questions to which there were no answers. The source of the turmoil was an Italian rail workers strike. It had been planned beforehand but I had not received the memo. The Italians were quite considerate about such things, they let you know when they were going to strike and when they were going to get back to work in advance and the chaotic system kept everyone happy and if you read the papers you would have known, but you hadn't, so you didn't. Of course, physics told you that the universe always veered towards entropy, only you could see it better in the Mediterranean than in a lecture hall in North America. The Italians respected disorder and embraced it as a simple fact of life.

I looked at my watch. Five hours to our plane in Milano and no trains to take us there. I had Sophie wait there and jogged up the Grand Canal to the Piazzale Roma where there were car rental places and walked into the first one I saw without a line.

A signature on a credit card slip and fifteen minutes later, I had a little silver Audi station wagon waiting next to a bratwurst stand in the parking lot and I rushed back to get Sophie.

It was the first time I'd driven a station wagon but this was a little European one, sprightly and with a surprising amount of pickup and well designed for the autostrada that went straight to Milan. It had been a long time since I'd driven, almost a year, and it was nice to be behind the wheel again and even better to be doing it in Italy where there were never any polizia on the sides of the road and very few speed limit signs which no one paid any attention to anyway.

All you had to do was point west on the A4 autostrada and go as fast as you could and make sure to get out of the way when someone blinked their brights at you, which, even though I did about 160 kilometers an hour, about 95 mph, was still more often than you would think. We drove without stopping for lunch or the bathroom, which endeared her even more to me. That and the fact she never once told me to slow down boded well for our new relationship. In Venice, I had reveled in the absence of cars in my life but I was overjoyed at the briskness of our pace and how the intimate confinement of a road trip inspires the sharing of stories and secrets.

Maybe the absence of things was the only way to learn to appreciate them. Either way, we were moving and I was glad that we were there in that domestic little Audi wagon together. And thankful that Malpensa was outside of Milan's busy inner city traffic. We pulled up to the modern terminal that looked a little like JFK, only smaller, in just under three hours, the same time a train would have taken for just a bit more than twice the cost.

I checked in the car and we both had the adrenaline surging excitement that comes with hurrying to catch a plane that was going to whisk you away somewhere new and exciting in absolutely no time at all. Only the young girl at the Alitalia counter told us it was not going to all, not today and probably not tomorrow.

There had been a bomb threat in the new Athens airport and no flights were going there that day, and probably not the next. The Greek police striving hard to show the moneyed travelers of the world that their country was safe and secure against any terrorist threat, not only the cradle of democracy but also the setting for the millions of dollars to change hands during the upcoming Olympics. Security had become everyone's first priority. To me, being too secure meant you couldn't go outside and play and climb a tree or pack up your things and go wherever you wanted, whenever you wanted. Those ideas were far more precious to me than security, which, not having been personally bombed or terrorized, was not of paramount importance to me and my own way of refusing to be terrorized. Sometimes you fell out of the tree and hurt yourself and the tree was still there, it didn't mean everything had changed, it just meant you learned the wrong way to climb a tree.

The world was a dangerous place and you either recognized that or you didn't and there were things that weren't worth trading for the impossible elusiveness of safety. I guess you could give up climbing trees, but then you lost the views and the excitement and most everything. Too much security could drain life of all that lent it splendor.

The world wanted beauty and joy but also safety and security and war, and depending on which way you looked or listened, you saw everyone following a different beacon. They weren't all going to get their way and some were going to get in everyone's way. Mostly what you could see was that people were going to do what they wanted, secure only in the righteousness of their own path. My uncomfortable communion with the God that was supposed to have resided in the Church of San Trovaso next to my apartment had left me feeling that if there was a God there or anywhere, he or she was but a troubled and helpless parent watching his offspring make the same mistakes, helpless to save them.

I wasn't willing to dwell any further on trees or bombs or terrorists or divinity; I was, in the way of my people, supremely self-interested and merely inconvenienced. And not willing to be so, not then, not there. It's hard, if you are not practiced at it, to be utterly self-interested, but anything can be learned with the proper motivation.

Without a flight where we wanted to go, the poetry of the Greek ferry was still enticing, but a decision that should have been made in Venice, not after quitting my job and leaving the apartment and the keys and driving across the breadth of Italy. We had no place to stay in Venice any longer nor reason to do so and a little villa in Greece waiting for us and I was not going to backtrack to catch a slow boat, not for poetry's sake. I had somewhere to be, even though the road I'd wanted to take could not, it seemed, be taken.

In Europe, if you can't fly, you take a train. Only there were no trains leaving Italy for the next week due to the planned strike, and no flights to Athens in the foreseeable future. Milan was not a place to while away a few days awaiting adventure unless you were a banker or businessman or a young model, and we weren't.

I did then what you have to do while trying to take a trip that won't seem to take you.

"Coffee?" I said.

No matter where you are in Europe, you're never more than a few steps away from someplace to have a coffee, which in the end seems the height of civilization.

So we took our bags and ourselves to an airport bar and sat down.

Sophie ate a small pizza with prosciutto and mushrooms and I watched her pick at it while I finished my coffee and thought and strategized and tried to pull a plan out of the ether, feeling rather like an ineffectual and ill-informed field marshal not knowing which way the battle lay. Napoleon said an army traveled on its stomach; I should have had something to eat, but didn't. What did Napoleon know anyway, trying to take Russia in the winter? Then Hitler failed to learn and made the same mistake. Even when it seemed that all the mistakes there were in the world had been made, there were still more. There would always be more emperors, chancellors, and dictators of all sorts and you could trust that they would find further egregious acts to commit.

I rolled around possible solutions in my little brain. Return to Venice, get a hotel, wait for next week's boat, that was no good. I could take the matrimonial bull by the horns and fly to Prague and get things done at the Embassy with Denissa, but that would delay us for the idyllic little house on the island that had just moments ago been right in my grasp and now seemed so elusive, making me want it all the more. Besides which it wouldn't be so cheap either, and I was, after all, newly unemployed. And if my wife and Aaron and their group there in the Czech Republic had already committed themselves to paying for tickets down to Greece, I didn't want to ruin that.

I tried to think of another airport that was nearby Athens and shorn of its security breach. What was closest to Athens? Thessaloniki, Sparta, Istanbul, Dubrovnik?

Driving across the Italian border for another international train where they weren't striking meant a long trip. How many days to Athens, did they even go through the war torn sections of former Yugoslavia and where else did you have to go and how long would it take?

That all this ran through my mind while we could have been ensconced in a little island hideaway didn't sound right or seem fair.

Though I had seen enough of life to know that most things weren't right or fair, it is a hard illusion to let go of.

She looked at me and waited.

I noticed her pizza was gone.

She went to get us two more coffees.

I had grown used to being easily whisked around Europe by trains and planes to places I had never even planned on going and now all of a sudden I had a place I planned on, I wanted to go with all my heart, and nothing was doing.

It was sort of funny that time was not really an issue for either of us, I mean we didn't have any place we had to be or anyone awaiting us anywhere except a waiter we didn't know with the keys to a house we hadn't seen that I'd rented from an American company I'd never heard of. We had the house, fully paid, for a whole month after all, and the season was over, we would undoubtedly be the last guests, the agency had said. But somehow I had the feeling, like a shark, that if we stopped moving for too long, all the magic and romance of our new adventure would die or disappear and I wasn't willing to let that happen.

I had to move. We had to move. I had to move us. How?

I left her there with our bags, saying I had to go to the bathroom, but didn't and went to look at a map of Europe on the wall, seeking a sign, getting the lay of the land, determined to get us out of there and in Greece, or nearby, that very day.

The only thing going anywhere nearby were flights to Sofia, Bulgaria and Thessaloniki, Greece, both later that week. Nothing that day. And no information on getting to Hydra, nor even Athens, from either of those places, not there in workaday Milano who wasn't so narcissistic as Venice but was just as utterly unconcerned with the outside world. Perhaps self interest is not as hard to achieve as I'd thought. Not for cities or countries who didn't have girlfriends or lovers they needed to woo.

Could you still say woo? Where the hell did I pick that up? It was most certainly not a word from the vocabulary arsenal of my Lieutenant Colonel father, nor from a former girlfriend, nor another man's wife. There it was rearing its pithy little head in my small brain, nonetheless. Pith, the inside skin of an orange, also the name of a safari helmet like I had at Princeton, though New Jersey was not a place for safaris. It had been a good hat for college precisely because it was so out of place from its setting. Which was how I was beginning to feel now, trapped there in the wrong place. Milan Malpensa.

I saw brief possibilities in a flight to the island of Corfu, where my poetic Venice-Greek ferry went, however, it was already over booked and not another one for a week. I felt the black hole of us being stranded in an airport sucking me in and wasn't going to stand for it. Perhaps Stephen Hawking was right about matter and light not being able to get out of a black hole, but I was not going to follow laws of physics I didn't understand.

I'd spent much of the past years traveling and had been stuck in many other airports in other places and other times on other trips. But not with her and not at the beginning of adventure. Not now, not this time, I said, to myself, staring at the lines of people at the crowded airline counters and the map of Europe on the wall adorned with the blue flag and yellow stars of the EU but well delineated by political borders and boundaries. I'd always preferred looking at maps made from satellites, where every place appeared as its own proper and real colors instead of the hues and tones and thick borders that politicians, generals, and mapmakers drew, a political paint by numbers landscape, but you worked with what you had.

I figured out the smart thing to do. Movement, good. Waiting, bad. Milano, bad; backtracking to Venice, bad. Always forward.

The smart thing was to get a car and drive down to Rome, then you were at least heading in the right direction and you could wait for the airport situation to be cleared up enough to fly to Athens. I knew Rome and some good places and it was a city you could wait for almost anything in, hell, maybe that was why it was The Eternal City. You could sip wines from the hills of Lazio, eat pasta, finish meals with limoncello, listen to the buzzing of the Vespas scooting around the city, go and look at St. Peter's again and wonder why Moses' statue had horns, or wander up the Spanish Steps which didn't of course go to Spain but were there all the same.

I'd learned from experience that the smart choice is not always the most enticing and it just didn't feel right. The sensibility of living in Venice was a slow one; the adaptation to the busy industrial cities elsewhere, the cars and noise and traffic, were big changes and abrupt. Abrupt change and traffic noises would not be conducive to staring in a stunning woman's eyes and forgetting about the rest of the world.

One had to be careful about selecting the right methods and setting the right mood in making your way through the world.

I considered the idea of renting a car and driving along the Adriatic coast, something I'd wanted to do for some time since seeing Zagreb during a conference and spending a solitary afternoon getting drunk afterwards on an excursion to Opatija, a charming little pastel colored town on the ever-shifting Italian-Croatian border, at a little dockside drinking hole called Hemingway Bar. It had seemed a place to go back to.

The coast would be nice and driving gave a sense of control and movement, all desirable. But I had seen and felt the sadness that drenched the splintered lands of the former Yugoslavia. It had too long been a battlefield of violence and hatred and not recovered. The stench of horror and hostility was still too strong there and it imprinted on you, like the red roses of Sarajevo that made you want to cry.

Especially once you found out, while aimlessly wandering the sidewalks and staring up at still shattered buildings, that the little red marks, the "roses" left on the cement walks, were there because they were where someone had been shot during the war. You had to stop staring at the gaping buildings and look down at the sidewalk to make sure you didn't step on one of them, each measured footfall a reminder of man's inhumanity. Right there in the middle of what had once been a beautiful city, where the winter Olympics had been held and where Muslim minarets stood beside Orthodox basilicas and had lived in harmony before ethnic cleansing had ruined all that. Maybe it would be beautiful again, but it wasn't yet, not now. Talk of a new war had of course made everyone forget about the Balkans and I wondered why those who made war had such short memories.

And I knew that there would be problems in Montenegro, plus Albania, with visas needed in advance and border crossings that meant bureaucratic delays and the ugly head of officialdom in Europe's most undeveloped and isolated region that was en route overland to Greece. I wasn't worried for our safety, Croatia was indeed becoming a popular tourist locale again. But the still disarmingly sad devastation of Croatia and its long rows of gravestones and emptied Muslim villages, it just wasn't a place you wanted to take a girl who had thought a bit too much about life and death recently, wasn't a place to tear through on the way to reinventing life.

What you wanted to do was fly over the Balkans somehow and get down to Greece, to your peaceful little island. That's what you wanted.

You wanted to forget about wars and sadness and killing and hatred. Maybe that's how they felt when they were there too, but you couldn't tell who was a patriot and who was a war criminal and who was a pacifist. Or if there were any pacifists left alive. I guess they killed the pacifists first in a good war. Forget about death and appointments in Samarra, I told myself. You can't dwell on things like black holes and war and killing if you cannot understand them or find them too large and too ugly to think about.

Think life, movement, escape. Think little plans, achievable goals.

∞ ∞ ∞

I sat at a confusing juncture. I had solved many problems before, much larger ones than this one of getting to another place, and knew I was perhaps imbuing this one with a shade more importance than it needed but couldn't help it nonetheless. And I turned and saw the Cypriot Airline counter and was glad that I had studied up and knew that Cyprus, though sort of Greek and sort of occupied on its upper half by Turkey, was at least a big island with its own airport, a historical crossroads of the Mediterranean. If you wanted to cross Homer's wine-darkened sea, you could do worse than to make it there, out of the way, but also well connected and far beyond the Balkans, though much closer to the Middle East. Also glad to remember that they were trying to make peace in Cyprus. They had had their war in the Seventies, so it was easier to forget.

Cyprus made me think of Lawrence Durrell and how he'd learned to love the bitter lemons that island life there bestowed upon him. There had been many islands in Durrell's messy affairs, also Corfu. With so many islands sprinkling these fabled seas, it was compelling to think that he should have lived on two of them that were now before us, in a manner of speaking. Or might be.

I left my thoughts alone and walked up to the Cypriot Air counter. Yes, they spoke English. Yes, there were still several flights to Cyprus that day: to Nicosia, Europe's last divided city, though she didn't call it that, as well as Larnaca and Limassol, towns I had not heard of. Could you get anywhere near Hydra from any of them? Well, there were the problems with the Athens airport, the best you could do was get a flight to Limassol—the very next flight leaving, actually, still seats available—and then make your way to Larnaca, from whence that very day, you could fly to Mykonos where you were well connected by ship to almost all of the Greek islands, perhaps Hydra. Those Cypriot ladies knew how to take care of things.

I reserved two seats for the whole deal, didn't even ask the price, and ran off to get Sophie's passport to complete the transaction. I stopped for a moment when I saw her sitting there, serene and beautiful and so willing and ready for new places and better times. Times that I might be intimately connected to, if things unfolded properly; if I was so blessed to be a part of her time.

"Here's the deal, no flights today are going to get us to Athens," I said.

She pursed her lips.

"But, I have a plan. I have a plan so cunning."

"Do tell," she said.

"Well, it's a little complicated and necessitates a bit of leg work and hopping around and rather out of the way and perhaps it's a bit rushed, and…"

"What about the down sides?"

"Almost none."

"Sounds perfect."

"Okay then. I will need your passport and I shall return momentarily. Meanwhile, you have another drink of something of a relaxed alcoholic nature. Get me one, too. And prepare to be whisked off to brief visits to out of the way places in the off season," I said. "So your passport and a kiss will seal the deal."

She took her passport out of her little suede purse and held it up.

"Wait," she said.

Uh-oh. She was going to think I was crazy, I couldn't explain all this, didn't have time and besides which, I knew it wasn't the kind of thing that could stand up to analysis.

"I was going to pay for the tickets," she said.

"How about this? I pay for these, I've been so greatly over paid for so long with nothing good to spend it on, and you, well, you can pay for our tickets when we leave."

She looked up at me.

"I don't know. You let a guy pay for a vacation house and your plane tickets and he's likely to get the idea that you owed him something."

"Oh, yes, he most definitely would."

I snatched her passport out of her hand.

"Okay," she said, "just so we're clear on that. Can I have that kiss now?"

She had it.

I rushed back to the dark-haired, green uniformed lady of Cypriot Airlines, trying to calculate along the way how many days, was it five, this would give us to settle down in our little house and get comfortable and acclimated before having to go to Athens and meet my wife. Those two words had started to take on a more ponderous weight of late, especially when they had initially struck me as so small while I was drunk and happy and jumping off bridges and dancing in conga lines in Prague.

I knew Sophie and I needed time together before things were thrown too far asunder and didn't want to risk any irreparable damage. There's no insurance, though, for these type of important things, not even Lloyd's covers it. Why can't you insure any of the important things like love or happiness? I should have asked that damned actuarial guy from my long ago past. He probably had a study. He was probably sitting in an airport somewhere right now talking about it. What was the percentage of happy people in love?

I scurried through the throngs of people running about on their own pressing airport errands. The messy missions of elsewhere that herded together unrelated species: drones off to do corporate bidding, makers of merry off on holidays visiting family or getting away from family. People that pined for new places, eager to be transported by experience. The different desires were processed with the numbing sameness of the cattle-herd corralling that humans put up with in order to be jetted away from things.

I was pretty sure right then that my mission, ill-thought out though it was, might well have been unique. I wasn't getting two tickets to unplanned places to see them or enjoy them—Cyprus or Mykonos, though they were probably as good a places as any—just to pass through and get me, get us, to a quiet and comfortable spot that was new. A spot we could make ours and grow to fit. Where nothing would be expected of us but to become closer and enjoy this slice of retirement. Perhaps my mission was just like everyone else's. I didn't ask.

The line moved, I with it. A couple came up and stood behind me, relieving me of being last in line, which made my position seem better even though it didn't change it. Moments passed and my turn came. Passports and tickets were pushed back and forth on the green plastic counter, a credit card slip signed, seats assigned, and the thing was done.

We hurried to the boarding gate and awaited the little bus that would take us out on the tarmac. A German Shepherd, trained to sniff out bombs or drugs or terrorists or maybe even besotted lovers, made his way eagerly to me. I was asked to take off my shoes and empty my bag and did. I was glad I was wearing sporty little socks. I patted the German Shepherd on the head and was well chastised by his trainer in Italian who had clearly been offended when I called his ferocious assistant cucciolo, puppy. The shepherd liked the attention until he was dragged off, the trainer disappointed that I wasn't carrying anything like drugs or bombs, and they went away to sniff out greener pastures. I hoped for the dog's sake they might be rewarded by sniffing out a terrorist, whatever terrorists smelt like. Dogs deserved whatever satisfaction they sought.

We got off the bus and boarded the small airplane. I tried to give her the window seat but she insisted I have it. I wasn't sure if it was generosity or so she could lean on my shoulder, but they both seemed pretty good. I stowed our bags in the overhead bin, surprised at actually getting space right above our seats, and scooted in and raised the arm between our two seats.

Not long after take off, before we had left the shore of Italy, Sophie was asleep on my shoulder. I remained vigilant.

The flight was longer than I'd expected, over three hours, made lengthier by me expecting it to end before it was even halfway anywhere. The seat front magazine, in English and in Greek, had a map that showed me that Cyprus was way down there, further east and south than I'd thought, and it might not have been the very best plan but I was ever so relieved to be moving again, carried along above the foamy shaving cream clouds that dotted the deep blues of the Mediterranean. I put the magazine back carefully so as not to disturb her sleep or attract her attention to my poor geographical solution. I sat there, her head leaning on my shoulder, looking out the little window and it seemed like it would have been a very tough jigsaw puzzle to put together and I wondered who had, or if it had just happened.

We stepped out of the plane and walked down the stairway to Cyprus. It was hot, like the heat of the Las Vegas desert in September when it won't let go. Even the airport had a flavor of the Middle East, dark complexions contrasted with pink and ruddy fair-skinned Brits on package holidays, the colorful medley that made up a crossroads. Getting to walk across the tarmac was a simple pleasure that larger airports denied you, and even though the bright sun reflected so hotly off the black asphalt, I was happy to do it. It's good to walk in the path of airplanes. When you turned your head to the right, just beyond the airport, you could see the minarets and white dome of a mosque, shiny and shimmering in the heat waves, penetrated only vaguely by long rows of palm trees and silhouetted against a long, low line of brown mountains.

There was customs, which was quick and easy, and outside a green airport bus to take us to Larnaca. They drove on the English side of the road. We skirted along through beach resorts and the place was much bigger than I'd expected, it didn't feel like an island was supposed to feel, somehow. It was thoroughly over-developed and crowded with English tourists and beach bars boasting of dart boards and English Premier League football and bitters and drink specials. Unlike the beaches of the Pacific, I noticed that the bars did much brisker business than the seashore. Cyprus had been an English colony for a long time and it showed everywhere, despite the dark-haired Cypriots and the hot weather and the flavor of the Middle East, which, not having visited the Middle East, I wasn't sure if I was right about anyway. I knew it was hot, though. I had another theory about the English, that their colonialism was driven by looking for better weather, but I didn't share it with her because we were moving and it was good to move and there would be more time later for theories and maybe she wasn't interested and maybe she was, but you never knew. Besides which, it could have easily been proved false by the fact that it didn't look as if any of them were enjoying the weather, just the drinks.

In Larnaca, another plane took off with us on it, and even our baggage, headed for Mykonos. The plane was full—more than usual for this time of year, we were informed—due to people trying to make it back to Athens and her closed airport, and we were part of the group, lemmings going along with a plan that people other than myself had thought of.

We arrived in the early evening, though it was still light, at the Mykonos airport on the desolate interior of the island. I had thought we might have had to change some euros but had forgotten that Greece too had joined up with the EU and agreed to use the bland and bureaucratic new euros, so it wasn't necessary. In front of the little airport, there was a greeting party of taxicabs, a colorful caravan of Mercedes and other makes, interspersed with brightly painted hotel vans and buses. One of the buses was pink and said Hard Rock Mykonos in turquoise letters. We grabbed the second taxi, an older black Mercedes. I don't know why exactly the second one is always better, but if you believe it, it is.

Yes, he could take us to the port, of course there were ferries still leaving. Everything was working well.

He dropped us off at the port just north of the main town which was all white cubist buildings and colorful crowds in their late summer clothes, just like the pictures said it would be: curving around a little bay and rimmed by a hillside topped with a row of still white-washed windmills that weren't in service any longer, though there was plenty of wind.

There were several travel agencies near the port, along with a herd of old Greek ladies, widows I guessed, all dressed in black and carrying pictures of their rooms for rent, as well as several English and Australian blokes touting their hotels, or the hotels that employed them, to snare new arrivals. I passed blithely through them all and made my way to the second travel agency, Prometheus Ships and Tours, a mythic name painted on a blue sign graced with a flaming yellow and orange torch, the fire that Prometheus gave mankind after stealing it from Mount Olympus. Poor Prometheus who had been so mistreated for his good deed.

There were two choices, the Greek man told me while he toyed with his string of orange worry beads. A fast hydroplane ferry leaving in less than half an hour, which would get us to Athens' port then on to Hydra the most efficient and inexpensive way possible. Or, if there was no rush, there was a fine boat leaving, The Odysseus, in an hour and a half. It happened that he had some lovely staterooms left and it took much longer, overnight, but would deposit us safe and sound on Hydra's shores early the next morning. If you've ever wanted to get someplace with a new woman you wanted to impress, you know then which tickets were purchased. I believe the Greek approved of my decision too.

We left our bags with him and went to eat. There wasn't time to walk all the way to town. It wasn't far, less than a mile, but there was a boat coming for us. Besides, I believed in the importance of first impressions and didn't want to cloud our first feeling of Greece by seeing too much in the wrong place. So we went to the first restaurant, since we didn't see a second choice close by, and sat down and had Greek salads of tomato, cucumber, onion, and olives and grilled chicken and some wine, which they brought out all at once. A simple and refreshing meal and then we walked, hand in hand, back to the dock.

Night descended around us slowly as we got on the boat, starting an adventure and putting to rest a day of dashing about the Mediterranean. We got the keys to our room from a heavily mustachioed man wearing a white uniform and dropped off our bags in the elegant stateroom, which was lacking in elegance or stateliness but did have a nice double bed and a little bathroom and a porthole, all of which I hoped to put to good use. I put the key in my pocket and we went together out to the prow of the large ship to watch the sunset, admiring the disc as it sank slowly below the edge of the sea and turned the white buildings of Mykonos all aglow with oranges and yellows as we pushed into the night, and the town slowly disappeared and was replaced with only a flattened horizon.

It got a little chilly outside and the rest of the people made their way indoors as the sun sank and everything turned purple, then gray, then blue and there was nothing to see, just the quiet sounds of The Odysseus cleaving the sea, us alone at the stern of the boat. Or was it the bow? I remembered port was left, because they both had four letters, but front and back, well, it didn't matter, we were in the front and alone and it was dark and we were heading for Hydra while the chill night air of the still sea shrouded us.

The deck was sparsely lit from the bridge up above and a giant steel anchor sat there, about twelve feet long, alongside a large pile of coarse rope and some oily chains.

"You cold?" I asked.

"A little."

She put her arms around me, and probably we should have gone inside to the warmth of our stateroom, but then maybe she wouldn't have needed my warmth. The pile of rope made a comfortable seat and we sat down together and she leaned her head on my chest. I knew we were in the Aegean Sea now, a different sea, the waters of Ulysses and Homer and everyone who came before us, and I felt a part of an old story. Happy is the man, I thought, who has the good fortune to accidentally find himself sailing the Aegean with the right girl's head lying on his chest.

We lay there in silence broken only by the brushing of the waters on the ship and we dropped off, it had been a long day of traveling for not actually getting anywhere.

I woke with a start, thinking I had dreamed something, someone was talking to me, but I looked over and Sophie was still asleep. Then I heard it again.

A voice over the loudspeaker said, "Give her a kiss," and she stirred but didn't wake, and I looked up and there was a small group of white uniformed, black-haired, bearded men on the bridge, back lit by a yellow light, staring down at us from above.

I couldn't decide if it was amusing, if I was insulted or offended, or proud or debauched. They stared down at us.

I kissed the top of her head and pretended I didn't hear them.

The voice sounded again, "Give her a kiss."

"Soph, you awake?"

"No," she said.

They stared down at us some more, laughing. We were part of a little game.

I felt a strange stirring of wanting to be part of a game, to perform well. Everything should be a game, I thought, even if it's one you aren't exactly sure why you're playing.

"Soph, they're not going to be happy unless they get a kiss," I said.

"So you want me to just run up there real fast and kiss them all?"

"No, I want you to stay here and kiss me real slow."

She looked up at them, stood up, and kissed me deeply and then all of a sudden dipped me backwards and we fell stumbling and laughing on the pile of rope. Then she hopped up and did a stripper-style spin around one of the poles that supported the upper deck, turned toward them and executed a theatrical bow and grabbed my hand and led us away, and as we ran off together, they sounded the loud foghorn in celebration of our performance, which had little to do with me but also certainly nothing to do with fog either.

We made our way as quickly as we could to our small room and decided not to go to dinner and not to have drinks. The game we didn't know we were playing continued as we undressed each other, still exploring the newness of each other's bodies and sharing the pleasure of it that was accentuated by being off balance by the small stirrings and rolling of the ship.

There was this liberating anonymity in being alone together in a little room floating on a strange sea on a ship that you hadn't even heard of that morning, making its way to your destination while you made love and perhaps you do some things together you might not usually do, which we did. And then we slept in the little room where the porthole didn't open and you couldn't see anything out there in the blackness and where it got too warm and we sweated on each other and stuck together in a sticky, sweet way as we slept.

We awoke with the sun and I looked out the little window and saw the brown, arid hills of a little island float by us. We dressed and she put on a hat and sunglasses, her disguise for being a wanton woman in more ways than one, she said, and I liked that, but then I liked everything about her, more than I even told her and had the feeling that she knew and understood and was maybe a bit tired of hearing it, so didn't say it.

Not knowing exactly what time we were due to arrive in Hydra, we left our bags and went and had Greek coffee in plastic cups in the dining hall, thick liquid laced with the heavy grounds that sat in the bottom of the plastic cup and which made you miss the fine Italian coffee, but part of traveling was that you drank what everyone else drank, and even if you didn't like it so much, you liked it in a different way, not for its taste but for it being the right thing to drink in the right place at the right time.

Our boat stopped at the island of Aegina and lots more people got off than got on, which I was pleased about, the less people that followed us the better. I didn't need or want anyone else in our path.

It looked pretty in the bright morning sunlight, all crisp and sharp, white-cornered, sugar-cube buildings, a few red tiled roofs and the sparkle of some hotel pools. It was busy and crowded and there were cars, and I sensed it was not a place of magic, not our destination, and was relieved when I found out it wasn't. In less than ten minutes, our ship set forth. Foghorns sounded, though there was no fog and, as far as I knew, no beautiful chestnut-haired artist performing a simulated striptease. But you didn't know, not really.

Strange and surprising things had a way of happening en route to other shores.

TWENTY

SIREN'S CALL

WHEN WE WENT OUTSIDE TOGETHER, the morning was still cool with the sharpness of the sea breeze. The fast plane and the slow boat had brought us further from the harsh heat of the lower Mediterranean.

We stared at the bright blueness of the sea, which had a crisp and clean opacity and was green and darker down below. I remembered at one of the tourism council meetings, having heard that the Saronic Gulf had some of Europe's best beaches and cleanest waters. I wondered what Hydra and our little house would be like and if everything would be right and determined that it would, that was definitely the way the wind was blowing.

"It feels," I said, "sort of like Christmas morning."

"Hmm," she said, "bright cerulean seas, skies awash in Prussian blue, summertime on a ship. I see what you mean."

She did, though. She did.

"For not knowing each other very long, you know," she continued, "we've been a lot of places but we haven't seen any of them yet."

"Ah, I've seen other places before, you've seen other places before. Hydra is going to be our place, our little perfect place with a month of retirement. You'll paint, I'll…" What exactly I would do besides be with her, I wasn't sure. Maybe there was nothing else I had to do for awhile.

"Will we drink like pesci and eat like porci? Is that what he said? Bruno?"

"That is exactly what we'll do."

"And then?"

"Well, we'll be happy homemakers, we'll swim in the sea, we'll make our visit to Athens,"

"Really your visit."

"But you are going to go with, right?" Why it seemed important to me, I didn't know. I had not yet been alone with Denissa, my new wife, once yet and was determined not to be. I didn't want to risk fracturing our togetherness or any of the magic I hoped we would build on the little island of dreams.

"We'll see."

The Odysseus pulled slowly into the edge of the port of Hydra. The ship was far too big for the port, though she made her way right up to the rim of it, turned slowly in the sea where there was no space to do so, and reversed her engines and backed gracefully up to the dockside, a maritime marvel of parallel parking. There was the sound of heavy chains being unwound and shouting and a clang as the metal door unfolded on the cement dock. White buildings adorned the curve of the harbor, stacked one above the other, sprinklings of red tiled roofs, and sea-facing patios blushing with bougainvillea. It was was smaller and more idyllic than I'd hoped, rich in romantic potential.

There were four or five restaurants, tavernas actually, with chairs right there on the waterside promenade of the little harbor. The gentle curve of the shoreline was a semi-circle of sea, maybe all of a half mile across, not so long but just the right size. The skirt of the single shoreline street supported everything, buttressing the layers of island homes that dotted the browns and greens of the hillside above.

There are panoramas too great for one viewing: Venice has them, Paris has them, the Grand Canyon, the large horizon of an empty shining sea. Sophie said she saw them in Turner's sunsets. Panoramas with so much to see and so much beauty that you can't take it all in and something is lost in the magnitude. This was bite-sized, a small amuse-bouche that whetted the appetite and tantalized the palate. It being manageable in size somehow made it more delicious in scope.

At the first curve of the quay, there was a little group of donkeys with baskets of fruit and packs of luggage and some lines of people waiting for our spot on The Odysseus. The little harbor was dotted with about twenty brightly painted fishing skiffs and a row of five or six matching catamaran yachts and two larger private motor yachts with little groups of people sitting on the decks in swimsuits.

We gathered our bags and made our way off the ship, and this time many more people got on than got off, which was nice. I retrieved the little confirmation paper from the American company that I'd printed out so long ago last week in Venice and hoped that things would proceed apace with such hastily contrived plans. There had been no phone number to call and alert them to the fact that, though it was early in the morning, we were a day late, which was one-thirtieth of our allotment of precious Greek island days and thus a much more valuable day to lose than most.

We strolled off the ship and were confronted by a few hoteliers touting their rooms, all of which looked nice enough but which I was glad not to need, that is if the house thing really existed and really worked out.

The Delfini Taverna was just beyond the dock. The street was paved with white and gray flagstones and a little truck filled with produce drove off of the ship and was unloaded by some donkeys, or mules, I never knew the difference. The Greek ferries were in and out quickly, and by the time we had made our way to the café, I looked back and the now empty truck was being driven back into the large cargo hold of The Odysseus.

The Delfini was the third bar, though they were lined up one after another and were demarcated more by the colors of their seat cushions than the locations of their tables and chairs. There were glass top tables and low slung bamboo chairs covered with blue and yellow flowered cushions. A small group of men were playing backgammon near the door, where there was a soccer match being watched and complained about, as there always is in Europe. Somebody, somewhere, was always rooting for the wrong side.

We took a table at the far end of the little gathering, furthest from the backgammon players, and sat down our luggage and ourselves. I wondered when someone would come up to us and if he would be Panos and have the keys to a lovely little home as I had been told in an email. Was he a xenophobic old Greek who would dread the arrival of incoming foreigners, or a young charismatic playboy who would try and steal my woman, or even, if he had the keys to a villa, the wealthy owner of the little café? You never knew what kind of guy the key master would be. Ask Lloyd Dobbler.

I looked at the drinks of the backgammon players—a light, coffee-colored beige filled with ice cubes—and got us two of those. Frappes, they called them.

"Sweet or Medium?" the young waiter asked in English. He didn't look like he held the keys to a villa, but one never knew in faraway places and there was an order to things I wanted to follow or design.

"Sweet," I said.

"Medium," she said.

"Me gala?" he asked.

It was a lot of questions to drink what the locals drank.

"Me gala? Milk?"

Ah. "Yes," we said simultaneously and he went inside, about as slow as you could have moved and still kept in motion.

It was good to be in a place where you didn't even know how to order your first coffee properly, and though I'd thought I'd miss my newly developed skills in Italian, I shed them easily and embraced ignorance and the opportunity to learn new things. The sun was bright but there was a light loose wind coming in off the sea.

Sophie took out a sweater, a baggy cable knit affair of red with one large white stripe across her breasts when she put it on.

We sat and drank our frappes, which were delicious and different and new, as was everything else. I looked around up the slope of the town, wondering where our house would be and what this place and this month would hold. Across the way from the bar, there was a street just wide enough for the passing of several people or two donkeys at a time and a bank a small stone's throw from where we sat, the National Bank of Greece. Next door to it was a jewelry store, then a little souvenir and postcard shop, then a restaurant and some more tables, then another street leading up the hill. There weren't many people about and it was deliciously slow and quiet and serene.

"I'm still sleepy," Sophie said.

I went inside and asked after Panos.

The young waiter stared at me, glanced out at Sophie and our bags, then back at me.

"Panos?" was all he said.

It flashed through my mind that this was an awful lot of trouble we'd gone to getting here if there was no Panos and no house and no keys awaiting us. I didn't like to worry and didn't want to worry and nothing could go wrong, there wasn't time.

At last, relieving me of some anxiety, he glanced down at the watch on his wrist.

"It's too early for Panos. He don't come until lunch."

So there was a Panos, which meant that there was a house, or at least pointed that way, and because we were early in the morning but a day late with our arrival, he was off somewhere else and there was no number to call him at and there was no longer any sense of urgency, so I went and sat back down across from Sophie.

"Panos sleeps. The red penguin walks at midnight. The walker is abroad," I said, solemnly.

"Are we spies now? First you want me to be the other woman, this I can handle. Then I have to help you take care of a painting you stole from a church and I can handle this too. I'm easy going enough.

Now I have to play spy games so early in the morning? Nothing doing. A girl has to draw the line somewhere," she said. "Wake him up. Stop sleeping, Panos. Wake up, Panos!"

From a table on the far side of the café that shouldn't have been able to hear us or care what we were saying, an older man—skin leathered by the sun, all wrinkles and whiskers and well-marked with the scars of a sun-drenched life—called out in hearty British English that matched his appearance.

"Cheers. Say, are you two looking for Panos?"

"Yes," she said.

"That wanker ought well to be up by now anyway. Kept me up half the night playing cards and backgammon and drinking ouzo then crept off to bed when I wasn't looking. He owes me for three games of backgammon. Never play backgammon with a drunken Greek, I tell you."

"If you say so," I said, which seemed to assure him that we were wise and willing to heed his good counsel, which was clearly going to be offered anyway, as he leaned forward toward our table to make himself heard, though I was sure everyone along the quiet little street could hear everything he said. You could tell he was used to being listened to.

"He only lives about fifty steps from here, I'll show you the way. Come along."

He stood up and I heard his joints crack and he sighed with age or pleasure, you couldn't tell.

∞ ∞ ∞

I got up and left Sophie there with the bags and went with the stranger, who turned out to be Nigel. He said he had been captain of one of the boats in the harbor, and when I questioned which one, he gestured casually out toward the small inlet bay but didn't say.

We made our way along, me following Nigel, him wearing scuffed blue boat shoes, khaki shorts and an unbuttoned guayabera shirt that made him look like a deposed dictator in a Banana Republic and a little worse for all the wear. There was a pleasant abandon or nonchalance, perhaps, about his appearance. An Englishman's long practiced ability to feel himself and be himself wherever he was. With his rumpled and tousled British expertise, he planted his sea feet down firmly upon the ground. There was still the sway of the sea in my own uneasy steps that reminded me of wearing a hat, how when it was there you didn't notice it and then when it was gone you could still feel its presence. We strode past the National Bank of Greece and went onward up the small slope of the hill. We passed a couple of little shops, one with a display of metal fish on a bed of fake ice cubes, another adorned with small seascapes and bright panoramic paintings, and it seemed an appealing and artistic place and a good choice. A place I was glad to be, where the catch of the day might be anything.

He brushed brusquely by these spots and then stopped and banged heavily on a yellow wooden door on the right-hand side of the small street.

"Panos, old man! Get the bed off your back, man. People here to see you. Foreigners. Important business."

It occurred to me that he, too, was a foreigner and that somehow he managed to convey otherwise with his indictment of me.

He looked down at me from the top of three little steps carved out of stone.

"It is important, aye?"

"Uh, it could wait, I guess, I mean we're in no real hurry," I said, not confident that my matter, being my own, was indeed important to anyone else. Something about the certainty with which he approached everything served to make me feel less sure of things.

"Panos, hurry up! Good god, man, are you going to sleep the whole day away, you lazy cunt?"

I'd been around enough Brits to have heard them toss around the dreaded c-word that being American wasn't available to you, but it sounded right on his lips and no one even gave us a second look. It was that kind of place, where you could bang on a yellow door in the early morning and call someone a lazy cunt and no one even gave you a second glance.

"A shiftless, lazy, good-for-nothing old Greek, Panos is," Nigel said, "Panos, man, make haste!" he yelled to the door.

I stood there on the street, all gray slabs carefully trimmed by whitewashed circles outlining the stones, Captain Nigel hovering menacingly atop the three little steps above me, looking as if he might, and could have, kicked down the yellow door. I knew red meant stop and sometimes yellow meant hurry up and sometimes it meant stop and that Marilyn Chambers, or was it Linda Lovelace, had been behind the green door. What this closed yellow door meant, I was not sure.

The door opened slowly, and there was a man with long black hair down to his shoulders and sleep in his eyes and pillow creases along the side of his face and he was wearing baggy white pants and no shirt and hadn't shaved and had clearly just been jarred awake and wasn't going to be happy, and it didn't seem an auspicious way to begin our month, but there we were.

"Enough. I'm up, I'm up," he said.

"Bloody hell, man, wake up, won't you? Day's half gone," Nigel said.

I looked down at my watch, it was nearly eight-thirty.

"Your Yank's here for you."

"I'm Mark Vandermar, we were, uh, supposed to be here yesterday to pick up the keys. To the house. The house we rented. From the agency in America."

He stared at me for a second until his eyes slowly dilated with daylight and comprehension.

"Ah, you were supposed to be here yesterday, to meet at the café."

"He's already after saying that," Nigel said, "clear your head, man, here he is, sure as Bob's your uncle."

"You are late. Where are your things?" Panos said, "I thought you were supposed to be two people."

"Where in bloody hell do you think they are? At the café. He left a pretty young woman all alone in your miserable café," Nigel looked down at me, "you shouldn't ought to have left her there. Nothing but trouble. I once left a girl sitting in a café in Cairo and never saw her again, you know."

"Moment, moment, I'm coming. I'm Panos," he said, sticking out his hand.

I repeated my name and shook his hand.

"Come on, malaka," Nigel said, "he hasn't got all day. I shouldn't wager one of your swarthy cohorts is making designs on his woman right now. You haven't all day, have you, man?"

"No rush, really, we can just wait down at the café."

"Fine Greek hospitality, Panos, splendid, absolutely brilliant," Nigel said, winking at me.

I wondered about Sophie at the café. He was kidding. But you couldn't help wondering. He was kidding? Had there been a girl in Cairo? I tried to remember if Cairo was even a seaport and couldn't and would be damned if I was going to take the bait and ask. I was only a little stupid, not a lot. But still.

"Come down for breakfast and try your revenge at backgammon. Hurry it up, old man, we haven't got all day," Nigel said.

The door closed and we were off heading downhill toward the café and the harbor with the promise of slowly awaking Panos to be along momentarily.

It wasn't, I thought, quite like checking in at the Ritz, though I couldn't be sure, not having ever checked in at the Ritz. Perhaps it was exactly like that, who knows?

As we walked down, Nigel interrogated me.

"Bit late in the season to be here, no? Been here before?" he asked.

"No," I said, to both questions.

"Nothing much going on this late. Every day something else closes, another few weeks and they'll be only a few places left to eat and drink. Bloody tourists all going home and good riddance to them, I say. What're you doing here?"

If you meet an Englishman on a small Greek island in the early morning who may or may not have been the captain of a ship and who may or may not have left and lost a girl in Cairo, you didn't tell him you came to a Greek island to fall in love.

Maybe you didn't tell anyone. I hadn't told Sophie again since that first day on finding her again. Both of us had carefully avoided the word and I wasn't sure quite why or even how or when it would end or begin.

"A month's holiday."

"Good for you, old man," he said, pounding me too hard on the back. "Near every time I meet a damned Yank traveling abroad he's off running around trying to see everyplace in Europe in ten days. Bloody blustering crazy, it is. You're not doing that, then?"

"Nope. I, uh, we," I said, staking a little territory, a bit of cautionary preventive measures, "were living in Venice and decided to come here. A little slice of early retirement."

"You left Venice for this place?" he said with incredulity, as if perhaps I was the stupidest man he'd ever met. It occurred to me that maybe I was.

"Well, damned fine idea. I've left some fine places myself, in my time. Of course everyone else is leaving here now, but to hell with 'em, I say, right?"

"To hell with them," I agreed, without his mastery of bluster and bravado, but in full agreement with his sentiment. To hell with all of them. Except her.

We got back and I invited Nigel to join us, mostly because you could tell he was going to anyway, heading as he was directly for my table and my girl. We sat down and ordered up three more frappes. Well, more accurately, Captain Nigel hurled some Greek words over at someone playing backgammon and a moment later, three more frappes appeared before us.

"So, what's this, huh?" he said, "Your man President Bush, what he's starting World War III, is it? Acorn didn't fall to far from the tree, there, huh?"

It was early in the morning for politics abroad and I had little interest in engaging him or defending American policy I didn't agree with. It was, in the words of Yogi Berra, déjà vu all over again.

I heard some shouting and quicker than I knew what was happening, the quiet little café was suddenly galvanized into action.

Panos arrived, striding proprietarily down the hill beside the café and talking into his cellphone and smoking a cigarette, with his hair now tied back in a ponytail. He lowered the phone and shouted at one of the men standing next to a donkey near the café who strode over and hastily grabbed our bags.

Panos yelled at the backgammon tables and some people ignored him, or went inside to do what he said, you couldn't be sure, not in Greek, but it had some effect, and he went back into the bar and came out with a coffee and threw out his cigarette on the stones and then lit another one and reached for his phone again as he sat down at our table. He exhaled deeply, spoke quickly into the phone and then closed it up and leaned back heavily in his chair.

A young boy appeared, Panos talked to him briefly and then to us.

"Dimi will show you the way. The donkey has been paid, you can tip him if you want, but not Dimi. If there is anything you can't find or need, just come here before dinner some time, after lunch anyway, and I can come up and show you. There is a package, some wine and food and toilet paper, and you have to turn on the hot water heater before you shower if you want hot shower. Americans are always wanting hot showers, no?"

∞ ∞ ∞

And we were off, trailing along behind a mule or donkey laden with our bags and being prodded by an old Greek man with a stick, walking alongside a little brown-haired boy of some eight or ten years, Dimi, who stopped and leaned his head quickly in at every store and shouted greetings of "yia sou."

As we made our way up the hill, the boy Dimi shared with us his small smatterings of English.

"Dimi speak English very well. In the school. Go someday America. Uncle Chicago. Very big man."

"Chicago is a nice place," I said.

"Chicago great city," he said reverently, "you know it?"

"Yes, I used to live there," I said.

His eyes opened wide.

"So you will tell me more of Chicago, yes?"

It was a pleasant little walk up the slope of the hill and it occurred to me that you never know which of the little meaningless moments in life might be pivotal moments in another life.

I could tell him Chicago was awful, that his home on the island was better, but he wouldn't believe me because little boys don't listen to what they don't want to hear. I could tell him more of how wonderful it was or how cold the wind off the lake in the winter was, how deep the snow was, how the Cubs could never win a World Series, how the waters of Lake Michigan were dull and gray compared to the bright blue sea surrounding his island.

But you never knew, perhaps you might inadvertently say something that would cause a stirring in a child's daydreams that lingered on past youth. In Greece, there and then on that sunny morning, it seemed that some elements of mythology were necessary, some grandiose tales. I thought about telling him about the Sears Tower and how fast the elevators went and how you could feel the building sway in the wind, but had the idea he might not believe me, somehow, even though it was true. Walking with a beautiful woman alongside a little boy under the island sun of the morning, you wanted him to believe you.

"It burned down once, the whole city, Dimi," I said.

"No. Impossible," he said, but looked at me to go on.

"It's true. A long time ago. There was this cow."

"Caw?" he said.

"Moo-moo," I said, pantomiming the milking of a cow and wondering if he would get it. Did not the Greeks get all their milk from goats?

"Yes, cow, I see it," he said, stretching out the word.

"This was the cow of Mrs. O'Leary."

"Who was the Missus? You knowing her?" he asked.

"No, this was a long time ago, before I was born, before you or your uncle were even born. Before everyone alive today had been born."

He reached up and placed his hand in Sophie's and slowed down, looking up at me, waiting.

"One morning, it had been a hot summer, no rain, and Mrs. O'Leary went to milk her cow," I said, mimicking milking again. He nodded his head solemnly.

"And the cow kicked over a lantern," I said, but lost him of course with that word, so had to take out my lighter and show him fire until he understood. I wanted to ask about Prometheus but would have been terribly saddened if the Greek myths weren't alive in the minds of modern young Greek boys, and didn't.

And I told him about the cow and the fire and how it was the night Chicago died and he was astonished and truly amazed and wanted to hear all about it and how they put it out and how they rebuilt the city.

"Don't scare him," Sophie said.

He stood up straighter and puffed out his little bare chest and patted it with his hand that wasn't holding on to hers.

"Dimi no get scared. Dimi strong boy."

"I believe you, Dimi. I think you are."

"Yes, true," he said, pleased, but he kept holding on to her hand.

"How is the cow called? What's name cow?" he said reverently.

Damn that boy if he didn't uncover right away my ignorance with the grace and enthusiasm that only young children have. When in adulthood does it happen that educated people lose the ability to get to the heart of the matter, the urge or need to know the important facts? Did Mrs. O'Leary's cow have a name? She must have, but had it been recorded in history? Why hadn't I paid more attention so I could tell this little Greek boy what he wanted to know?

"Mrs. O'Leary's cow was named…" I said, "Dimi."

He looked up at me.

"No, it's no true. Dimi, like me?"

"He's lying," Sophie said.

"I think so too, missus."

"She was called Bessie," I said, feeling that the odds of that were pretty good and it would do for now. Wasn't Bessie what you were supposed to name a cow?

"Missus Oh-Leery. The cow of Missus Oh-Leeery, Bessie, make fire." he said.

"Yes, the greatest fire ever. Ask your uncle. He will tell you."

"When you live Chicago, you have cow?"

"No, I never had a cow," I said, happy to be able to report something else truthfully.

"Neither me," he said.

"The cow of Mrs. O'Leary," I said, picking up his English syntax, "is very famous cow, maybe most famous cow in all America."

"Really? You tell truth?"

They both looked up at me.

"Yes, ask anyone," I said.

"I will ask my teacher of English at the school. He very smart. Teach me all the English. First I must tell my friends all of this cow of Missus Oh-Leery. May I have this story for myself?"

"Yes, Dimi, you may have this story. It's true. It's all true," I said, hoping and wishing that he wouldn't uncover the name of the cow and prove me a liar.

"Okay, Dimi show you house, this way, come, and then must go and tell friends this story. Let's go. Quickly now, come on, this way," he said, trotting forward with two little steps for each of our longer strides, but keeping right up with us, leading us, actually.

And on we went, winding our way through the little maze of streets.

He unlocked a blue wooden door with a heavy skeleton key and opened it and stood there on the little stoop waiting for us, and I wanted to carry her over the threshold, but didn't and wondered if I ever would, sometime, somewhere else. I looked over at her and none of us moved. I guess I was thinking about firemen from the story. I reached out and grabbed her little purse and handed it to Dimi.

"Dimi, we have an important tradition in America for good luck in a new house. Will you help me?" I said.

"Yes, I help," he said, taking the purse.

I turned toward Sophie and grabbed her arm and ducked my shoulder and tossed her over it fireman style and put one arm around both of her legs while she thumped me on my back, laughing. I spun us around in a circle for no reason at all but enjoying the makeshift celebration and excited about the new house and the presence and sincerity of the little boy who had brought us here and asked to have a story and who laughed with us as we spun around.

"Dimi, before we go in, now you must yell the name of the cow of Mrs. O'Leary to make sure that fire never comes to this house forever," I said.

"Bessie," he said.

"You must say it three times."

"Bessie! Bessie! Bessie!"

An old lady leaned out from her porch just up the way and snapped some words to him I didn't understand. I guess there were things you couldn't yell there, even if lazy cunt wasn't one of them. There were lots of rules for young boys everywhere the world over. Maybe you just had to be a ship captain or a foreigner. The old woman turned away and went back inside shaking her head, perhaps we weren't noteworthy new neighbors.

I put Sophie down and he smiled and she punched me on the arm.

"The poor kid is going to think we're crazy, you know."

"Artists and Americans are supposed to be crazy, it's part of our charm," I said.

Dimi's dark eyes lit up again.

"We have something for make good luck of house," he said.

"How do we do it?" I asked.

He made a face and squinched up his eye and pointed at it and then spat on the ground. I didn't quite get it, but copied him anyway, though it turned out that was the wrong thing to do. He meant something else and was suddenly carried away with the importance of it and more than a little frustrated with us that we didn't understand him properly.

"Dimi show you, I come back," he said, and ran off and left us standing there.

I turned to go in and hoped the house would be nice.

"Mrs. O'Leary's cow, is that true?" she said.

"So they say. Shall we?"

We walked in and closed the blue door behind us. There must have been another key, because our bags were sitting there in the little courtyard already, somehow, which seemed magical and easy and something like the Ritz. The courtyard had a small bright blue metal table and three chairs and one side of it was covered in vines and red bougainvillea flowers, and though it was small, there were stone walls of about ten feet high on both sides and then two stone steps and another blue wooden door to the house, the key to which was on the heavy key ring Dimi had left us. I unlocked it and we left our bags out there in the sun and went in.

Inside, there was a modern kitchen, strangely out of place in the old house with its whitewashed walls of stone, but I noted a dishwasher, a small washing machine, a small sink of white porcelain, and a refrigerator and a kitchen bar of sorts, on which sat a straw basket with a bottle of local wine and some fruit, toilet paper, and a greeting card signed by the American company and a number to call for emergencies, though there was no phone. Past the kitchen, there was a light-colored, heavy pinewood dining table for four and a built-in couch covered with stuffed red and yellow cushions and a small television. Off to the left was a little bathroom and beside that some steep wooden stairs of blonde wood.

Upstairs was one large room running the length of the house with a cushiony little green sofa, two soft yellow armchairs, another dining table, and a large bed with yellow sheets and a blue bedspread that matched the color of the doors and a diaphanous white mosquito net hanging down either side, and two wooden nightstands. At the front of the upper floor, there were two large windows and French doors, blue again, that opened out onto the balcony, where there was another blue metal table.

I opened up the doors and sunlight streamed into the room and cut a long diagonal swath across the wooden floor and you could see the little dust motes floating around aimlessly in the light air, hurrying around nowhere very busily.

We stepped out onto the balcony and below us the little port town spread out like a well adorned tablecloth, all white walls and roofs draped with red and purple flowers, blue shutters and doors, red tiled roofs, all of it arcing gracefully around the curve of the harbor. The masts of the ships in port striped the bright blue of the sea which stretched out on the horizon as far as you could see, dotted here and there with small white specks of boats and a few faraway whitecaps and the hazy line of the distant shore that might have been the mainland, I wasn't sure. Off to the left of our view, where the buildings skirted the edge of a hillside, just beyond the promontory of land, there was a patio café overlooking a small, brown rock island outcropping with no trees, just some dirt and stones and a tiny white cross jutting out from the water.

She stood there next to me while we took in all the views, there were so many even though it all was part of one whole. And she reached up and brushed her hand along the back of my neck and sent little shivers down my spine with her fingernails.

"What do you think?" I said.

"I think it's perfect. It is like Christmas."

While we stood there, I wondered how many times you could make love in 29 days and nights on an island and if you could really make love, the way you could make a painting or a press release or a perfect circle. And if it could be made, could you wrap it up somewhere safe and take it with you anywhere? Even to Athens, to meet your wife?

I was jolted out of my reverie when the blue door to the patio below us opened up and in rushed Dimi carrying a small white tissue papered ball.

"Kalimera, hallo, it's me, Dimi, here," he called out, "I have good luck with me."

"Up here, come inside Dimi," she said.

He ran up the stairs, I guess he knew the house or maybe he ran everywhere, one never knew with little boys, they always knew much more than you thought they did, and even though they had more free time than anyone, were always in a hurry.

He came up to us out on the balcony and didn't even look at the view, the way you can ignore beauty when you are too much surrounded by it and when it is what you know well and take for granted, and I hoped the world would always be so beautiful for him that he could take it for granted always. Hell, I hoped that for myself even though I was old enough to know better.

He proudly handed the tissue papered package to Sophie.

"Present, missus, from the Mama of Dimi," he said, smiling and I could see where he was missing a tooth and wondered if he had lost it and was awaiting a permanent tooth to fill the gap and if there was a tooth fairy in Greece.

She carefully opened the package and unwrapped a large, flattened dollop of blue glass, all dark sea blue on the outside, ringed on the inside with lighter blues and an opaque white circle with a black spot in the middle. There was a little hole at the top with a black string of leather circled through it and tied carefully together.

Dimi scrunched up his left eye again and spat on the balcony.

"See, it keep this, evil eye, away, always. Put on front of house, I show you, Missus, Mister," and he grabbed her hand and led us back down the stairs.

He showed us how to hang it up beside the door and stepped back and surveyed it with pride.

"You safe now here. No evil eye, no cow make the fire," he said.

I believed him too, no matter what they say about Greeks bearing gifts. Having protected us, he ran off to tell people about the cow of Missus Oh-Leery, eager with the enthusiasm that is a young boy's domain when he has special new dangerous stories to tell of faraway places and destruction.

Alone in the little house, there was anything we could have done and with all the possibilities, the feeling left us not knowing which to pursue. It was too early for lunch. She took a red apple out of the little basket and took a large bite out of it, and it was crunchy and the sound seemed to pleasantly fill the little house, and she handed it to me and I took a bite just below hers and I don't know if she was thinking about the Garden of Eden, but I was and didn't care. It was a damned good apple and very sweet. I handed the apple back to her and went out to the patio and brought in our bags and took them upstairs and she didn't offer to help and I wouldn't have taken it anyway.

TWENTY ONE

PAINTING PARADISE

HOW WE WELCOMED THE PASSIONATE EMBRACE of these open-armed island days. The slow-paced sweetness of being intentionally stranded on a small island in the Saronic Gulf, so far from everywhere, spoke to us.

How simple our little world became, how filled with hidden pleasures we had not known existed. The secrets of each other's bodies we uncovered under the billowing mosquito net upstairs, the things we whispered to one another before and after we made love in every way I'd known and some I hadn't, the meals we shared and the bottles of wine we drank, the plans we played with in the languid luster of the starlit nights.

What I discovered there on that island was that we were seductively secluded from the machinations of the real world. The slow rhythm of the island in the waning days of the season became ours. It was something like the feeling of being at an intoxicating party where the host had specifically requested you to stay on after everyone else left. Like being chosen for preferential treatment, deemed worthy of an exclusivity that had escaped others. Every day, more people departed and there were less new faces to replace them. The number of boats and tourists and foreign newspapers dwindled with each day's dawn. With the lack of other newcomers to the island, our presence there together took on a larger scale in the proportion of things. We were a healthy and significant piece of the island population.

Our expansion caused other things to diminish before us.

The sun started shining less strongly, the days grew slowly chillier and shorter as they melted into longer nights.

The set of each sun was ceremony, we didn't miss one of them, though we invested extravagant amounts of effort seeking the perfect spot to watch them: the balcony; the port promenade, where you couldn't quite make out the final dip of the fiery star as it melted into the sea but could see the traces of cathedral-glass colors it painted on the waters; our favorite taverna, where we went into the kitchen and picked out whatever was made for us that day; the quiet hilltop above the town with the silent little church that had no bells and a rounded blue dome. We watched the colors of peaches and nectarines paint the horizon until the light dwindled and made way for eggplant and plum-colored purples.

And we feasted on them, these special moments.

They were always well-lubricated sunsets, the last rays shimmered on the sea as we drank ouzo and water. We watched the clear ouzo turn milky white when we poured in the water or sometimes had it just on ice and waited for the cubes to melt and stir up the color, and it was like making a magic potion every time, a secret alchemy. In those anisette laced instants lied little mysteries, like how it tasted of black licorice and neither of us liked black licorice, but we drank it and it was the right thing to drink, the flavor of enigma. Other nights, we slaked ourselves with wine. As the season dwindled and visitors vanished, so too had the varietals. The finer bottles imported from Arcadia gathered dust in the tiny grocery just beyond the house where the donkeys carried up supplies with the scarcer ferry arrivals. We sipped more frequently from the locals' tangled, blushing blends of whites and reds; whatever grew on those rocky ridges.

After ceremonial sunsets, we finished appetites with Metaxa brandy and worked our palate and appreciation up from three stars to seven, which was the most and the finest. We sipped the stars while the potent light of the heavens distilled itself above us, so many that they could not be counted even when we lay on the cool cobbled stones of the balcony all night and tried. There was an infinity of beauty and we were blanketed by it, became a part of it.

There was all that and it filled up the space of all that was not.

No phones, no one to call, no computers, no internet and no email, no obligations.

We lived well on what I thought of as nineteenth century days: reading, sleeping, eating, talking, loving. Doing all the things the twenty-first century had forgotten or not yet learned to do and we learned to do them together, the first time I understood how to do them properly. I was maybe a late pupil to be learning such lessons but was buoyed with the dedication that is lent only by knowing how elusive and unnamed happiness can be.

Living within the limits of the island's shores, we learned to
embrace the beautiful imperfections. The lack of distractions and
the pine and sage scented hills seasoned our self-indulgent days.
Choices grew simpler.

We ate yogurt and honey laced with sunset-colored fruits for our
ritual breaking of the night's fast and called it breakfast even if it
was lunchtime. In the days, she sketched and painted and I read and
started writing for the first time, about all the things I had learned
and the many I did not understand.

In the afternoons, we walked to the west side of the island and
stripped down to our swimsuits, both to just our bottom parts,
contentedly topless if there were people, or both bared down
completely if there were not, and we swam on our own select pebbled
beach to work up another appetite, and I always licked the salty briny
delicious flavor of the sea off the back of her neck beneath her
dampened hairline. We found ourselves, more than once, wet and
loving with sand and sea-polished pebbles stuck everywhere on our
sweating bodies and had to jump in the cool evening sea to clean
ourselves and then we set forth to rush home, so starved for hot
showers that it seemed we didn't have time to stop for a drink, we
were so cold. But we usually found it, the time, and the thirst. Those
things could be found if you searched in the right places, and in a
small world, there were less places to search.

The timeless questions of when and why paled before the simpler
ones of what and how.

Like the somber starless night she cried and sobbed to me about
nothing in particular and about everything in general and how I cried
with her, but then the tears washed away some of the sadness. How
I plucked a drop off of her cheek and it tasted like the sea and then
another tear left the same salty taste in her mouth. How the quiet sobs
led to an exhaustion that earned the rejuvenation of sleep. How the
next morning, I woke up and found her sitting on the toilet peeing
and tying her white tennis shoes at the same time, and there were
the light sounds of rippling water as she smiled when I caught her,
and I loved her for this modest display, even if I didn't understand
it and didn't know why or how completely.

Then the awareness that there would be another day and it would
be without any tides of tears.

Or the trip to Athens and the American Embassy, and how Pavel
couldn't make it due to some important political meeting of the
type that kept revolutionaries from lesser missions. How Aaron had
indeed rustled up a girl all the way from New Zealand, an investment

banker on holiday in Prague, of all things. How Denissa and her bad-tempered behavior bothered everyone while we let that ill-chosen favor of a paper marriage interfere with our halcyon island days. How that first unnecessary nuptial would forever be the last first marriage but not the last mistake, and that anyway there would be other firsts.

How I decided that Terra Firma was fraught with all manner of different dangers, that medieval mapmakers may have had it right, that on the unknown borders of Terra Incognito might be dragons, and if you could not see them or train them, you might learn to stay away from them, to seek security.

How I became an island, how we became one together, Sophie and I. How the sum of our parts became a new entity that overshadowed our separateness. How from she and I, we found we, and the forging of this creation contained us, all of us.

How the strange celebration of that Athens' night in the Plaka ended with Denissa and Sophie yelling at one another for no real apparent reason, except for maybe because I was there and Sophie was there and it was a place that Denissa had not ever planned on being, and maybe none of us should have been there at all, in places we were not supposed to have been. And how sharp the stinging sound was when Sophie slapped Denissa across her wide, rouged Slavic cheekbones and the way Denissa cursed me out in Czech words I didn't understand and then said, "I am very angry," but none of us knew exactly why or at what, and how Aaron and his rustled up female friend from another hemisphere laughed until they cried and found it terribly amusing and just so like her. And how my wife, Denissa, went home to Prague to pack and go off to find her way in America, to seek out the American Dream that she'd heard of from her brother and seen on television.

How on that dangerous trip to the mainland, after we were done with the Embassy, and Aaron and the Kiwi investment banker and Denissa—the little sister of a revolutionary seeking another revolution—had flown away, how we tracked down the distant remnants of Sophie's real father's family and found out the man she'd never known had died without her ever meeting him. That he had never talked of her nor sought her out, and she had tried too late. How she didn't cry, maybe she'd run out of tears, and we went back to the Hotel Omiros and stayed there all afternoon, and for some reason ended up later, drunk and laughing and marching behind the skirted soldiers in front of the former palace of King Otto in Syntagma Square and drinking champagne in the trendy Kolonaki neighborhood, and both purely alone in the world, were drawn closer.

And how Sophie and I, the island of us, headed back to Hydra. How relieved we were to leave behind the problems of the busy city of Athens, the paperwork of the embassy and the disappointment of discovering unknown death, and how we watched all of it, everything else, recede into our distant wake.

How we pined in just those short few days for our adopted island home and were so happy to return to it that we even arranged to stay there longer, having rented it for an off season pittance from Panos, us still together or perhaps together again, maybe together for always, and referred to Denissa never by name and only as "that Czech girl," or sometimes, other times, when Sophie had drunk several ouzos after sunset and the winds off the sea were bitter, "that miserable, ungrateful Czech bitch," and how I loved her for that too, and how I never disagreed with her, not about anything important like that. Just about lesser things we fought over and how the fights made us closer. Like how we both solemnly agreed to squeeze the toothpaste from the bottom and how she never did, and I grew to appreciate these minor differences that became a part of us.

And how she yelled at me when she was perturbed over something and then it dissolved into laughter, and how I delighted in seeing her passion and emotion be reborn because her passion fed my passion, had become a part of me. And how we busied ourselves inventing theories about everything under the sun, even ourselves, and they were all insightful and ponderous and silly and just our own and wouldn't have worked for anyone else. That was the beauty in them. They were ours.

How we carefully planned a going away party at Panos' bar for Captain Nigel, our firmest off-season island friend. A party everyone else disdained because no one believed he was going to leave anyway. But still everyone came and several of us, thirsty for more liquor than we could hold, threw up in the sea and then drank more because if he didn't leave, the party would last forever. But how the next day, a sleek 150-foot yacht sporting a British maritime flag pulled out of the harbor and he was gone, leaving behind but the many memories and the trail of a transient wake that dissolved into elsewhere.

How if you sustained yourself from the bare bounty of a small island, some things left you and other things replaced them.

Like how we were adopted by an island dog, a sad and beautiful stray that was skinny and needed tending—or saw that we did—and we called him Fritz, even though we didn't know why, but he didn't look like a Sancho. He followed us everywhere all the days and then slept upstairs on the couch in our bedroom until sometime during the chillier nights, when he decided it was time to migrate to the bed. There was room for everyone. After Fritz helped one of us paint or write, the three of us walked to the beach in the afternoons while the island slumbered during siesta silence, and there was only our voices and the lapping of the waves against the stones until his animated barking told us it was time to return, because no matter which way we went home, the walk took us by the butcher shop of Spiros and some days we would stop and go inside to buy a big lamb shank bone for Fritz.

On those days, Spiros would tell us that we were crazy foreigners for wanting to waste money on a bone that should have been used for soup, that he should charge us double if we were going to waste it on that filthy beast. Then he would reach down to where he had put a bone aside that he'd saved for Fritz and give it to us for free and tell us to get lost. And we would, but less and less, because by then we knew our way on the winding island streets that had no names. Even Fritz understood that there were not bones every day. But there was the hope for them.

And we learned hope.

How there were mysteries to solve about how things worked and if you did not always understand them, the small world around you, in its growing generosity, might explain them to you. If you were in the right place and your mind was open. If you were there, all there.

How there were many different delights, even if some of them became routine.

Like the mornings spent at the table in Panos' bar. Always the same table. I had fallen in love with that table too. I had found so much love to give away. That table, my table, was where I sat while I waited for Sophie to finish painting and meet me for lunch.

From that round table, you could watch the whole island pass you by, always a few new tourist faces from the ever less-frequent ferries, though fewer and fewer with the slow passing of every day. You could watch the colorful cadre of fishing ships creep into the little harbor trailing their yellow nets in the water, and then the men beating their catch of squids on the stones to tenderize them, as they always had, before they took them up to the restaurants that were staying open for the off season.

How if there was a newspaper on the island, you could sometimes finish the Herald Tribune crossword, if you were ambitious, before the last fishing boat floated in sometime in the afternoon. How sometimes it was the most satisfying thing you accomplished the whole morning, sometimes the only thing, or how there were many other days with no regular ferries from the mainland, when there were no English newspapers and no news of fires or wars or murders or politics, and how you didn't miss them, and so you let Panos beat you at backgammon again instead, and it was just as good, maybe better, even though it was just as routine as the news or the crossword.

How there was always at least every day one new boat, a luxurious yacht, in the harbor and how you waited to meet them, the beautiful people on the boat, and how you did, invariably, because on a small island they all passed you by sometime. How you sat there at your table and watched everything and it all came to you, you didn't have to go anywhere else to find it, all of it slowly passed by you right there on the shore and waited for you to absorb it.

How you grew to appreciate the well-orchestrated nuances of the performance, how it was like a symphony only you couldn't see the conductor.

But you began to admire his prowess nonetheless.

How you grew to know the same island faces. The donkey man with his cell phone and his copy of Dante in demotic Greek and his bushy moustache and ever-present scowl, and how he wouldn't drink with you, and how he always had the book with him but you never once saw him read it and thought that terribly wonderful, somehow. The young French couple with their baby that had taken a house for the whole winter on the other side of the island, whom you always meant to meet but never did, even though you saw them most everywhere. The storekeepers, the widows in black, the young Greek children that came to the café to let you buy them ice cream in the afternoons after school. How they all knew, now, about Mrs. O'Leary's cow, Bessie. How sometimes they sat with you at your table and marveled at the fact that you didn't know basic words in their language, like salt or water or chair or smile, and how you all delighted in your ignorance, the ever-growing bounty of how much there was to learn.

How some days, in the sameness of simple routine, you found significance, found magic in the things that would have remained unknown if you were not there to bear witness to their lessons.

Like this one day marked by the indelible stamps of overflowing others, when it was early afternoon and you sat at your beloved table as the play of the self-contained island stage was being performed for you, how Panos came and sat down and said it had been his birthday the day before.

And why hadn't, you asked, there been a party?

How instead of answering, he went inside and took out a bottle of seven-starred Metaxa, even though you were drinking coffee and not brandy that early afternoon, and how he poured out two glasses and shared blunt-spoken, big-hearted thoughts in which you found wisdom, though he never claimed to be a wise man.

How you stared at the amber liquor in the glass, slowly swirling it against the backdrop of the blue waters of the bay while he talked.

How he looked at you from across that table and spoke.

"Do not believe you need a reason to celebrate, my friend. You are no longer a tourist on a trip. The trip is finished but you are still here now. Do not be a tourist in life. Let me tell you the secret: here we celebrate because it is today and we are alive. This is enough."

And so glasses were raised to Panos' words and to his unmissed birthday, an unexpected celebration. Then he stood and went inside, taking his brandy of seven stars with him, off to clean the bar, though there were no boats due that day and not many customers that had made any mess or were likely to, since most all of you took your dishes inside.

And then you sat at your little table and stared at the horseshoe-shaped bay before you and realized that maybe you had understood it all for a moment, this thing called life. That if you had ever done anything any differently, no matter how many mistakes you'd made, you might not have understood, but you hadn't, not before.

How the immensity of all that you had not understood diminished before all that you had in that moment.

And how you thought about this while sipping your frappe, your daily dose of afternoon iced coffee that followed the serendipitous cocktail of midday Metaxa and old world wisdom, while your dog, Fritz, lay there at your feet, lazily swishing flies away with his long tail, marshaling his energy for a late afternoon trip to Spiros' butcher shop. Because whether it was a day for bones or not, there was the belief that every day was such a day. The hope.

And how you knew that before you finished this coffee, because it had been true every day on that island in that new life that you'd built, or maybe discovered, that Sophie would walk down past the National Bank of Greece and be wearing something casual but radiant and still have flecks of paint on her hands and sometimes her face, and how you could read her mood by the colors of what she had painted that marked her skin, and how more and more they were brighter and luminous, like the sea and the large island sky.

How in the prism of her paint-freckled skin, you could see all the colors that ever existed, or ever would.

And how she would sit down beside you, and without being summoned, Panos would appear with two more iced coffees and set them on the table, and before you asked her about what she had painted or told her what you had written, that she would tell you, as she always did now, that she loved you. That then there would be a kiss that would last for a small but sublime slice of eternity. That you realized you had traveled all this distance to get to these moments and this place.

And how you would report to her on what had gone on in the port that day and tell her before she counted, the number of ships in the harbor.

How even these little things could be important, could be an indispensable part of everything else.

And how you knew that sometime you would have to leave this perfect place, and you would, and you could, you might just, go somewhere else, and do something else, some tomorrow. But that you would do it together and it wouldn't matter where you went, you would always go together.

Here and now, you were. Alive.

ABOUT THE AUTHOR

Scott Stavrou was born in Chicago then raised in San Diego and Las Vegas before graduating from Georgetown University. Since then, he has lived and worked as a writer in San Francisco, Venice, Prague, and the Greek islands where he and his wife presently call home.

Stavrou has written fiction and non-fiction for numerous publications in the U.S. and Europe. He is the author of the award-winning travel book *Wasted Away*, the original stage play *Picketing with Prometheus* as well as two original screenplays. He is a long time member of the International Food, Wine & Travel Writers Association and the Georgetown Entertainment & Media Alliance.

He was awarded the PEN America International Hemingway Writing Award for his short fiction *Across the Suburbs*.

In addition to writing, he serves on the Board of Advisors for Write Away Europe and he is also a Creative Writing Instructor. More of Stavrou's writing can be found at ScottStavrou.com and on Medium and Twitter.

His next book is scheduled for release in 2019.

Free Reading Group/Book Club Guide for *Losing Venice* is available at RogueDogPress.com.

If you enjoyed this book, why not take a moment and leave a review on Amazon or Goodreads.